BELOVED BETHESDA

The provenance of this rare and valuable portrait of the Rev. George Whitefield has been traced by Nita (Mrs. Pomeroy) Williams, of the Bethesda Museum Committee of the Woman's Society. It originally belonged to James Whitefield, brother of the founder, and it passed to his daughter Elizabeth Johnston, to her daughter Eliza Morrison, to her daughter Jane Fullerton Morrison Grigg, to her daughter Eliza Grigg who gave it to the Georgia Historical Society in 1888. (Courtesy Georgia Historical Society.)

Beloved Bethesda

A History of George Whitefield's Home for Boys, 1740–2000

by

Edward J. Cashin

Mercer
University
Press
2001

6316 Peake Road
Macon, Georgia 31210-3960

ISBN 0-86554-722-X
MUP/H542

First Edition.

∞The paper used in this publication meets the minimum requirements of American National Standard for Information Sciences—Permanence of Paper for Printed Library Materials, ANSI Z39.48-1992.

Library of Congress Cataloging-in-Publication Data

Cashin, Edward J., 1927-.
Beloved Bethesda : a history of George Whitefield's home for boys / by Edward J. Cashin.
p. cm.
Includes bibliographical references and index.
ISBN 0-86554-722-X
1. Whitefield, George, 1714-1770. 2. Bethesda (Orphanage : Savannah, Ga. (1740-1809) 3. Orphanages—Georgia—Savannah—History. I. Title.

HV995.S45 C37 2001
362.73'2'09758724—dc21 2001018018

CONTENTS

PREFACE

George Whitefield, the "Great Itinerant," changed the religious character of Colonial America more than any of his contemporaries. Many of today's Christians, especially those who think of themselves as "born again," are his theological heirs. Only a few Americans realize that the religious history of this country would have been remarkably different had it not been for the institution Whitefield loved dearly enough to call his "Beloved Bethesda."

Whitefield's purpose in coming to the colonies was to care for orphaned children. He embarked on that mission with all the considerable talent and zeal at his command. Sure of himself and confident that he was doing the will of Providence, he stirred controversy wherever he went, first in Georgia, then throughout the colonies. He might have gone on his "progresses," as he called his travels along the eastern seaboard and into New England, even if there were no Bethesda, but the establishment of the home and his ambitions for it made fundraising excursions a necessity. On these tours, Whitefield's unprecedented practice of preaching outdoors extemporaneously annoyed many of the traditional clergy and thrilled multitudes. His listeners found it enormously comforting to learn from him that the emotion stirred by his preaching was in fact the very saving election of God. The Itinerant spoke about Bethesda in England, Scotland, Wales, and everywhere he collected money for the orphan home; as a result, Bethesda became one of the most famous places in all of Colonial America.

This is the story of George Whitefield's founding and nurturing of Bethesda. Even readers who are well acquainted with Georgia's history will find a number of surprises in this account. For example, a case is made that Bethesda sustained Georgia during the dark years of 1740–1742, when Spanish invaders threatened the infant colony and many Georgians fled to the safety of Carolina. When Whitefield realized that his orphan house would not survive unless Georgia succeeded economically, he became a major force in persuading the trustees to change their policies. The most controversial of his decisions was to advocate the introduction of slavery into the province, partly because he thought Georgia would not thrive without plantation slavery, but mostly because he needed a plantation as an additional source of revenue for Bethesda. Essential to Georgia's success were the contributions of the "Bethesda Connection"—James Habersham, Francis Harris, and Jonathan Bryan, among others—whose names are well known in Georgia's colonial history, but whose relationship with Bethesda is not nearly so well known. Neither do many people realize that Bethesda alumni proudly bearing the title "Bethesda boys" helped establish the Union Society that in time took over the custodianship of the home.

Whitefield's effort to transform the orphan home into one of America's first colleges is an essential part of the story. So is the involvement of the Countess of Huntingdon, a dynamic figure in England's religious history who attempted to make Bethesda the base for the conversion of American Indians. Her agent, the Reverend William Piercy, remains a man of mystery; one who, strangely enough, professed loyalty to the countess while stealing her money and declared allegiance to the king while associating with American revolutionaries.

An intriguing question is, why did Bethesda survive? Why did it outlast the Revolution and the many crises since then? The most plausible answer is that George Whitefield's commitment to the home ran so deep that Savannah's gentlemen of the revolutionary era felt inspired to maintain the facility. Meanwhile, successive generations of Savannahians have inherited and accepted the same responsibility. For more than two centuries, Savannahians have cared for the home, while generations of Bethesda alumni have contributed both specifically to Savannah and, more broadly, to Georgia as a whole. Even today the abandonment of Bethesda is not even considered an option by the people of Savannah. In this way, we can understand why this is not only Whitefield's story, but also Savannah's story. For the Great Itinerant, as for friends and supporters, this is the story of "Beloved Bethesda."

Research about Bethesda has taken me to a number of interesting places: the Library of Congress Rare Book Room and the Countess of Huntingdon Collection at Westminster College in Cambridge, England; the Lambeth Palace Library, the Library of the Royal Academy, and the new British Library in London; the Emory University libraries, the Georgia Department of Archives and History, and the Atlanta Historical Society in Atlanta; the South Carolina Historical Society in Charleston; the Georgia Historical Society in Savannah; and, of course, the extensive Bethesda Archives. I am indebted to the gracious assistance of the staff at all those places.

The research has been as interesting as the story. My wife and I visited the tomb of Selina, Countess of Huntingdon, at the ancient Church of St. Helen's in the Leiscestershire town of Ashby de la Zouch. Ashby is not an unattractive town, although it lacks the panache its name implies, and tourists prefer the more charming villages of the Midlands. The town derives its identity less from the distinguished Hastings-Huntingdon family, who have lived in or near the town since the time of William the Conqueror, and more from its being mentioned in Walter Scott's novel *Ivanhoe.* On the day we visited, locals bedecked in the garb of medieval knights cavorted about amid the impressive ruins of the castle adjacent to the church. A few miles to the north stands the restored Donnington Hall, the ancestral home of the Hastings. Now the headquarters of an airline company, Donnington Hall retains its dignity despite the roar of racing cars just beyond its manicured lawns at a track called Donnington Park.

We also visited Newburyport, Massachusetts, and the Old South Church where George Whitefield's body is interred beneath the altar. Bustling, wealthy Newburyport, its historic district recently restored and spruced up, seems unaware of the international fame of the preacher who converted thousands. It occurred to us that he died the death of an itinerant, God's salesman, away from the place he thought of as home. His bodily remains lie in the New England town, but his spirit resides in Bethesda.

I admit to having caught some of George Whitefield's infectious fondness for Bethesda. My wife Mary Ann and I have been pleasantly received on our visits to the home by David Tribble, Bill McIlrath, and John and Heather Gehrm. We enjoyed meeting Glaen Richards and the "old" Bethesda boys on Anniversary Day as well as participating in the nostalgic annual banquet. We felt the heart warming experience of watching the boys receive their awards, understanding the transforming effect of the historic grounds on those who have lived there. The massive oaks, some there since Whitefield's day, the Spanish moss, the marsh, and the ever-flowing river—all inspired a dawning appreciation for those who have preserved Georgia's oldest institution.

I have come away from this study with admiration not only for the members of the Union Society for their unselfish dedication to Bethesda over the decades, but also for the members of the Women's Advisory Board for their eighty-five years of exercising a civilizing influence on the men and boys of Bethesda. I thank Nita Williams for her interest in this project, for her assistance with the illustrations, and for the valuable information she provided along the way. I am also grateful to Nancy Edenfield, my student assistant, for her arduous work on the word processor.

Edward J. Cashin
Augusta State University

CHAPTER ONE

THE BIRTH OF BETHESDA

Our story begins when twenty-four-year-old George Whitefield, still in the first fervor of his conversion, stepped ashore on Tybee Island on May 8, 1738. He thought he "might" establish an orphan house, but in any case, he expected to be God's instrument in some grand plan. He could not have known what we know today: that his influence would help overturn the trustees' plan for Georgia and, incidental to his building an orphanage, that he would ignite that religious fire known as the Great Awakening, a phenomenon that changed the character of religion in America from Whitefield's day to ours.

Why Whitefield knew about the need for an orphanage before coming to Georgia and why he thought of himself as an agent of the Almighty requires a brief explanation and, in the process, introduces into our narrative the brothers Wesley, John and Charles. Both sons of a clergyman, the Wesleys had formed a prayer group at Oxford when George Whitefield first met them in 1734. Charles and a few others began the meetings, but it was John—"a born organizer," as his biographer called him—who suggested that they live by a set of rules. People began to call the pious youths "Methodists," members of the "Holy Club." George Whitefield, only twenty, and a student at Pembroke College, had seen enough of the world's wickedness at his parents' tavern in Gloucester. He admired the members of the Holy Club, joined them, and even outdid them in extravagant acts of penance and self-denial. He practically starved himself to death and wore rags, yet experienced no approving consolation from heaven. Meanwhile, John Wesley felt called by God to go to the new colony of Georgia and convert the Indians there. He persuaded his reluctant younger brother, Charles, and two others, Benjamin Ingham and

Charles Delamotte, to accompany him. The Georgia Trustees, headed by John Percival, Lord Egmont, and represented in Georgia by James Edward Oglethorpe, appointed John to the Savannah ministry and Charles to Frederica. Charles also had the tedious and unwelcome task of performing secretarial duties, spending most of his time in the unapostolic job of writing reports.[1]

In Savannah John Wesley gathered disciples into a Georgian version of a Holy Club, although members lacked the educational advantages of their Oxford counterparts. Wesley started a school with Delamotte as teacher, and for a short while Benjamin Ingham conducted a school for Tomochichi's Yamacraw Indians at Irene, several miles up the Savannah River.[2]

While the Wesleys were in Georgia, George Whitefield assumed leadership of the Methodists at Oxford. In June of 1735, he experienced a profound conversion that changed his own life and, through him, the lives of thousands. He believed that the palpable consolation he felt meant that God had called him to salvation, that he thus became a new Adam, now capable of doing virtuous deeds.[3] His subsequent theology and the central message of his ministry derived from his personal conversion. Humans came into the world doomed by the original sin of Adam and Eve, with wills darkened and unable to choose the good. However, God had seen fit to save certain souls. He made known this election by personal emotional communication. Whitefield called this phenomenon a "new birth." The "born agains" of modern Georgia know what he meant; many of them follow in the way Whitefield first led. If a person did not have that personal experience, he or she remained in a state of sin and would end up in

---

[1] Frank Baker, *John Wesley and the Church of England* (New York: Abingdon Press, 1970) 22–26; John Gillies, D.D., *Memoirs of Rev. George Whitefield* (Middletown CT: Hunt and Noyes, 1837) 16–18; Charles Wesley Flint, *Charles Wesley and His Colleagues* (Washington DC: Public Affairs Press, 1957) 29.

[2] Wesley's Georgia adventures are found in the *Journal of the Reverend John Wesley*, 4 vols. (London: J. Kershaw, 1827).

[3] Gillies, *Memoirs*, 17–18.

hell, despite any outward conformity to Christianity. His absolute certainty of his own election gave George Whitefield an authority and confidence that seemed like arrogance to those who did not agree with him.

Shortly after his spiritual rebirth, Whitefield received a letter from Georgia, written by John Wesley. God's work needed to be done in Georgia. The harvest was great and laborers few. Who would heed the call? "What if thou art the man, Mr. Whitefield?" Wesley asked.[4] This clear summons, coming so soon after his conversion, Whitefield took to be God's clear message. A message from Charles Wesley made his mission even clearer. Charles Wesley explained that the fever raging in Georgia had left many children orphaned. These little ones needed a home. George Whitefield credited Charles Wesley with the idea of a Georgia orphanage: "It was first proposed to me by my dear friend Mr. Charles Wesley, who with General Oglethorpe, had concerted a scheme for carrying on such a design, before I had any thought of going abroad myself."[5]

George Whitefield completed arrangements for going to Georgia. The bishop of Gloucester ordained him as deacon in the Church of England, and he obtained an appointment from the Georgia Trustees to the Savannah Church, replacing John Wesley. It is tempting to relate the account of John and Charles Wesley's brief and unhappy stay in Georgia, but ours is the story of Whitefield and Bethesda. We will simply quote John Wesley's own statement that he had gone to America to convert Indians and was not himself converted: "All the time I was at Savannah I was there beating the air."[6] His own "new birth" occurred in 1738, after he returned from Georgia. On December 22, 1737, Wesley took leave of Charles Delamotte and left Georgia. Benjamin Ingham and Charles Wesley proceeded him to England. Charles Wesley's subsequent career in England as hymn-

---

[4] Gillies, *Memoirs*, 21.

[5] George Whitefield, *A brief account of the Rise, Progress and Present Situation of the Orphan House in Georgia* (New York: Pudney and Russell, 1855) 329–31.

[6] Wesley, *Journal*, 1:95.

writer and preacher is well known. Less known, but just as pertinent to our story, is the career of Ingham. While in the course of preaching in Yorkshire, Ingham attracted the attention of the sisters Anne and Margaret Hastings. Lady Margaret invited him to her home, Ledstone Hall, to expound the Gospels. Ingham not only converted the lady, but he also married her. It happened that Lady Margaret Hastings was the sister of Theophilus Hastings, Earl of Huntingdon. The Earl's wife and the dear friend of Lady Margaret was Selina, Countess of Huntingdon, about whom we will hear a great deal in this narrative.[7] Lady Margaret felt such peace and joy after her conversion that she made a profound impression on Selina, who soon embraced the Methodist theology herself.

Now, we return to John Wesley, who left Georgia under a cloud. A grand jury, composed primarily of persons who disliked Wesley's strict preaching, indicted him for refusing to give communion to Sophy Williamson, a lady to whom he had once (in fact, more than once, according to Sophy) proposed marriage.[8] "I shook off the dust of my feet and left Georgia," he wrote, "after having preached the gospel there (not as I ought, but as I was able) one year and nine months."[9] By coincidence his vessel sailed into the Thames as the *Whitaker,* with Whitefield aboard as well as soldiers of Oglethorpe's 42nd Regiment, sailed out. Wesley had adopted a practice of the Moravian Brethren whom he admired in Georgia, namely the casting of lots to ascertain God's will in important matters. Wesley had cast lots when trying to decide whether to marry Sophy. When Wesley learned that Whitefield's outgoing vessel was held up by contrary winds, he cast lots to discover God's will regarding Whitefield's mission to Georgia, sending over the urgent answer, "Let him return."[10] George

---

[7] Gilbert W. Kirby, *The Elect Lady* (London: The Trustees of the Countess of Huntingdon, 1772; rev. 1990) 10. The document can be found on the internet at <http://www.cofhconnexion.org.uk/electlady.html>.

[8] Wesley, *Journal,* 1:52.

[9] Wesley, *Journal,* 1:57.

[10] Gillies, *Memoirs,* 27.

Whitefield, secure about everything since his recent conversion, did not require lots to know God's will. He disregarded Wesley's lots and sailed for Georgia.

During the few months while he prepared for his mission to America, George Whitefield discovered that he had a gift of eloquence. Blessed with a strong, resonant, melodious voice that he could play with the skill of a born actor, he began preaching with the assurance of one of the elect—with astounding results. His sermons were printed and widely read, and by the time he reached London to board ship, he had become quite a celebrity. He marveled at his sudden fame: "I could no longer walk on foot as usual, but was constrained to go in a coach from place to place, to avoid the hosannas of the multitudes."[11] Among his advisors were the brothers James and Joseph Habersham. Originally from Beverly in Yorkshire, the brothers had come to London to work in their uncle's store. Twenty-four-year-old James showed an aptitude for business, and George Whitefield told him he could use his talents and experience in Georgia. Many years later, Habersham wrote that he met Whitefield soon after the young clerk left Oxford for London and they liked each other from their first encounter. Whitefield lodged with the Habershams in London. Habersham said he "couldn't bear to part" and asked to go to Georgia "without having any particular design in view."[12] Whitefield knew he would need a teacher once he started an orphanage and arranged for the Georgia Trustees to pay Habersham's way as a prospective schoolmaster. Among George Whitefield's contributions to the colony and State of Georgia, tangible and intangible, the introduction of the Habershams ranks high.

George Whitefield's conduct aboard the *Whitaker* tells us much about his typical attitude and behavior. His fellow passengers consisted mostly of irreligious soldiers among whom hard drinking and constant cursing were considered the norm. George Whitefield

---

[11] Stuart C. Henry, *George Whitefield Wayfaring Witness* (New York: Abingdon Press, 1957) 30.

[12] James Habersham to Countess, December 10, 1770, Georgia Historical Society *Collections*, 6:102–103.

both challenged and changed them by the time they reached Georgia. "Bad books" and decks of cards were thrown overboard and replaced with pious tracts handed out by Whitefield. The newly reformed captain assembled the entire ship's company for daily prayers. George Whitefield had a way of intimidating people, even hard-bitten soldiers and sailors.[13]

Whitefield's theology influenced his pedagogy, also an important fact in view of his intention to assume responsibility for rearing orphans. Unless and until children had personal experience of salvation, their natures remained wicked. An excerpt from Whitefield's journal records an example of what he called "the Benefit of breaking Children's Will:"

> I asked one of the women to bid her little Boy that stood by her, say his Prayers, she answered... she could not make him. Upon this, I bid the Child kneel down before me, but he would not till I took hold of its two feet, and forced it down. I then bid it to say the Lord's Prayer (being informed by his Mother he could say it if he would) but he obstinately refused, till at last after I had given it several Blows, it said its Prayers as well as could be expected, and I gave it some Figs for a Reward.[14]

Modern readers might be surprised that a four-year-old could have memorized the Lord's Prayer and aghast at the thought of giving "it" several blows to produce the prayer. Evidently, George Whitefield regarded young children in the same way trainers regarded wild horses; they had to be broken before you could get their attention.

Now that we know why George Whitefield planned to start an orphanage before he landed in Georgia, our story can resume. The Wesleys had prepared the way; all Whitefield needed was to see the situation of the Georgia children himself; as he put it, he required only

---

[13] Gillies, *Memoirs*, 29.

[14] Henry, *George Whitefield*, 34.

"an ocular demonstration."[15] As God's messenger and instrument, he expected to accomplish great things.

George Whitefield and James Habersham took a boat at Tybee and proceeded upriver to Savannah. May is a beautiful month in Georgia and the climate must have smiled on the newcomers. The town itself sat upon Yamacraw Bluff, once the home of Tomochichi's band. Five years before, James Oglethorpe had laid out an ambitious town plan consisting of six squares, each surrounded by forty lots and occupied by the people brought to Georgia at the trustees' expense, not debtors (despite the persistence of that old myth), but poor persons screened and selected by a committee of the governing trustees. When Whitefield climbed the sandy bluff, he saw a clustering of cottages grouped around the six open spaces. Some Savannahians had come over at their own expense and their dwellings were more substantial. The town looked tentative, uncertain. Failure was as likely as success. Truth to tell, Georgia in 1738 was sustained largely by the will of its founder, James Edward Oglethorpe. Most of the activity centered in Frederica on St. Simons Island, where the newly arrived 42nd Regiment had its barracks. Across from Frederica on the mainland, the Scots of Clan Chattan were trying to survive while waiting to do what they had come to Georgia for three years before, namely to fight the Spaniards in Florida. Their river, the Altamaha, marked the southern boundary of Georgia, although Oglethorpe had hopes of extending it into Spanish Florida.

Oglethorpe had deliberately settled families at strategic places in the hopes that they would form permanent villages. Actually, most of these hamlets were disappearing as the families either died or moved away. Highgate, five miles below Savannah, still had nine French families, and a sister settlement a mile distant called Hampstead had five of the original twelve German families. Upriver from Savannah near the trading post of Oglethorpe's Indian interpreter, Mary Musgrove Matthews, was a place called Irene, where Benjamin Ingham had conducted a school for Indian children until he got discouraged and returned to England. A group of Moravians lived there in 1738. Above

[15] Gillies, *Memoirs*, 31.

Irene was the village of Abercorn, where ten families had lived, but all were gone by 1738. Farther upriver, at the limit of tidal action lay the German settlement called Ebenezer. Sixty neat cottages, each with its own garden, testified to the industry of the inhabitants. Ebenezer marked the northern limits of the land allowed for settlement by the Creek Nation. The Creeks considered the Savannah River the dividing line between the English and themselves, but in 1736 they allowed Oglethorpe to settle his people in the narrow region between the Savannah and the Altamaha as far inland as the flow of the tide. The Creeks allowed an important exception. The town of Augusta, 140 miles above Savannah, lay on the right bank of the river at the fall line where several old trails crossed the river. In 1735 Oglethorpe persuaded Parliament to pass an Indian Act, giving him control of the Indian trade west of the Savannah River. In 1738 Roger Lacy of Thunderbolt carried out his assignment to build a fort at Augusta, and already Carolina traders were taking residence in the town on lots surveyed by Noble Jones who lived on the Isle of Hope. Augusta's layout was meant to resemble Savannah's, squares surrounded by forty lots. However, only one square and its forty lots were surveyed; the town then straggled out on the main Indian trail.[16]

Whitefield's dear friend from Oxford, Charles Delamotte, greeted him in Savannah and was introduced to Habersham. Characteristically, Whitefield believed that God had planned things that way; he wrote that Delamotte was "providentially left behind at Savannah against my coming."[17] They quickly agreed that Habersham would take over the school, freeing Delamotte to return to England, which he

---

[16] John Wesley provided a sketch of the first Georgia settlements in his journal, 59–61; for Augusta, see Heard Robertson and Thomas H. Robertson, "The Town and Fort Augusta," *Colonial Augusta: Key of the Indian Country,* ed. Edward J. Cashin (Macon GA: Mercer University Press, 1986) 59–74. The standard on Oglethorpe is Phinizy Spalding, *Oglethorpe in America* (Chicago: University of Chicago Press, 1984).

[17] George Whitefield, *A Continuation of the Reverend Mr. Whitefield's Journal from His Arrival at Savannah to His Return to London* (London: W. Strahan, 1739) 1.

did on June 2, 1736. Meanwhile, he introduced Whitefield to Wesley's little circle of converts. On the day after his arrival, Whitefield met with Thomas Causton, the chief magistrate and prosecutor of John Wesley. Causton and the other magistrates greeted him civilly enough, but already Whitefield noticed signs of factional discord.

Partly to get acquainted with the surroundings and partly to look for orphans, Whitefield visited the outlying families at Hampstead and Highgate. As early as May 19, 1738, less than two weeks after his arrival, Whitefield completed his "ocular demonstration." There were many orphans (children with only one parent were included in this category) who he decided needed care. "Nothing can affect this but an Orphan House," he wrote in his journal.[18]

Whitefield paid a visit to old Tomochichi, but neither the chief nor his wife, Senauki, could speak English, so they merely shook hands and parted. A few days later, when the chief's nephew, Tooanahowi, acted as interpreter, Whitefield called upon the old man, now scarcely more than skin and bones. Whitefield got right to the point, asking where the chief intended to go when he died. "To heaven," Tomochichi answered. The cleric did not record what he said in response, but he thought, "Alas, how can a Drunkard enter there?"[19] He told the nephew not to get drunk, for if he did, his sin would be greater since he spoke English.

In July, Whitefield went to visit the industrious Lutherans at Ebenezer. He admired the piety of the people and "contracted an intimacy" with their pastors, Martin Bolzius and Israel Gronau. More importantly, from Whitefield's point of view, Ebenezer had an orphanage with seventeen children under care. Pastor Bolzius lined them up and led them in a hymn; then they prayed together. Whitefield loved it; in his journal he recorded that "the little Lambs came and shook me by the hand one by one, and so we parted, and I scarce was ever better pleased in my Life."[20] Georgia historian Kenneth Coleman said of the incident, "Whitefield's mind was defi-

---

[18] Whitefield, *A Continuation*, 3.

[19] Whitefield, *A Continuation*, 3.

[20] Whitefield, *A Continuation*, 6.

nitely made up now. He must have little lambs of his own."[21] The cleric had already decided to start an orphanage; clearly, he was reassured by witnessing a successful one.

During August, Whitefield ventured to the south. He went to Frederica, a town greatly swelled in population by the five hundred men of Oglethorpe's regiment and their families. Then, he called on the Highlanders at Darien and the Reverend Mr. McLeod, their minister. Many of the Scots talked openly of quitting their frontier outpost in favor of Charlestown, where they had relatives.

After three month's observation, Whitefield was surprisingly generous in his opinion of Georgia and Georgians. He thought that, despite appearances, the infant colony might very well succeed. The Georgia experiment was still popular in England; Whitefield thought that he could easily raise money for an orphanage. "I was really happy in my little foreign cure, and could have cheerfully remained among them, had I not been obliged to return to England to receive priest's orders, and make a beginning toward laying a foundation to the Orphan-house."[22] Curiously, after succeeding in establishing himself as minister in Savannah, he would resign his ministry before returning to Georgia. Already he had formed larger views than Savannah. He meant not only to build and support an orphan house, but also to make a success of the colony of Georgia. He had already decided that the trustees' regulations would not work. The trustees were well intended, but impractical nonetheless. People were assigned land regardless of its potential for fertility, and women were not allowed to inherit property. By two acts of Parliament in 1735, rum and slaves were forbidden. "So that in reality, "Whitefield wrote, "the people there on such a footing was little better than to tie their legs and bid them walk."[23]

---

[21] Gillies, *Memoirs,* 32. Kenneth Coleman, *Colonial Georgia* (New York: Charles Scribners' Sons, 1976) 162.

[22] Gillies, *Memoirs,* 31.

[23] Gillies, *Memoirs,* 31.

Whitefield departed from Georgia on August 28, 1738, to the tearful good-byes of some of his flock. He left to James Habersham the responsibility of keeping the prayer meetings going in the Methodist manner, of taking in orphans at his Savannah school, and of preparing in any way he could to build a proper orphan house. Alexander Garden, commissary of the Church of England in Charlestown, greeted Whitefield warmly, sympathized with him about how badly John Wesley had been treated, and assured his guest of his support should Whitefield suffer the same treatment Wesley endured. These were nearly the last pleasant words that passed between the two. Whitefield sailed for England on September 8, 1738, and after a perilous crossing, landed in Ireland. From there he made his way to London, arriving on December 8, 1738.

So far in his Georgia ministry, Whitefield's affairs had proceeded smoothly, in contrast to John Wesley's contentious stay in Georgia. That happy frame of circumstances, however, came to an end shortly after the cleric's return to England. The Reverend William Norris, sent to Georgia by the trustees to replace Wesley, wrote the trustees soon after his arrival in Savannah to complain about James Habersham and his friends. Wesley had formed a group who called themselves "the faithful," and Whitefield enlarged it. James Habersham, in particular, found fault with Norris for not stressing the need for a spiritual rebirth. Norris thought it particularly bold of Habersham to wonder aloud whether Norris was saved. Norris thought "the faithful" were all guilty of spiritual pride.[24]

Another source of irritation to many members of the Church of England, including the Archbishop of Canterbury and the Bishop of London, was the recent publication of Whitefield's journal of his voyage to Georgia, in which he had made disparaging remarks about the clergy. After his arrival in London, several pastors refused to let him use their pulpits, and "some of the Clergy, if possible would oblige me to depart out of these Coasts," he wrote.[25] Previously, he had been

---

[24] Norris to Egmont, December 12, 1738, "Journal of the Earl of Egmont," *Colonial Records of Georgia*, 5:76–77.

[25] Henry, *George Whitefield*, 43.

the object of acclamation by throngs of people, but now every crowd included hecklers who denounced him as a pious fraud.

Lord Egmont and the gentlemen of Georgia Trust wondered about Whitefield when he indicated that he wanted to return to England after only three months on the job. Lord Egmont noted that "this resolution of returning so soon to England shows him of a roving temper."[26] Whatever else Whitefield might be accused of, he certainly *was* of a roving temper. Five days after reaching London, Whitefield paid a courtesy call on Lord Egmont at the office of the Georgia Trust. He spoke bluntly, as he usually did, noting that many people in Savannah ignored the trustees' prohibition of rum and were lewd in their behavior. At a subsequent meeting, he added that the Georgians were lazy and the people at outlying villages were "mere heathens." He even complained that Thomas Causton objected to his taking charge of orphan children above seven years of age. However, Whitefield had spoken to Colonel Oglethorpe on that matter and believed Oglethorpe sided with him.

All inconveniences aside, Whitefield was willing to return to Georgia if only the trustees would agree to certain conditions. He wanted a house and garden plot, and asked the trustees to reimburse him and his friend Delamotte for the cost of their travel. He also requested a letter from the trustees to the Bishop of London endorsing his ordination to the priesthood and his assignment to Savannah. Finally and most importantly, he wanted the trustees to commission him to go about the country to collect money for his favorite project: the orphan house. He made it clear that if he could solicit money, he would bear the full costs of the orphan house and its upkeep; in other words, the trustees would not need to pay so much as a shilling.[27]

The noble gentlemen of the trust must have marveled at the boldness of this son of a publican, a bit awed by his assurance. They agreed to his terms, but they could not give up final authority over the people of Georgia, including orphans. As the weeks passed, the trustees

---

[26] Egmont's "Journal," July 1, 1738, *CRG*, 5:45.
[27] Egmont's "Journal," December 13, 1738, *CRG*, 5:83.

must have felt that they were losing control of this particular Georgia clergyman. The trustees did as Whitefield wished, writing letters to the bishops, making out the commission for him to collect for the orphan house, and in due course, deeding him 500 acres for the precious orphan house.[28]

On January 17, 1739, Whitefield returned from Oxford, where the Bishop of Gloucester had ordained him to London to report that he had collected £46 for the orphans. By May 9, 1739, he surprised the trustees by announcing the collection of £700, and then he told the flabbergasted gentlemen that he was returning the commission they had given him to solicit funds. He told the trustees, as Lord Egmont noted, that "he was not able to collect a farthing by virtue of it, but rather that it everywhere met with contempt." Furthermore, he declined the £50 per year salary the trustees offered for his Savannah ministry.[29] We can only imagine the trustees' reaction: astonishment certainly, indignation probably. However tempted they might have been to dismiss the bold young cleric from their service, they refrained. He had become too much a celebrity. Besides, he had friends in Parliament and the trustees were desperately afraid that the Walpole administration would surrender Georgia to Spain in order to avert a war with that country, or at least that Parliament would withhold the annual subsidy for Georgia. So, Egmont bided his time, but he concluded in his journal that Whitefield wanted to be accountable to no one.[30]

Whether the preacher knew it or not, the trustees' commission performed an essential service for him. When the crown solicitor inquired of the trustees whether they had authorized Whitefield to go about collecting money for Georgia, they vouched for him. Otherwise, Whitefield would have been arrested and we would not be telling the story of Bethesda at all.

---

[28] Egmont's "Journal," May 2, 1739, *CRG*, 5:164.
[29] Egmont's "Journal," May 9, 1739, *CRG*, 5:166.
[30] Egmont's "Journal," May 9, 1739, *CRG*, 5:166.

A Sensation, Then a Revolution

In the process of collecting money for the orphans, Whitefield caused a religious revolution. Rather, first he created a sensation, *then* a revolution. There was the affair of St. Margaret's Church in Westminster on a Sunday in early February 1739. Whitefield attended service in the old church adjacent to Westminster Abbey, expecting to be called on to preach. However, the resident minister refused to allow the visitor in the pulpit. Then, some unruly members of the congregation locked the pastor in his pew and triumphantly conducted Whitefield to the pulpit. The publicity did little more than make Whitefield look like a bully.[31]

Next, there was the Bristol affair. Whitefield wondered why an invitation to preach there had been withdrawn. We can guess it was because Whitefield had said publicly that he could produce two cobblers who knew "more of true Christianity than all the Clergy in the City" of Bristol.[32] Whitefield complained to the dean of the Bristol clergy, yet received the equivalent of the modern "Don't call us, we'll call you" rejection. Whitefield wrote a letter to the Bishop of Bristol, asking, "What evil have I done?" He answered his own question in his journal: "It is not against the Orphan-house, but against me and my Doctrine, that their Enmity is levelled."[33]

Next came the revolution. With churches and pulpits denying him, Whitefield did the unprecedented: he spoke in the fields! On February 17, 1739, he went out with a friend named William Seward and preached to a gathering of about two hundred coal miners, most of whom had never heard a sermon before in their lives. Some of them were moved to tears, the tears causing white streaks on their blackened faces. Whitefield knew he had done something revolutionary by speaking outdoors without permission and extemporaneously. "Blessed be God. I have now broke the ice; I believe I never was more

---

[31] Henry, *George Whitefield,* 45–46.

[32] Henry, *George Whitefield,* 46.

[33] Whitefield, *Journal,* 1:28–29.

acceptable to my Master then when I was standing to teach those Hearers in the open Fields." The first open-air sermon resulted in a flood of invitations to speak in places other than churches. "I now preach to ten times more people than I should if I had been confined to the Churches," Whitefield noted.[34] No longer confined to buildings, his audiences numbered in the thousands.

Whitefield won another battle in this curious religious warfare when John Wesley joined him at Bristol and showed unusual courage in following his friend's example. "I could scarce reconcile myself at first to this strange way of preaching in the fields of which he set me an example on Sunday." Wesley wrote, "I should have thought the saving of souls almost a sin, if it had not been done in a church." Wesley reflected that the Sermon on the Mount was "one pretty remarkable incident of field-preaching."[35] On April 2, 1739, Wesley "submitted to be more vile" and preached to about 3,000 people on a hill outside of Bristol. Those were exciting days when John Wesley teamed with George Whitefield and Charles Wesley in preaching outdoors. All three emphasized the necessity of spiritual rebirth, insisting that without it, religion was a sham. The listeners grew to astonishing numbers. On June 14, 1739, as many as 14,000 gathered to hear Whitefield and Wesley. Soon, Wesley noticed another phenomenon when Whitefield preached: some people went into convulsions, moaning and crying aloud. Wesley recorded similar reactions to his own sermons, people quivering and quaking, some to the point of hysteria.[36]

An important difference between the two leaders of Methodism resides in their aspirations. Both hoped their messages would spur on conversion and salvation. Wesley, the organizer, formed lasting societies in the places he preached. Whitefield collected money for his orphan house. Wesley's legacy would be the Methodist Church, Whitefield would have Bethesda.

---

[34] Henry, *George Whitefield,* 48.

[35] Wesley, *Journal*, 177; Henry, *George Whitefield,* 177–78, 195.

[36] Henry, *George Whitefield,* 177–78, 195.

Whitefield's fame or notoriety attracted the attention of Lady Selina, Countess of Huntingdon, who had become a disciple of Benjamin Ingham, her brother-in-law. An aggressive Christian herself, she admired the courage as well as the piety of these Methodists. She had heard of Whitefield from Ingham and expressed support for the Itinerant as early as 1739, even before she met him. The Bishop of London had also heard about the Methodists, and as such, he issued a letter to the clergy, admonishing them to avoid extremism. He might have had Wesley in mind, and he was certainly thinking of Whitefield.[37]

While waiting in London for his ship to sail, Whitefield continued to attract crowds. The difference between this departure and the last is that many of the people demonstrated against him. George Whitefield was not perturbed. These disturbances could be attributed to the Devil's machinations. "My master makes me more than a conqueror," he wrote. Another reason for his satisfaction is that he had collected almost £1000 for his orphan house.[38]

On October 30, 1739, Whitefield and his party arrived at Philadelphia. His success in the experiment of open-air preaching in England led him to try the same technique in Philadelphia, preaching to crowds from the courthouse balcony for four nights in a row. Benjamin Franklin, a shrewd businessman, decided to exploit Whitefield's popularity by printing his sermons. Whitefield agreed.[39] Forbidden the pulpit in New York, Whitefield preached to crowds outside the city before moving on to Boston.

Benjamin Franklin heard Whitefield and felt moved—not to conversion, but to empty his pockets for the orphan house. His description of the occasion in his autobiography is quite familiar:

---

[37] Henry, *George Whitefield*, 44; Gillies, *Memoirs*, 42.

[38] Henry, *George Whitefield*, 50; Egmont's "Journal," May 30, 1739, *CRG*, 5:173.

[39] Frank Lambert, "Subscribing for Profits and Piety: The Friendship of Benjamin Franklin and George Whitefield," *William and Mary Quarterly*, 3rd sermon, 1/3 (July 1993): 529–54; Thomas P. Haviland, "Of Franklin, Whitefield, and the Orphans," 29/4 *Georgia Historical Quarterly*: 211–16.

> I happened soon after to attend one of his sermons, in the course of which I perceived he intended to finish with a collection, and I silently resolved he should get nothing from me. I had in my pocket a handful of copper money, three or four silver dollars, and five pestles in gold. As he proceeded, I began to soften, and concluded to give the coppers. Another stroke of his oratory made me ashamed of that, and determined to give the silver; and he finished so admirably that I empty'd my pocket wholly into the collector's dish, gold and all.[40]

Practical Ben Franklin wondered why Whitefield wanted to put his orphan house in an unpopulated frontier when he could build it in Philadelphia where there were plenty of orphans. Franklin argued with Whitefield openly on this issue, even as he offered to print the sermons of the evangelist. Whitefield agreed to the business transaction, but he never wavered in his commitment to Georgia. Perhaps surprisingly, he had taken a personal interest in making a success of the Georgia colony. It is interesting to notice that the epochal religious revival of which Whitefield was a chief instigator was a by-product of the subscription of funds for the orphan house. Whitefield was concerned with saving souls, of course, but his reason for canvassing the country was to build and staff the orphanage. Ben Franklin marveled at Whitefield's oratorical ability, pacing off the ground covered by the sound of Whitefield's captivating voice and calculating that 20,000 people could fit within earshot. Franklin wrote that the evangelist "tried indeed, sometimes to pray for my conversion, but never had the satisfaction of believing that his prayers were heard."[41]

---

[40] Haviland, "Of Franklin," 212.
[41] Haviland, "Of Franklin," 212.

The Great Awakening

The revolutionary feature of Whitefield's preaching, other than his not needing a church, was that he spoke extemporaneously. The established custom called for carefully researched and meditated written sermons. Even Jonathan Edwards, the Massachusetts divine who separately initiated a Great Awakening among his own listeners, spoke from notes. The idea of speaking from the heart appealed to the preachers of the Great Awakening. The old Puritan ministers stressed the necessity of a personal conversion, but they expected this experience to follow long intellectual preparation and to occur individually. The exciting aspect of the Great Awakening lay in the mass conversions that took place with practically no preparation. And, to make things even easier, the new preachers agreed with Whitefield on the "once saved, always saved" doctrine. Among others whom Whitefield met and encouraged during this initial thrust into the northern colonies were the Tennents, father William and sons William and Gilbert, all Presbyterian ministers.

Whitefield received so many gifts for the orphan house that he purchased a sloop to convey them to Savannah. Several persons who wanted to associate more closely with Whitefield went south aboard the vessel, newly named the *Savannah*. Among these recruits were 16-year-old Mary Bolton and her sister Rebecca. Their father, a Philadelphia merchant named Robert Bolton, admired Whitefield so much that he allowed his daughters to enroll in the as yet nonexistent orphan house. Whitefield even persuaded the father to start a school in Philadelphia.[42] The Reverend Jonathan Barber, a born-again congregational minister, volunteered his services and went to Georgia aboard the *Savannah*, arriving in December. Whitefield planned to employ Barber as spiritual director of the orphan house.

Whitefield bade farewell to the new members of his family as they set sail, and he made his way southward overland the better to save

---

[42] Erwin C. Surrency, "Whitefield, Habersham, and the Bethesda Orphanage,"34/2 *Georgia Historical Quarterly*, 94.

souls and raise money in the process. However, Whitefield found Maryland and Virginia disappointing. Women were "as much enslaved to their fashionable Diversions as Men to their Bottle and their Hounds." South Carolina ranked even lower, for there, he wrote, "they have many Ministers both of our own and other Persuasions, but I hear no stirring among the dry Bones." On January 10, 1740, he noted in his journal, "I am come to Georgia."[43]

The biggest single difference between Georgia in 1740 and the Georgia Whitefield had left in 1738 was the fact that Spain and England had gone to war with each other in the curiously named War of Jenkin's Ear.[44] James Oglethorpe welcomed the war as an opportunity to expand Georgia's boundary southward beyond the Altamaha. In fact, he spent most of 1739 preparing the defenses of Frederica and recruiting Indian allies. He had taken the unusual step of traveling overland to Coweta town on the Chattahoochee to cement an alliance with the Creek Nation. He knew that he had to contend against the intrigues of the Louisiana French. On November 16, 1739, Oglethorpe informed his colleagues of the Trust: "We are here resolved to die hard and will not lose one inch of ground without fighting." [45]In December 1739, Oglethorpe invaded Florida and captured a fort on the St. Johns River, leaving a garrison there before retiring to Frederica to prepare a larger invasion.

Habersham Finds the Right Place.

This war seemed a nuisance to George Whitefield, brought on by God's displeasure with the licentious living of certain persons in Savannah. He ignored it as best he could, allowing Oglethorpe to do the world's work while he devoted his attention to God's. Meanwhile,

[43] Henry, *George Whitefield*, 53.

[44] Coleman, *Colonial Georgia*, 63.

[45] Mills Lane, ed., *General Oglethorpe's Georgia*, 2 vols. (Savannah: The Beehive Press, 1975) 2:420–22.

James Habersham had done everything his friend could have expected. He had been instructed by Whitefield to "get boards" for the orphan house, but as he pointed out in a letter, Whitefield had not specified any essential details such as where to build, how large a house to scope out, even what size boards to use. Habersham had to use his own imagination and initiative. When he learned that the trustees had decided to allot 500 acres for the orphan house, he did not wait out the usual delays. Instead, he located a likely place on a backwater of the Vernon River, later known as Back River, about ten miles southwest of Savannah; then asked Oglethorpe to assign 500 acres there. Oglethorpe did so, making the grant to Habersham. The place was not as isolated as it might seem. The Vernon River offered easy access from the sea, and people had begun to settle nearby. The property abutted on William Stephens's plantation called Beaulieu (pronounced "Bewlie") on the Vernon River. Noble Jones, the surveyor, had established his residence across the Back River on the Isle of Hope. On the far side of the Vernon River, some French and German immigrants formed the Vernonburg settlement. [46]

Habersham borrowed £80 to begin clearing the land, fencing in a portion, planting a vegetable garden, and building a house. He hardly could have been more enterprising. Whitefield was surprised and pleased at the progress. The only feature he did not care for was that the 500-acre grant bore Habersham's name. He later had the trustees re-issue it in his own name. [47]

Habersham had been less successful in winning friends for the orphan house. William Stephens, as the trustees' resident secretary, kept his superiors posted. He tried to be fair. Habersham did a good job as schoolteacher, less so as a preacher. The little society formed by Wesley and nourished by Whitefield, who referred to themselves as "the Fraternity" or "the Faithful," too obviously considered them-

---

[46] Habersham to Whitefield, November 29, 1738, in *Minutes of the Union Society Being an Abstract of Existing Records from 1750 to 1858* (Savannah: John M. Cooper and Company, 1860) 21–22.

[47] Egmont's "Journal," January 28, 1740, *CRG*, 5:291–92.

selves saved and others not so. Stephens claimed they assumed "the power of opening and shutting the Gates of Heaven." If Habersham and his friends had limited themselves to ostracizing known sinners, of which Savannah had a sufficiency, they might not have been so controversial. But they also condemned the clergy, attacking specifically the Reverend William Norris, John Wesley's replacement, as pastor of the Savannah parish. When George Whitefield arrived in Savannah on January 10, 1740, Norris moved to Frederica where Oglethorpe invited him to go along on the invasion of Florida as chaplain.[48]

Until the orphan house could be occupied, the children lived in a rented house in Savannah. The new arrivals from Philadelphia, including the Bolton sisters and three little German children from nearby Highgate, raised the number of dependents to twenty. On January 24, Habersham showed Whitefield the property he had selected. Whitefield liked what he saw, not doubting in the least that God had inspired Habersham to choose this particular site. He noted in his journal on that date, "I called it Bethesda, that is the House of Mercy."[49] Now and evermore, the orphan house had a name. Its future residents might have been comforted by Whitefield's conviction that Providence inspired James Habersham to pick the location.

It is worth mentioning again that Whitefield thought of himself not only as the founder of a House of Mercy, but as a promoter—even as a founder—of the colony of Georgia. His commitment to Georgia is made clear in his letters and journal. A few days after visiting the site of the orphan house, he noted in his journal that he hoped the ambitious building program he had in mind would "make Savannah lift up her drooping head." To a friend he wrote, "God, I believe, is

---

[48] Henry, *George Whitefield,* 59; Egmont's "Journal," December 20 ,1738, *CRG*, 5:84.

[49] George Whitefield, *A Continuation of the Reverend Mr. Whitefield's Journal After His Arrival in Georgia until His Return thither from Philadelphia* (London: W. Strahan for James Hutton, 1741) 3–4.

laying a foundation for great things in Georgia."[50] He hired thirty artisans and others to begin work at the site and would have hired more if workers had been available. Already, after such a short sojourn, he had decided that the trustees' regulations threatened to drive people out of the colony. He considered the prohibition of slavery to be particularly damaging, echoing the prevailing belief among planters in South Carolina that plantation work required slaves. Whitefield later wrote about the desolate condition of the colony in the year 1740 and blamed it on the "badness of its constitution, which every day I expected would be altered." [51] Never very tactful, Whitefield wrote a letter to the Georgia Trustees, the lawful governors of the colony, to tell them that if it were not for his orphan house, its growing family, and the work it provided, Savannah would be deserted. He even chided the trustees for not providing a parsonage—not to mention the fact that he had to buy candles himself for church services. He added a threat that "if the affairs of Religion were not better regarded, he should be obliged to inform the world how little is to be seen for all the money good people contributed." Lord Egmont considered the latter statement "an impudent paragraph, tending to blame the trustees for want of religion." [52]

Whitefield chose not to wait for the completion of the orphan house to begin recruiting children. He rented a large house in Savannah for an amount he considered exorbitant as a temporary lodging for the dependents he brought down from Pennsylvania and New England. On January 18, 1740, he took in his first Georgia orphans, Richard and Elizabeth Milledge, who were passengers on the historic first voyage to Georgia aboard the *Ann* and whose father had died several years before. He began an aggressive canvass for children in February, convinced that his authority to manage an orphanage included jurisdiction over the children of Georgia. On February 4, 1740, he

---

[50] George Whitefield, *A Select Collection of Letters of the Late Reverend George Whitefield M.A.* (London: Edward and Charles Dilly, 1772) 1:150.

[51] Gillies, *Memoirs,* 45.

[52] Egmont's "Journal," 28 January 1740, *CRG,* 5:291.

wrote a friend that he thought he could take in fifty children in the near future. [53] Of course, he soon became involved in a controversy that distracted the attention of James Oglethorpe from his imminent invasion of Florida.

---

[53] Whitefield to Rev. Mr. D. R., February 4, 1740, *A Select Collection*, 1:149.

Chapter Two

A Seminary of Methodists

On February 11, George Whitefield set out for Frederica in order to pay his respects to General Oglethorpe and, as he put it, "to collect more orphans."[1] The dignified Oglethorpe, who saw the need for an orphanage even before Whitefield's arrival, received the minister graciously and wished him success. Whitefield returned to Savannah, recruiting a few orphans at the Scottish settlement of Darien along the way, and Oglethorpe went to Charlestown on a recruiting mission of his own. He needed a regiment of Carolina militia for his impending invasion of Florida. When he returned to Frederica, busy with a host of details, he learned that Whitefield had taken children from homes where they had been well cared for. The case in point concerned Richard and Elizabeth Milledge, ages thirteen and twelve, who lived with an older brother and sister. Oglethorpe knew the brother, John Milledge, eighteen years old and a cadet in Oglethorpe's service. When John Milledge complained to Oglethorpe, the general agreed with him and ordered the two children to be returned to their home, explaining to the trustees that, in his opinion, orphans who had adequate care should not be delivered over to Mr. Whitefield against their will. The trustees agreed with him.[2]

George Whitefield, however, took issue with Oglethorpe and the trustees. He sometimes forgot that his legal authority over the orphans, in fact, came from the trustees; he usually considered God his

---

[1] George Whitefield, *A Continuation of the Reverend Mr. Whitefield's Journal after His Arrival at Georgia to a Few Days after His Second Return Thither from Philadelphia* (London: W. Strahan for James Hutton, 1741) 6; Whitefield to Trustees, March 10, 1740, *CRG*, 358–60.

[2] Egmont, *Journal*, April 2, 1740, *CRG*, 5:330.

authority. When he received orders from Oglethorpe's messenger to send the Milledge children home, he told the man that they already were at home in his house "and he knew no other Home they had to go to." He instructed the messenger to give that answer to the general. John Milledge bided his time. When Whitefield left Savannah, John took his brother and sister away from the temporary orphanage in Savannah. When he discovered what had happened, Whitefield wrote an angry letter to the trustees about the whole affair. Lord Egmont called in an "invective" against Oglethorpe, while Whitefield further annoyed the gentlemen of the trust by threatening to transfer his orphanage to Pennsylvania and by telling the trustees not to bother sending a minister to Savannah.[3]

The flurry of complaints by and complaints about Whitefield caused Lord Egmont to call a special meeting of the trustees to decide what to do about the contentious cleric. Mr. Burton said it was clear that Whitefield meant to be completely independent, that in taking care of orphans, "he meant only to breed them up Methodist." Mr. Digby said that it was unforgivable that he should write so "saucily" to his superiors. Egmont blamed Whitefield's "youth, inexperience, un-mannerly education, and indiscreet Zeal." He confessed to his journal that he "was willing to excuse the fool the best I could" because he did not want to lose the orphan house.[4] For the time being, the trustees deferred taking any action. For one thing, they needed Parliament's support in defending Georgia against Spain, and they knew all too well that Whitefield had several admirers in Parliament. They hated to imagine the damage Whitefield could cause if he so chose.

It wasn't only with Oglethorpe and the trustees that Whitefield quarreled. When he went to Charlestown in March to meet his brother, a sea captain, Commissary Alexander Garden received him coolly. Whitefield recorded their remarkable conversation. He understood, he said, that Garden wanted to ask certain questions. The commissary, growing more heated as he talked, charged his guest with

---

[3] Egmont, *Journal*, May 19, 1740, *CRG*, 352.
[4] Egmont, *Journal*, April 16, 1740, 332–35.

"Enthusiasm and Pride." Why, he wanted to know, did Whitefield denounce his fellow clergymen of the Church of England? Whitefield blandly replied that he had scarcely begun to denounce them. Why, what had they done? Whitefield answered that they failed to preach justification by faith alone. Whitefield believed that Garden was as ignorant as the rest and implied as much. In a rage, Garden forbade Whitefield any pulpit in his jurisdiction. Whitefield calmly replied that he would obey that as readily as he would orders from the pope of Rome.

Having defied the highest-ranking churchman in the colony, Whitefield then reproached Garden for not denouncing the frequent "Assemblies and Balls" in Charlestown. Garden objected to being catechized, but managed to reply that he saw no harm in social gatherings. "Then, Sir," said Whitefield, "I shall think it my Duty to exclaim against you." Thereupon, the exasperated Reverend Commissary told the preacher to get out of his house.[5]

It was typical of Whitefield to arouse such indignation while remaining secure in the knowledge of his own righteousness. He left the interview, as he noted in his journal, "pitying the Commissary." He had thought his superior above such behavior. Alexander Garden did his best to silence Whitefield. The South Carolina ecclesiastical court decided that Whitefield violated canon law and suspended him from his clerical privileges. Whitefield paid no attention to the court's decree, but Whitefield and the orphan house had thenceforth to contend with one more redoubtable enemy. Garden printed a scathing critique of the "crude Enthusiactick Notions...now revived and propagated by Mr. Whitefield and his Brethren Methodists." Whitefield's sermons contained "Truth and Falsehood Sense and Nonsense." Garden believed that the enchanting sound of Whitefield's voice swayed weak minds.[6]

---

[5] Whitefield, *Journal*, 2:10–11.

[6] Alexander Garden, *Regeneration and the Testimony of the Spirit* (Charlestown: Peter Timothy, 1740); Boston *News and Courier*, February 4, 1901, clipping in Bethesda Archives; Stuart C. Henry, *George Whitefield Wayfaring Witness* (New York: Abingdon Press, 1957) 141.

During March, Whitefield informed the trustees that he had the care of forty children in the rented house in Savannah. They had settled into a routine, though not yet as monastic as they would experience at Bethesda. They attended school four or five hours a day and did their lessons for Mr. Habersham. The rest of the day they worked and prayed. Whitefield liked to stress the value of his home to the colony of Georgia. He provided work for over forty artisans out at Bethesda, and in Savannah, his school trained future "Planters and Mechanicks."[7]

The First Brick

March 24, 1740, proved to be a minor landmark in Bethesda's history. On that day, Whitefield, his extended "family," and the many workers gathered at Bethesda for the ceremony of the laying of the first brick for the great house. Twenty acres had been cleared for planting, two small houses constructed, the timber sawed, and the foundation dug. Whitefield informed Howell Harris at Treveca in Wales, "God, I believe, is laying a foundation for great things in Georgia." He wrote his Methodist colleague Benjamin Ingham on March 28 that the orphan house only prospered while the colony itself declined.[8]

Whitefield regarded his creative impulses as heaven-sent inspirations. Among others during the Spring 1740, perhaps the most surprising was his decision that the still unfinished Bethesda would become a university. Very late in his career, he returned to this objective, but clearly he had it in mind all along, intending Bethesda to be a university of learning as well as a house of mercy. He seemed to face the

---

[7] Whitefield to Trustees, March 10, 1740, *CRG*, 2:358–60.

[8] Whitefield to Howell Harris, February 4, 1740; Whitefield to Rev. Benjamin Ingham, March 28, 1780, *A Select Collection of Letters of the Late George Whitefield, M.A.* (London: Edward and Charles Dilly, 1772) 1:150, 158.

reality at the very beginning that there would never be enough orphans to make his home viable.[9]

Whitefield described yet another inspiration in his letter to Ingham: "I believe it is God's will I should marry." He made it clear that he himself did not require a wife; in fact, he explained that he did not want to have a wife unless he could live as he though he had none. Within the month of this expressed thought, he wrote out a proposal that must have seemed strange to the lady he had in mind: Elizabeth Delamotte. He explained in his letter to her parents that he was "free from that foolish passion which the world calls love." However, Bethesda needed a mistress "to take off some of that care which at present lies upon me." Then he wrote directly to the young lady herself, promising only "to keep my matrimonial vow, and do what I can towards helping you forward in the great work of your salvation." Evidently, Miss Delamotte was completely "underwhelmed," so to speak, by the great preacher's proposal, so much that she declined. Whitefield confided to a friend that the lady must have lacked faith: "Surely that will not do. I would have one that is full of faith."[10]

On March 20, 1740, Whitefield noted in his journal that "Providence calls me toward the Northward." With nearly a hundred mouths to feed, he had to embark again on a fund-raising, soul-saving tour. He actually made two forays into the north country, both aboard his sloop the *Savannah*. He left Georgia with William Seward as his companion on April 2, spoke to thousands in Pennsylvania and New York, and returned to Savannah on June 5, 1740. He left again on August 17 for a four-month tour of New England and was back in Savannah by December 13, 1740.[11]

---

[9] Whitefield to James Habersham, June 7, 1740, *Select Collection*, 1:184–85.

[10] Whitefield to Benjamin Ingham, March 28, 1740; Whitefield to Mr. and Mrs. Delamotte, April 4, 1740, *Select Collection*, 1:158–60; Henry, *Wayfaring Witness*, 74.

[11] Whitefield, *Journal*, 2:14, 52; *A Continuation of the Reverend Mr. Whitefield's Journal from a few days after his Return to Georgia to his Arrival at Falmouth on the 11th of March 1741* (London: W. Strahan for R. Hitt, 1741) 13, 77.

The Great Itinerant

It is difficult for moderns to appreciate the impact George Whitefield made wherever he went. He stirred emotions of all kinds and degrees: excitement, consternation, fear, exhilaration, hope, dread—the whole gamut, we might say. He strove for an emotional reaction in his listeners, insisting that only in the supreme emotion of spiritual rebirth could they find salvation. According to him, they would *know* they were saved because they would *feel* that they were saved. This kind of preaching, this preying on the emotions—outdoors and extempore alike—stirred the Great Awakening in the American colonies even as Whitefield's colleagues stoked the fires in Britain. For his central role in the Great Awakening, George Whitefield is known in history as "the Great Itinerant" and the "Awakener."

We can glimpse the reaction of the regular clergy in letters addressed to the bishop of London, who had jurisdiction over American affairs, correspondence now housed in the Lambeth Palace Library, London. One letter, written on May 9, 1740, by a worried cleric, reported that Whitefield "who is the occasion of much debate and inquiry among us is expected the next Fall." He wanted to know how to behave toward Whitefield. Another correspondent described Whitefield's reception in Boston on December 1740. When the great preacher landed in Rhode Island, crowds gathered along his route. Preachers of the congregational churches announced his coming, calling him "the Wonder of the Age." He wore his clerical gown while in Boston, and "while he was here little business was done; people were always flocking towards him." Thousands gathered to listen to him speak; in fact, on one occasion 20,000 people heard him![12]

Perhaps we have cited enough of the correspondence to make the point that anyone who could put a stop to business in Boston, where

---

[12] Roger Price to Bishop Gibson, May 9, 1740, Fulham Papers V, 259; Timothy Cutler to Bishop Gibson, 5 December 1740, Fulham Papers V, 269–70.

the pursuit of money was frantic and incessant, surely must have been the wonder of the age. George Whitefield felt convinced that many souls were saved through his mediation. Historians recognize that the course of American religious history was radically altered by his efforts. In Whitefield's wake, self-appointed preachers, some without education or training, set out to rouse people into salvation. The message appealed to frontier people who had no time for learning and lived far from any churches. The message that the feeling generated by a fiery preacher meant that they were saved once and for all brought great comfort. "New light" congregations multiplied as Baptists, Methodists, and Presbyterians espoused the Great Awakening. For those who are following the history of Bethesda, one line in the letter cited above stands out: "He always reminded us of the Orphan House at Georgia, and obtained a collection in one place and another of above £3000 this currency." To stop business and to collect £3000 from Bostonians was more so the marvel.[13]

After his triumphant visit to Boston, Whitefield traveled to Northhampton, Massachusetts, to pay his respects to Jonathan Edwards, whose description of the stirrings of the Spirit in his own congregation Whitefield had read. The Congregational minister Edwards and the Anglican priest Whitefield admired each other hugely. Edwards, famous in American religious history for making his hearers weep with emotion, cried himself when Whitefield preached. Whitefield doubly admired Mrs. Edwards. He considered her the ideal wife, possessing the twin virtues of piety and meekness. Witnessing the happy couple, Whitefield renewed his prayers to God to select a proper mate for himself. The spontaneous Whitefield and the intellectual Edwards, the two giants of the Great Awakening, would have created a sensation if they had teamed up, as Whitefield and Wesley had done in England. But Edwards was not an itinerant, and besides, Whitefield needed no help in causing a sensation. After they parted on October 20, 1740, Whitefield and Edwards never met again.[14]

---

[13] Timothy Cutler to Bishop Gibson, 5 December 1740, Fulham Papers V, 269–70.

[14] Henry, *Wayfaring Witness*, 66.

Georgia historians have paid scant attention to Whitefield's campaign through New England because James Oglethorpe's military campaign through Spanish Florida happened at the same time. In May the general invaded Florida with a formidable force composed of five hundred men of his own regiment, the Scots of Darien, five hundred Carolinians, and about a thousand Indians. When the Spaniards refused to come out of the Castillo de San Marco, Oglethorpe began a lengthy siege. Unfortunately, a Spanish force staged a surprise night attack on Fort Mosa, to the west of town where the Scots were posted and killed or captured most of them. It was a crippling blow to Oglethorpe and an equally devastating one to Darien. In the absence of their fathers, several Darien children went to live at the orphan house in Savannah, among them Lachlan McIntosh and his sister Ann. The South Carolinians went home, grumbling about Oglethorpe's mismanagement of the campaign, and by the end of July, Oglethorpe and his regiment were back at Frederica, expecting a Spanish counterattack.[15]

The only bright spot in an otherwise dismal year for Georgia was Bethesda, and Whitefield seemed almost jubilant. "I really believe Savannah will yet become the Joy of the Earth," he noted in his journal on June 6, 1740. He had brought volunteers from the north to teach and supervise the children. They worked industriously at their studies, they spun and wove cotton, went on walks, sang hymns, and overall, behaved in an edifying manner. Whitefield managed to see a benefit in Oglethorpe's war; he believed the Lord was "purging the Province apace." On June 27, he added, "Providence seems to smile upon the Orphan House."[16] The occasion for his remark introduces to this story Jonathan Bryan, already a "wealthy, moral civiliz'd" South Carolina planter, as Whitefield noted, and a major figure in Georgia's colonial history. Jonathan Bryan's career has been well documented in a biography by historian Allen Galley. Bryan and his brother Hugh became Bethesda's most generous benefactors. When the Spanish

[15] Coleman, *Colonial Georgia* (New York: Charles Scribners Sons, 1976) 66–67.

[16] Whitefield, *Journal*, 2:55.

threatened to invade Georgia, for instance, the Bryans gave refuge to the children and staff. They also purchased a plantation for Whitefield in South Carolina to produce income for Bethesda. When slavery became legal in Georgia, Jonathan Bryan selected land for a plantation and secured slaves to work it. Hugh Bryan even donated a canoe and, when called on, counseled Whitefield on legal matters, including the purchase and sale of land.[17]

We will have occasion to wonder why Whitefield, the personification of a committed Christian, would argue for the introduction of slaves into Georgia and purchase slaves himself. While we can understand his line of reasoning, few people today would agree. However, it should be noted that, to his credit, he strove to awaken the conscience of planters regarding their treatment of slaves, going so far as to write an open letter to planters warning them of God's wrath if they did not evangelize their slaves. Hugh Bryan, in the first fervor of one newly reborn, outdid Whitefield. His letter of November 20, 1740, published in the *South Carolina Gazette*, blamed all of Carolina's ills—including the slave uprising of 1739, a recent drought, and the failure of Oglethorpe's campaign in Florida—on the sins of the people generally and on an unregenerate clergy specifically. He inveighed against the false leaders among the clergy and insisted on their being reborn as a qualification for preaching. Whitefield's bland admission that he had seen and approved Bryan's letter stoked the ire of Alexander Garden.[18]

James Habersham, the schoolmaster, also overstepped the bounds of decorum in an attempt to emulate the master. In the Itinerant's absence, Habersham conducted morning and afternoon church

---

[17] Alan Gallay, *The Formation of a Planter Elite: Jonathan Bryan and the Southern Colonial Frontier* (Athens: University of Georgia Press, 1989) 41; George Whitefield, *An Account of Money Received and Disbursed for the Orphan House in Georgia* (London: W. Strahan, 1741) 32.

[18] Hugh Bryan to a friend, November 20, 1740, *South Carolina Gazette*, Fulham Papers X:64; Alexander Garden to Bishop Gibson, July 30, 1741, Fulham Papers X, 86–87. Hugh Bryan became the laughing stock of Charlestown by attempting to divide the waters of a river as Moses had done the Red Sea; Garden chortled at the spectacle of "the famous Hugh Bryan sousing himself into the River Jordan in order to smite and divide its waters." Boston *News and Courier*, February 4, 1901, Bethesda Archives.

services in Savannah. To Whitefield, the graceful gesture, the dramatic posture, the wonderfully cadenced delivery came naturally and never failed to produce the effect he intended. Habersham, on the other hand, preached like someone doing a poor imitation of Whitefield. The puzzled William Stephens tried to describe the performance: "He affected a vehement Emphasis, frequently in the wrong place, too; and turning himself to and fro in several Postures towards different Parts of the Congregation, many people looked upon it as ridiculous."[19] Ridiculous it may have appeared; sincere it certainly was. James Habersham took his religion very seriously. As Whitefield's surrogate at the family's big rented house in Savannah, he worried about the effect of many of the townspeople's examples. In October he made a mature and responsible decision. He would not wait for the Itinerant's return from his second trip northward; in fact, he did not know when Whitefield would return to Georgia. So, on November 3, 1740, he moved the family to Bethesda. Did Whitefield feel a twinge of disappointment that Habersham had not waited for him? Master of the dramatic that he was, he would have turned the short trek into a biblical exodus with Bethesda as the New Jerusalem. Instead, the historic occupation happened without the master and without fanfare.

Whitefield arrived soon afterwards and spent a happy Christmas at Bethesda with his large family. The highlight of the season was the marriage of James Habersham, age twenty-seven, and Mary Bolton—formerly of Philadelphia—age sixteen, with the Reverend Whitefield officiating. Dependable, hard-working, pious James Habersham found in his student the kind of wife George Whitefield had been praying for, a woman both virtuous and clever. The marriage produced ten children, among them three remarkable sons, all of them revolutionary war patriots and one of them a member of President George Washington's cabinet.[20]

---

[19] James Ferris Cann, "Bethesda Its Founders: A Historical Sketch," *Minutes of the Union Society* (Savannah: John M. Couper and Company, 1860) 22.

[20] Whitefield, *Journal,* 3:77; W. Calvin Smith, "The Habershams: The Merchant Experience in Georgia," *Forty Years of Diversity: Essays on*

George Whitefield's Bethesda as it was planned in 1740. (Courtesy Georgia Historical Society.)

We Are All Removed to Bethesda

George Whitefield provided a detailed description of Bethesda in its first year of existence outside Savannah. His description, later printed and circulated throughout Britain and America, was intended to reassure his donors and silence critics who claimed he kept the funds he collected. "We are now all removed to Bethesda," he wrote. He went on to say how they lived in the outlying houses until the great house could be completed. As of the close of the year 1740, the building still needed about two months work on the interior. The house measured sixty feet by forty, contained sixteen "commodious" rooms and a ten-foot wide porch (or piazza) around the building. The house would have been furnished sooner if the Spanish had not taken a schooner

---

Colonial Georgia, eds. Harvey H. Jackson and Phinizy Spalding (Athens: University of Georgia Press, 1984) 198–216.

loaded with ten thousand bricks intended for chimneys as a prize of war. In addition to the main house, four framed houses also had been built, as well as a combination of stable and carriage house. Twenty acres of land had been cleared and a road laid out from Savannah to Bethesda.[21]

Whitefield counted forty-nine children under his care at Bethesda, twenty-three English, ten Scots, four Dutch, five French, and seven "Americans." (His use of the term Americans to distinguish those born in the colonies from the English, must have been among the earliest uses of that differentiation.) Twenty-two children had neither father nor mother, twenty-four had only one parent, and three—perhaps including the Bolton sisters—paid their own way. From the beginning, Bethesda has cared for children with at least one parent, even though they are not "true" orphans. The diversity of nationalities is a reminder of the multi-ethnic nature of colonial Georgia. Another characteristic of the Home throughout its existence is its revolving-door approach to operations. Children might stay a month, a year, or several years. Whitefield placed two boys in Savannah before he left the orphanage, one with a bricklayer, the other with a carpenter. One lad assisted the orphan house surgeon, one operated a loom, two worked at tailoring. Anyone deemed to be "sanctified"—that is, to have experienced a spiritual rebirth—Whitefield intended for the ministry. The Home housed girls as well as boys. Two or three had learned to spin, and several to knit. Girls were expected to do the house cleaning; Whitefield called it learning "Housewifery." Boys and girls alike picked cotton and did outside chores. Although the children were trained for specific jobs, Whitefield's first concern was "to build up Souls for God." He himself taught catechism during the intervals he spent with the children. He noticed that the girls especially seemed "tender-hearted," which led him to hope that the seed of grace had been sown in their hearts.[22]

Whitefield's family included the staff and workers: James Habersham; the superintendent and his wife; two schoolmasters and

[21] Whitefield, *An Account of Money*, 2–3.
[22] Whitefield, *An Account of Money*, 3–5.

their wives, who also taught; the surgeon and his wife; a shoemaker and seamstress; laborers and hired servants. In all, he had eighty persons to care for. The farm was stocked with two hundred hogs and one hundred heads of cattle. Whitefield employed a man and an assistant to tend to the livestock. His hired men and the older children could not manage more than twenty acres under cotton cultivation, and that amount would not produce a profit. He had determined, and would soon tell the trustees to their face, that Georgia needed the help of Negro labor.

An intriguing comment made in passing in Whitefield's description of Bethesda was that "in my Absence, when my family had little or no Provisions, the Indians brought in Plenty of Deer."[23] The Indians must have come sometime after the move to Bethesda on November 3 and Whitefield's return on December 10, 1740, so Bethesda had a Thanksgiving reminiscent of the Indians supplying the Pilgrims at Plymouth. The Indians likely belonged to Tomochichi's Yamacraw band. Though the old chieftain had died in 1739, his nephew had met Whitefield and lived close enough to be aware of Bethesda's needs. The event has entered into local lore and boys dressed like Indians have re-enacted the scene in 20th-century pageants at Bethesda.

James Habersham's careful account of receipts and expenditures appeared in print as an appendix to Whitefield's commentary. By the end of 1740, the orphan house had cost over £3150,[24] the entire amount having come from donations. That fact is witness enough to Whitefield's rare powers of persuasion. As he left Georgia, he noted that he was several hundred pounds in personal debt, but he relied on the Lord to supply Bethesda's needs. Having collected twice in the northern colonies, Whitefield returned to England in 1741 to raise more money. The incessant demand for funds forced him into a continual itinerancy. Because he sustained Bethesda by his tireless solicitations, Whitefield's activities are an integral part of our story.

---

[23] Whitefield, *An Account of Money*, 3–5.
[24] Whitefield, *An Account of Money*, 41.

The removal from Savannah to Bethesda fostered the separation Whitefield's followers had always sought. To the intangible, or spiritual, separation—the eternal separation of the saved from the damned—the relocation meant a physical separation from Savannahians. The problem with those who believe firmly that they are saved is that they often manage to infuriate those they regard as unregenerate and, as such, on their way to Hell. The addition to the staff of the new spiritual director, Reverend Jonathan Barber, a Presbyterian minister who accompanied Whitefield to Georgia in December 1740, injected an added fervor to the prevalent spirit at Bethesda.

The feeling of being beleaguered by sinister forces is evident in James Habersham's letters, even as he related good news to his friend Whitefield. On June 11, 1741, he wrote to Whitefield that the boys had moved into the house; that the children had made the bed sheets they were using; that they expected a plentiful crop; and that their benefactors, the Bryans, intended to procure a plantation in Carolina in Bethesda's name. However, counterbalancing these happy prospects, "Satan rages furiously against this Institution in this Province." By contrast, away from Savannah, "We live in love."[25] Habersham reflected the opinion of the residents of Bethesda; theirs was a holy place, if not quite a monastery, in the midst of a hostile world. Despite the controversy he caused, Whitefield exerted a calming influence when he resided at Bethesda. With him gone, the leaders became more frantic in their zeal than they would have been with Whitefield there. Habersham alone would not have felt so alienated from Savannah; in a few years he would be Savannah's leading merchant. Meanwhile, the Reverend Jonathan Barber, the spiritual director, set the tone. Barber resembled the Old Testament prophet: intense, grim, severe. While he directed the religious life of the family, the prevailing mood was one of tense anxiety. On the other hand, Joseph Periam, the schoolteacher, set the example of exaggerated enthusiasm. When first converted by

---

[25] Habersham to Whitefield, June 11, 1741, *A Continuation of the Account of the Orphan House in Georgia, January 1741 to June 1742* (Edinburgh: T. Lumesden, 1742) 8.

Whitefield in England, he prayed so loudly "as to be heard four story high."[26] Because he continued to behave erratically, the authorities shut him up in Bethlehem Hospital, better known as "Bedlam." Whitefield heard of his plight and had Periam released from the madhouse on the condition that he would take him to Georgia, entrusting him with the care of little children. Since then, Periam had found a wife and Whitefield had performed a double wedding ceremony for Periam and Habersham at Christmas before leaving Georgia.

To illustrate the kind of discipline the Reverend Barber demanded, we introduce the Tondee brothers to our story. Peter Tondee is one of the better known colonial Georgians because the Georgia patriots many years later gathered at his tavern to protest British taxation. In his first canvass for orphans in February 1740, George Whitefield recruited sixteen-year-old Peter and ten-year-old Charles. The boys had a good home with Henry Parker, and Peter was really old enough to take care of himself. Henry Parker made the same complaint to the trustees that John Milledge did, namely that children who had good homes should not go to the orphan house against their wishes. Peter spent almost a year helping the master carpenter James Papot build Bethesda. The trustees ordered Whitefield to allow Peter to return to Parker, and in December of 1740, Whitefield did so. When Whitefield mentioned in his published expense account that he had apprenticed one of his orphans to a carpenter, he meant Peter Tondee and James Papot.[27]

Many of the Bethesda children responded fervently to Reverend Barber's exhortations. Barber collected letters from the children to demonstrate their progress in holiness and sent them to Whitefield, who promptly published them. Among the letters was one from Mary Bolton Habersham's sister, Rebecca, who expressed gratitude that God had not already sent her to hell; two other girls wrote the same

[26] Henry, *Wayfaring Witness*, 50.

[27] Carl Weeks makes the point that Whitefield deferred releasing Peter until the great house was built; Carl Solana Weeks, *Savannah in the Time of Peter Tondee* (Columbia: Summerhouse Press, 1997) 69.

sentiment. Meanwhile, two boys were worried about the Devil devouring them like a roaring lion, while young Lachlan McIntosh, although he believed he had not yet been converted, felt the Lord knocking at his heart. As Carl Weeks described the episode in his fine biography of Peter Tondee, "[T]he only sentiment universally shared was a protest of unworthiness—your dutiful and unworthy child, your unworthy Boy, your unworthy servant—and William Bradley flirted perilously with pride by declaring himself the Unworthiest." Historian Kenneth Coleman suggests that the "remarkable similarity in content" means that Barber and Habersham might have orchestrated the letter-writing as a contest in edification.[28] Whitefield thoroughly approved of the contents of the letters, as evidenced by the fact that he published them. He strongly believed that a sense of one's wickedness was prerequisite to receiving God's saving grace. In fact, he agreed with the children's low opinion of themselves. He wrote Rebecca Bolton, Mary's little sister, "You may well wonder the God has not sent you to hell long ago." Whitefield was even more severe with "Mary A": "You may see what a poor wretch you are, how proud, how earthly, how sensual, how devilish."[29]

The desired result of this kind of self-deprecation was that the despairing would experience a spiritual rebirth. Joseph Periam, the same who spent time in Bedlam, witnessed a group conversion among the children. They were out in the field picking cotton, he wrote Whitefield, when one of the orphans proclaimed, "If we do not believe in the Lord Jesus Christ, we shall all go to Hell." One after the other fell to the ground, crying out. Other members of the family gathered around and prayed while the children continued to exclaim for "an Hour or two." Clearly, the children followed Periam's example of very "vocal" public praying.[30]

Charles Tondee, age thirteen, was not one of the letter-writers or one of the visibly moved children in the cotton field. Instead, he wrote a letter to Henry Parker complaining of harsh treatment. Parker, like

[28] Coleman, *Colonial Georgia*, 167; Weeks, *Peter Tondee*, 75.
[29] Henry, *Wayfaring Witness*, 88.
[30] Henry, *Wayfaring Witness*, 88–89.

many other parents and guardians, thought the child probably deserved the punishment he received. And, unfortunately for Charles, the Reverend Barber learned about the letter to Parker and called Charles in for chastisement. He struck the boy repeatedly with a rod from his shoulders to his knees, threatening to repeat the punishment if Charles refused to retract his complaint. The boy retracted, but at first opportunity, he ran away to Henry Parker at the nearby Isle of Hope. When William Stephens saw Charles Tondee two weeks later, the boy's lacerations still had not healed. Stephens wrote the trustees that the boy had been treated like a common criminal, stripped to the waist and lashed repeatedly, "[w]hereby his whole Back, Shoulders, Loins, Flank, and Belly were in a dreadful Condition."[31] The magistrates reprimanded Barber, but he denied their right to meddle in Bethesda's affairs, arguing that Bethesda was subject only to God's jurisdiction. It would be almost a year before the authorities began to carry out the trustees' order to inspect Bethesda for other incidents of mistreatment.

Clearly, an adversarial relationship between Bethesda and the town had developed by the time Whitefield's successor as resident minister to Savannah arrived. The trustees selected young Christopher Orton for the Savannah post on July 25, 1741. Orton was ordained in St. James Chapel, London. He seemed to be the gentle, inoffensive kind of person who would not make enemies easily. As Lord Egmont noted in his journal, "He seemed a good natured, harmless young man, but always on the smile, as if tickled with the thought of being Minister of a Parish." Egmont worried that Orton might be too gentle for faction-wracked Georgia. He finished his note, "I wish he may keep his Smiles when he comes here."[32]

With Orton on the *Loyal Judith* were two others who became involved in future controversies. John Dobell, a disenchanted former follower of Whitefield's who was newly appointed schoolteacher in Savannah, and Thomas Bosomworth, named clerk to William Stephens. Orton stopped smiling soon after taking up his duties in

[31] Weeks, *Peter Tondee*, 75–76.
[32] Egmont, *Journal*, September 10, 1741, *CRG*, 5:543.

Savannah when Barber, Habersham, and Joseph Hunter (the surgeon at Bethesda) accosted him, insisting flatly that he was no Christian, and it was their duty to warn their friends not to listen to him.[33]

The Savannah magistrates defended Orton. William Stephens explained the situation to the trustees in his report of February 4, 1742. Orton, he wrote, "behaved unexceptionally well to all, and done the Duties of his office with great Decorum and Diligence." However, he added, "were he an angel from Heaven, the Distractions about religion, which our Methodists have been so zealously fomenting, would stir 'em up to oppose him." Orton himself considered the Methodists rude and un-Christian and believed that many were turning against them. Newcomer Thomas Bosomworth demonstrated as much enthusiasm in criticizing Barber and the others as they did in preaching their message. After denouncing the Methodists to the trustees as "Desperadoes" who were "immers'd in the bottomless Gulph of Spiritual Pride and Obstinacy," Bosomworth reached new heights of unintelligible invective; the Methodists were, he said, "trasonical, vain-glorious Diotrepheses."[34] Bosomworth informed Stephens that he did not care to be his clerk; instead, he returned to England to be ordained. He would return after ordination and become better known as the husband of Coosaponakeesa, whom the Georgians knew as Oglethorpe's interpreter, Mary Musgrove. William Stephens considered Bosomworth an eccentric, "the Mercury being not yet well fixed."[35]

Magistrates Henry Parker and John Fallowfield arrested Barber and Habersham for harassing Orton and disturbing the peace. After a week in jail, the jury found them guilty, and they had to pay a token fine. George Whitefield complained to the trustees about the treatment of his people and asked to have his own magistrates at Bethesda. The trustees declined the request.[36]

---

[33] Whitefield to Trustees, August 17, 1742, *CRG*, 23:391–95.

[34] William Stephens to Trustees, February 4, 1742; Orton to Trustees, March 10, 1742; Bosomworth to Trustees, March 10, 1742, *CRG*, 23:201–221, 228–30, 231–50.

[35] Stephens to Trustees, June 9, 1742, *CRG*, 23:346–51.

[36] Whitefield to Trustees, March 17, 1742, *CRG*, 23:391–95.

Christopher Orton did not live long enough to witness the end of the controversy between Bethesda and Savannah. He died in October 1742. John Dobell, the schoolmaster, called him "a good minister but also a Gentleman who had the Good of the Colony to Heart."[37]

A visitor to Bethesda wrote a letter to his father dated June 1, 1742, describing the daily routine at the orphan house. The wake-up bell sounded at sunrise. The thirty-nine boys and fifteen girls sang a hymn upon rising from bed and prayed before going to the washroom. Next, the bell called all to public worship, consisting of a scripture reading and the singing of a psalm and a prayer. Only then was breakfast served. After eating, some of the older children went to work and the younger to school. Habersham and Periam instructed the boys, while their wives led the girls. Barber taught Latin to those boys who seemed destined for the ministry. At noon, the children and staff dined together, with a hymn before and after eating. After a half-hour recess, school or work resumed. Time for reading was provided before the bell rang for prayer and supper. And at the end of the day, the schoolmasters and mistresses conducted the children to bed and led them in prayer.[38] When Lord Egmont learned of the routine, he commented acidly, "Not a moment of innocent recreation tho' necessary to the health and strengthening of growing children is allow'd in the whole day." More than ever, he and the trustees believed that Whitefield intended "to establish a school or seminary to breed up those of his sect in."[39]

Everything we have seen so far leads to the conclusion that Bethesda resembled a reformatory more so than a house of mercy. The case of Charles Tondee only reinforces this impression. We know enough to judge that Barber was over-rigid and Periam given to an excess of enthusiasm. However, we are made to pause in reaching a severe judgment by Habersham's comment: "We live in love." The visitor outlining the above routine concluded, "Upon the whole, I think the

---

[37] Dobell to Trustees, March 11, 1742, *CRG*, 23:432–42.

[38] Whitefield, *A Continuation of the Account of the Orphan House*, 14–16.

[39] Egmont, *Journal*, June 4, June 6, 1740, *CRG*, 5:359.

institution to be of God; therefore it doth and will prosper." In fact, he wrote his letter to counteract the reports circulated by Whitefield's enemies, adding, "The family now consists of eighty persons besides labourers, who all contradict the wicked and false accounts of their being starved and cruelly treated, by the lively and hearty countenances they shew." Clearly, he hoped to become one of their number.[40]

British Lieutenant Colonel Archibald Campbell's 1780 map shows the "orphan house" across the tributary of the Vernon River from Vernonburg (Courtesy Augusta Museum of History.)

[40] The letter from "A young gentleman of Boston" (January 1, 1742) reprinted by Georgia Archives and resides in the Bethesda Archives

CHAPTER THREE

BETHESDA SUPPORTS GEORGIA

One reason for the besieged mentality of Bethesda residents in the years 1741 and 1742 was that everyone expected a Spanish invasion. George Whitefield was not particularly interested in earthly warfare, and he opposed any effort to recruit his workers for Oglethorpe's army, but his people at Bethesda could not help being concerned about the very real possibility that Bethesda, Savannah, and in fact, all of Georgia might soon be subject to the King of Spain and the dreaded Roman Catholic Church.

Historian Harvey H. Jackson has described the mood of the people and the condition of Savannah during the Spanish threat.[1] The town, writes Jackson, presented a dismal scene. Bethesda may have had more occupants than Savannah in 1741. Many of the town's one hundred forty-two houses stood empty, with weeds overtaking the deserted lots. Those who remained were discontented and uneasy. A malaise had fallen over the place, and no one seemed willing or able to reverse the steady decline. Savannahians represented their dire condition in a November 22, 1740, petition to the trustees: "Tis evident to every person in this place, to all our adjoining neighbors... that Georgia is going hourly to destruction." For the year past, the town had been almost wholly supported by the money expended in the building of the orphan house. The petitioners estimated that the sixty odd carpenters,

---

[1] Harvey H. Jackson, "Behind the Lines: Oglethorpe, Savannah, and the War of Jenkins Ear," *James Edward Oglethorpe: New Perspectives on His Life and Legacy*, ed. John Inscoe (Savannah: Georgia Historical Society, 1997) 71–91.

bricklayers, sawyers, plasterers, and common laborers drew wages amounting to £1500.[2]

In late June 1742, the news that a massive Spanish armada had been sighted off the Georgia coast alarmed the people at Savannah and Bethesda. As refugees from Frederica sought sanctuary at Bethesda, James Habersham took advantage of Hugh Bryan's hospitality and, in the schooner *Savannah*, transported his charges to Bryan's plantation on the Port Royal River. On July 4, between three and five thousand Spanish troops landed on St. Simon's. Oglethorpe had his regiment of roughly 500, some Indians, and the gallant few of Darien. Oglethorpe earned the lasting gratitude of Georgians that day, describing the action of July 7 as follows: "Learning that an enemy detachment was marching up the Frederica road, I charged them at the head of our Indians, Highland men, and Rangers, and God was pleased to give us such success that we entirely routed the first party, took one Captain prisoner and killed another and pursued them two mile to an open meadow or Savannah." He posted three platoons of the regiment and a company of Highlanders in the trees at the edge of the marsh. Over 300 Spanish troops advanced with loud shouts and fired at the partially concealed British. Two British platoons fell back toward Frederica, encountering Oglethorpe horseback riding to the sound of gunfire. He turned back the retreat and when he and his men reached the scene of the fighting, now known as Bloody Marsh, they found that one platoon of regulars and the one company of High-landers had held their ground and turned back the Spanish advance.[3]

Bloody Marsh is justly celebrated as a great victory, though only a few on each side actually fought. The important effects of the battle were that James Oglethorpe proved his courage, that the Spanish with-

[2] "From the Inhabitants of Savannah to the Trustees, November 22, 1740," *Setting Out to Begin a New World*, ed. Edward J. Cashin (Savannah: The Beehive Press, 1995) 68–69.

[3] Habersham to Whitefield, 22 September 1742, *A Continuation of the Account of the Orphan House in Georgia, January 1741 to June 1742* (Edinburgh: T. Lumesden, 1742) 21; Oglethorpe to the Duke of Newcastle, July 31, 1744, *Setting Out to Begin a New World*, 88–93.

drew from St. Simon's a week later, and that Georgia would be English rather than Spanish territory. The king made Oglethorpe a Brigadier General, whereas before he had been named general only by virtue of his command of the South Carolina and Georgia troops. Oglethorpe invaded Florida once again in 1743, failed again to capture the citadel, and then on July 23, 1743, left Georgia for good. His friend Lord Egmont resigned from the Board of Trustees at about the same time.[4]

Bloody Marsh as a Watershed

Bloody Marsh marks a watershed in Georgia history. A new optimism took root and slowly grew. The trustees' regulations started to fray, and people began to move into Georgia rather than move out. Bethesda changed, too. The holiday in Carolina on Hugh Bryan's plantation from June to August cheered and changed the children. Not all of them returned. Six went back to their homes during the Spanish alarm. Fifteen-year-old Lachlan McIntosh went to Frederica on April 26, 1742, to join Oglethorpe's regiment as a cadet and may well have been involved in the fighting at Bloody Marsh. Elizabeth Pitts left the home in June 1742, and by 1745 was married to "a considerable person in South Carolina."[5] Elizabeth was one of those letter writers of the year before who professed her unworthiness to Reverend Whitefield. However unworthy she might have been spiritually, she proved most worthy as one of Charlestown's leading citizens. It is not clear what seventeen-year-old Elizabeth did between 1742 and 1744, but in that year she married Thomas Lamboll, a prominent Charlestown merchant and a Quaker. She was Lamboll's third wife; his first had died in April 1742, his second in September 1743. Even Elizabeth

[4] Egmont's *Journal,* February 17, 1743, *CRG*, 5:619; Coleman, *Colonial Georgia,* 73.

[5] The list of children at the Orphan House for the years 1740–1745 is in George White's *Historical Collections of Georgia* (New York: Pudney and Russell, 1855) 332–35.

was outlived by her husband. She died in 1770 and he in 1774. Elizabeth's importance in Charlestown's history is that she kept the town's first noteworthy garden at her home on King and Lamboll Streets. She began a correspondence with John Bartram of Philadelphia, and they exchanged plants. John shared his information with European botanists such as Peter Collinson and Carl Linnaeus. When John and his son William visited Charlestown in 1765, they stayed with the Lambolls, and Elizabeth—only forty at the time—took a motherly interest in William and gave him provisions for his journey.[6]

We have singled out Elizabeth Pitts because we happen to know more about her than the other children of Bethesda. Most of the children who entered Bethesda at its inception left after a stay of one or two years. Of the eighteen original children admitted in 1739, only two were still there in 1745. Forty-six entered in 1740, eleven stayed a year or less, eleven two years, and only nine remained by 1745. Bethesda's numbers have always fluctuated; when children could return home, they did so. That principal has been true throughout Bethesda's history. It would be wrong for us to think that the most zealous masters of Bethesda, including Reverends Whitefield and Barber, prevented children from leaving when there was a place waiting for them. The case of Charles Tondee is an exception. Twenty-seven children were returned to their families in the first four years.

Another principal from the earliest days is that children learned employable skills and were placed with artisans or businesspeople when they were ready. Richard Warren, one of the very first orphans, went to work for James Habersham in 1744, as did Francis Milledge. John Feaster worked for Thomas Bailey, the blacksmith, joining Charles Tondee the runaway, who already worked for Bailey. Dr. Joseph Hunter, the surgeon, took in William Riley and Elizabeth Feaster. James Papot, the master carpenter who built the great house must have had plenty of work because he took in James Ballache, Richard Milledge, and John Mackay, who thus joined young Peter Tondee in Papot's shop. Thomas Salter, the brick mason, took in William Mackay, John's brother. Seventeen-year-old John Riley went

---

[6] Lamboll Papers, South Carolina Historical Society (Charleston SC).

to sea with William Grant, master of the *Savannah*. Meanwhile, John More took up the tailor's trade with John Teasdale.[7]

Marriage ended the stay of some of the Bethesda girls. Jane Dupree of Purysburg, after a sojourn at Bethesda, married the gardener Anthony Gautier and the two moved to Savannah. Mary Antrobus, whose aged father also lived at Bethesda, married Captain William Grant. We have mentioned the happy marriages of Mary Bolton to James Habersham and Elizabeth Pitts to Thomas Lamboll. Thus, at the outset Bethesda adopted principles that have persisted ever since, namely the care of needy children until they could return to their families, and the training in skills that would fit young people to make their way in the world. Bloody Marsh saved Georgia, provided a morale-booster to Georgians, and by coincidence, changed the lives of Bethesda's first children. Led by the example of James Habersham, relations between Bethesda and Savannah became more congenial. At the same time, important decisions affecting Georgia were being made in England, and George Whitefield had an important role in these decisions.

Bloody Marsh also helped the trustees raise money for Georgia, but their cause suffered from a devastating report written by dissatisfied former Georgians—"malcontents," as the trustees dubbed them—in 1741. The publication, titled *A True and Historical Narrative of the Colony of Georgia*, mocked Oglethorpe as "our perpetual dictator" and blamed Georgia's woes on the trustees' restrictions on the use of rum, limitations on land-owning, and prohibition of slavery. Lord Egmont wrote a rebuttal, but pro-Georgia sentiment in Parliament was weakened.

Then Thomas Stephens, the son of William Stephens, embarrassed the trustees still more by presenting to Parliament a petition signed by one hundred forty-one landholders in Georgia asking for the right to have a government like the other colonies, for the introduction of

---

[7] The numbers are from an analysis of the Bethesda census accompanying Whitefield's "A Brief Account of the Rise, Progress and Present Situation of the orphan House in Georgia," March 21, 1746, in George White's *Historical Collections*, 332–35.

Negro slavery, for land grants similar to those in South Carolina, and for permission to manufacture a variety of products. Lord Gage, a political opponent of the trustees, learned from Thomas Stephens that George Whitefield also advocated reforms in Georgia, particularly the introduction of slavery. In an effort to further embarrass Lord Egmont and associates, Gage moved in Parliament that Whitefield be invited to address the House. Egmont's friends, however, managed to block any overture to that "Enthusiastical Mad Man," as they called Whitefield.

Thomas Stephens addressed his complaints to the king's council on March 30, 1741, and on April 7, 1741, the House discussed what should be done about Georgia. The gentlemen of the House of Commons could not fail to notice that the Reverend George Whitefield himself sat in the gallery. More than the unknown Thomas Stephens, Whitefield represented the greatest threat to the trustees' continued control of Georgia. The Minister Robert Walpole refused Lord Gage's motion to ask Whitefield to speak. Then Lord Gage "[s]poke bitter things against the colony," demanding a Parliamentary inquiry as to why Parliament had "thrown away" £129,000 on Georgia. His motion lost because of the argument that such an inquiry would give comfort to Spain, a declared enemy engaged in war for the control of Georgia. The trustees battled in Parliament for Georgia even as their colleague Oglethorpe engaged in a military struggle for the colony.[8]

As a gesture of reform, the trustees adopted the resolution proposed by James Vernon, for whom Bethesda's nearby river was named, to divide Georgia into two districts: Savannah and Frederica, each with its own president. They named their loyal secretary, William Stephens, President of the Savannah, or northern district. Oglethorpe

---

[8] Coleman, *Colonial Georgia,* 99–100; Egmont's *Journal,* March 23, 1741 and April 7, 1741, *CRG,* 5:478–80, 489–93; for Thomas Stephens's activities, see Betty Wood, *Slavery in Colonial Georgia 1730–1775* (Athens: University of Georgia Press, 1984) 44–58.

was supposed to appoint someone in Frederica, but in the confusion of war, neglected to do so.[9]

The criticisms of the malcontents weakened the trustees' commitment to their own policies, and Whitefield's personal lobbying further eroded their convictions. The trustees permitted the use of rum on the day Whitefield made a personal appearance before the Board on November 30, 1742.[10] Egmont's resignation a year later, brought on by discouragement as much as ill health, terminated the prospect for the kind of Georgia originally envisioned by Oglethorpe and his friends. Oglethorpe himself paid less attention to Georgia and more to matrimony. He married a wealthy widow named Elizabeth Wright and moved from his ancestral home at Godalming to her estate at Cranham. Then he became embroiled in the Scots Rising of 1745 under Prince Charles Stuart. The Duke of Cumberland assigned Oglethorpe the task of cutting off the retreat of the fleet-footed Highlanders. Because Oglethorpe failed, the angry duke scolded him. Oglethorpe asked for a court martial, got one, and had the satisfaction of exoneration. However, he never held a military commission again because Cumberland, the King's nephew and military commander, never forgave him. He went on to other adventures, including fighting on the continent in Frederick the Great's army under an assumed name. His interests and energy no longer focused on the colony he, more so than any other individual, was responsible for founding.[11]

---

[9] Egmont, *Journal,* April 15, 1741, *CRG,* 5:494.

[10] Egmont, *Journal,* November 30, 1742, *CRG,* 5:672–73.

[11] Rodney M. Baine and Mary E. Williams, "James Oglethorpe in Europe, Recent Findings in His Military Life," in Phinizy Spalding and Harvey H. Jackson, *Oglethorpe in Perspective: Georgia's Founder after Two Hundred Years* (Tuscaloosa: University of Alabama Press, 1989) 112–21; Edward J. Cashin, "Oglethorpe's Account of the 1745 Escape of the Scots at Shap," *James Edward Oglethorpe: New Perspectives,* ed. John Inscoe, 92–104.

Whitefield as Georgia Booster

George Whitefield, on the other hand, seemed to intensify his interest in Georgia. Instead of pitting Bethesda against Georgia, he supported the two. As the trustees' concern decreased, his only increased. Considerations of Bethesda influenced one of his most personal and important decisions: the choice of a wife. On June 26, 1740, Whitefield confided to a friend, "My poor family gives me more concern than every thing else put together. I want a gracious woman that is dead to every thing but Jesus and is qualified to govern children and direct persons of her own sex."[12] He seemed to suggest that although he did not need a wife, Bethesda required a mistress. His search ended when he met and married a widow somewhat older than himself on November 14, 1741, at Caerphilly, Wales. He was twenty-six, she in her thirties. Elizabeth James, his bride, met the spiritual requirement. John Wesley thought well of her as a "woman of candor and humanity." Wesley visited Mrs. James the month before she married Whitefield and enjoyed her hospitality. Indeed, Wesley might have even recommended the lady to Whitefield himself.[13]

Some might wonder whether it was a good idea for Whitefield to recruit a housekeeper by marrying her. In Whitefield's case, perhaps not. The marriage was less than ideal. One of Whitefield's closest associates, Cornelius Winter, said flatly, "He did not intentionally make his wife unhappy. He always preserved great decency and decorum in his conduct towards her." However, Winter indicated that Whitefield made a somewhat fussy husband: "He was very exact to the time appointed for his stated meals: a few minutes delay would be considered a great fault. He was irritable, but soon appeased... Not a paper must have been out of place, or put up irregularly. Each part of the furniture must have been likewise in its place before [he retired

---

[12] Whitefield to William S., June 26, 1740, *Select Collection*, 194.

[13] Stuart C. Henry, *George Whitefield: Wayfaring Witness* (New York: Abingdon Press, 1957) 74–75; Wesley, *Journal*, 325.

at night]." The marriage produced a son named John, but the infant died four months later.[14]

In the year of his marriage, Whitefield and his friend Wesley argued publicly about predestination. Whitefield heard from one of his friends that both Wesleys preached a salvation open to all who would be saved: "With universal redemption, brother Charles pleases the world—brother John follows him in everything. I believe no Atheist can more preach against predestination than they."[15] Whitefield never let friendship deter him from stating his beliefs, and he published a pamphlet stating that Wesley preached an erroneous doctrine. Wesley noted in his journal Whitefield's comment, "He told me, He and I preached two different Gospels, and, therefore, he not only would not join with, or give me the right hand of fellowship, but was resolved publicly to preach against me and my brother, wheresoever he preached at all." Wesley reminded Whitefield of his earlier promise not to air his differences with Wesley. "That promise," Whitefield answered, "was only an effect of human weakness, and he was now of another mind."[16]

Wesley worried over Whitefield's reply and several days later saw him again, accusing Whitefield of "a mere burlesque upon an answer, leaving four of my eight arguments untouched." In going public, Whitefield had caused "an open (and probably irreparable) breach between him and me."[17] Wesley's premonition proved prophetic. Although he and Whitefield were reconciled with each other within the year, an irreparable breach between Whitefield's "Calvinist Methodists" and Wesley's "Arminian Methodists" had indeed occurred. After quarreling with Wesley, Whitefield accepted an invitation to travel through Scotland to Edinburgh, evangelizing and, as usual, soliciting for Bethesda. As before, astonishing scenes attended his

[14] William Jay, *Memoirs of the Life and Character of the Late Rev. Cornelius Winter* (New York: Samuel Whiting, 1811) 61–62; Henry, *George Whitefield: Wayfaring Witness*, 74–76.

[15] Wesley, *Journal*, 257.

[16] Wesley, *Journal*, 292.

[17] Wesley, *Journal*, 292.

passing. Even he expressed awe at the numbers who came to hear him: "Scarce ever was such a sight seen in Scotland. There were undoubtedly upwards of twenty thousand people." Waves of emotion stirred the throng, some wept openly, others cried out, and not a few collapsed in a swoon. In addition to the spiritual success he achieved in Scotland, Whitefield also collected £500 for Bethesda.[18]

In the meantime, Whitefield also raised an additional £500 in excursions through England, enough to pay all the debts he owed for building and sustaining Bethesda. He meant to return to Georgia, but because England's war with Spain had grown into a wider struggle—with Spain, France, and Prussia allied against Britain and Austria—Whitefield had to wait for a convoy of warships to escort his vessel and other merchant ships to America. He reached York, Maine, and after a short illness, repeated his earlier evangelizing tour of New England with the usual success both in conversions and collections.

By sheer coincidence, the war that threatened Bethesda in 1742 stirred New Englanders to attack French Canada in 1745. Whitefield had declined to cooperate with the military on the southern front, but found himself involved in the expedition bound for the French fortress of Louisburg at the mouth of the St. Lawrence River. An indication of Whitefield's stature and influence at the time was the appeal of the military leaders to Whitefield to bless their invasion; "otherwise the serious people would be discouraged from enlisting."[19] Not only that, they insisted, he must give them a slogan to inspire them. Whitefield suggested, "If Christ be captain, no fear of defeat," and huge numbers of volunteers promptly enlisted under that banner.

The episode is reminiscent of a quixotic version of the Crusaders of old. In Whitefield's theology, God blessed the elect in this life. Many of the volunteers felt confident in their election; therefore, they set sail to do battle with the presumably unconverted Catholics of Canada who "deserved" the disaster awaiting all those not born again. The remarkable fact about the 1745 assault on the supposedly impregnable

---

[18] Henry, 78; John Gillies, D.D., *Memoirs of Rev. George Whitefield* (Middletown CT: Hunt and Noyes, 1837) 71.

[19] Gillies, *Memoirs*, 95, 105.

fortress of Louisbourg was that it succeeded. General William Pepperall, one of Whitefield's most ardent admirers, sailed to Canada without artillery, without men who knew how to fire a cannon, and without so much as a battle strategy. The men landed on an unknown shore in a "picnic mood." The captain of a convenient British warship loaned them the services of experienced artillery men. The New Englanders captured an outlying battery and turned the guns on the fortress. The French defenders promptly surrendered. Pepperall and his men had no doubt that God was on their side. A postscript to this interesting event, the second important American battle after Bloody Marsh, was that the king's ministers gave Louisbourg back to the French in the peace treaty that ended this conflict in 1748.[20]

I Have Been Too Rash and Hasty

"Alas! Alas! In how many things I have judged and acted wrong," George Whitefield confided to a friend. "I have been too rash and hasty in giving characters, both of places and persons."[21] It would be too much to claim that George Whitefield mellowed as he turned thirty; it would also be misleading to say that he compromised with worldly ways, but we *can* say that he became more tolerant of his fellow humans. As for Bethesda, the home lost its monastic isolation and reached out to help resurrect a moribund Savannah. The chief architects of the new Savannah were Bethesda residents James Habersham and Francis Harris. Habersham gave up his managerial position at Bethesda and moved to Savannah in 1744. He had already incurred debt on Bethesda's account while Whitefield lingered in Britain. He paid for the improvements such as the planting vines, corn, and other crops. His own family grew year by year. He had been a successful merchant in London and he put his skills to work in Savannah. His friend, Francis Harris, frequented Bethesda and

---

[20] Samuel E. Morrison, *The Oxford History of the American People* (New York: Oxford University Press, 1965) 158–59.

[21] Henry, 82.

followed Whitefield's theology. There seemed to be a dawning realization that Bethesda would need a healthy Savannah. Indeed, Savannah would in time replace Whitefield as Bethesda's main source of support.[22]

Bethesda's détente with Savannah began in 1743 when James Habersham and Francis Harris took advantage of the availability of Bethesda's schooner, the *Savannah*, and opened a store in town. They transported goods to and from Charlestown in the schooner. William Stephens noted in his journal on March 17, 1744, that several of the Bethesda fraternity "think it not amiss to employ themselves in affairs of this world without being polluted." As a gesture of good will, Habersham allowed William Stephens to use the schooner for official business between Savannah and Frederica. Thereafter Stephens's references to Habersham in his correspondence with the trustees took on a more positive tone. He now thought that Habersham "would be a first rate storekeeper."[23]

In 1744 Bethesda acquired neighbors. As of January, thirty families—German and Swiss—lived at Vernonsburgh across the Vernon River. Others settled close by in a place called Acton. Thomas Bosomworth, newly ordained and a vituperative critic of Bethesda on his earlier visit to Georgia, arrived in Savannah on February 21, 1744, to replace the deceased Christopher Orton. After firing off a blast at "those superstitious zealots" in a letter to the trustees, Bosomworth seemed to realize that no one wanted to fight any more. Cooperation and a hitherto unpracticed Christian charity were now in vogue. A minor wonder occurred when Bosomworth and Barber conducted separate services in Savannah without denouncing each other. Bosomworth "seems to advance every day in the good opinion of his Congregation," William Stephens noted in March 1744. The brick foundations of the church had been laid by then. On Easter Sunday a hundred people attended services, the most in years.

---

[22] E. Merton Coulter, *The Journal of William Stephens 1743–1745* (Athens: University of Georgia Press, 1959) 81–82.

[23] Stephens to Trustees, October 17, 1744, *CRG*, 24:331; Stephens, *Journal*, 81–82.

Meanwhile, Bosomworth astounded his parishioners by returning from a visit to Frederica with his new bride, the celebrated Mary Musgrove Matthews, Coosaponakeesa, a relative of the great chiefs of Coweta, Chigilli, and Malatchi. Stephens described the public reaction, saying that people are "chattering on the late Surprising adventure of our Parson's attacking and carrying the Widow in a Short storm." Bosomworth gave a reception for his wife and a throng filled the parsonage for the happy occasion. Stephens expressed relief that "nothing happened that gave offense."[24]

For almost a year, an unprecedented Christian serenity prevailed between Savannah and Bethesda. The Reverend Bosomworth actually taught catechism to the growing numbers of former Bethesda residents and their children. Even Stephens expressed surprise that "Church Catechism was again allowed in that Family."[25] Three distinct congregations worshipped with relatively little rancor or interference. Bosomworth conducted services from ten to twelve o'clock on Sundays, and again from three to five for members of the Church of England. A newcomer, Reverend John J. Zubly preached to the large foreign community from eight to ten and again from one to three. Presbyterian Jonathan Barber preached to dissenters "where he thought most convenient."[26]

As Savannahians adjusted to the new spirit of accommodation, Bosomworth left for England in an effort to persuade the trustees to honor Oglethorpe's promises to his wife. He returned in 1746, but not as the resident minister at Savannah. Instead, he resided at Mary's trading house and Pipemaker Creek above Savannah and continued to lobby the trustees on her behalf.

Upon learning that George Whitefield had returned to America, James Habersham decided to meet the great man in Philadelphia. He took his sister-in-law Rebecca Bolton with him; she intended to remain in Philadelphia to care for her aged mother. They sailed in the

---

[24] Bosomworth to Trustees, May 7, 1744, *CRG*, 24:234–39; Stephens, *Journal*, 79–80, 132.

[25] Stephens, *Journal*, 207, 214.

[26] Stephens, *Journal*, 197.

Savannah, captained by William Grant, in mid-February 1745, and on the way dropped off fifteen thousand vine cuttings at Hugh and Jonathan Bryan's plantations on the Port Royal River.[27]

Six months later Habersham returned to Savannah with news that Whitefield was on his way to Georgia by land, accompanied by Mrs. Whitefield. Whitefield's preaching all along the eastern colonies from Massachusetts to Georgia had the effect of spreading the Great Awakening, and though he might not have intended to, he accelerated the splintering of the established church. Most of those who followed Whitefield's theology resented any attempt of the Bishop of London to enforce conformity. The separation from the Church of England proved to be a step toward political separation from England.

George Whitefield arrived in Savannah on November 14, 1745; paid his respects to William Stephens; and then received the warm welcome of his spiritual family at Bethesda. He had left over a hundred persons in 1740; now the family consisted of only twenty-six persons. Two of the boys were blind, one mentally retarded. A poor and aged widow had sought refuge at Bethesda as well. Stephens and Whitefield discussed the placing of several Bethesda boys as apprentices around town. Whitefield then went off to Charlestown to fetch his wife and introduce her to her life's work—as he assumed, the tending of Bethesda. The Whitefields' arrival permitted Jonathan Barber, his wife, and children, to return to New England, where he had distinguished himself in the ministry.[28]

The Most Delightfully Situated Place

We can hope as we watch the story of Bethesda unfold that Elizabeth Whitefield liked what she saw when she reached the end of the ten-mile road with its ten bridges and came out of the forest into the sweeping open space. There, facing away from the Back River (a

---

[27] Stephens, *Journal*, 236, 252–60.

[28] Frances Manwaring Caulkins, *History of New London, Connecticut* (New London: H. D. Utley, 1895) 460–61.

tributary of the Vernon River), she saw the stately three-story building where she would live with her husband. Four smaller-framed houses, each measuring thirty by twenty feet, stood in front of the great house, two on each side of the approach. During Whitefield's five-year absence, Habersham had beautified the grounds with gardens and orchards. Care had also been lavished on the house in anticipation of the Whitefields' coming. The twenty interior rooms were finished. The front door led into a hall twenty-six feet square and a stairway leading to the second floor. An inscription hung on the wall: "This House Was Erected in the Year of Our Lord 1739 by Contributions Collected by the Rev'd Mr. George Whitefield." Two handsomely paneled parlors stood ready to receive visitors. The main hallway led to the chapel, twenty-four feet long and twelve wide. To the left of the hallway were two rooms, plastered instead of paneled. One was intended to be used as a library, but in fact had been appropriated by Dr. Joseph Hunter as an infirmary. The next room on the north side was the dining room used by the children and staff. Stairs led up to a long hallway running the width of the house with eight rooms opening from it, each plastered and adorned with crown moldings. The two rooms on the south side were the Whitefields' private quarters. The other rooms and the six on the third floor were boy's dormitories, whereas the girls and women slept in one of the four small houses. The building opposite the house was used as a school. A kitchen and a washhouse completed the campus arrangement.[29]

Forty acres had been cleared around the buildings. To the east stretched the marshes, with the Back River winding through. Whitefield loved it, once saying that Bethesda was "the most delightfully situated place in all the southern parts of America." In a wistful moment during this sojourn, he thought of ending his travels. "I love to range the American woods," he wrote, "and sometimes think I shall never return to England any more." Of course, he would have to return to England. His Bethesda family, even reduced as it

---

[29] Lilla Mills Hawes, ed., "A Description of Whitefield's Bethesda: Samuel Fayrweather to Thomas Prince and Thomas Foxcroft," 45/4 *Georgia Historical Quarterly* (Winter, 1961): 363–66.

was, depended upon his fund-raising tours, or "progresses" as he called them. Whitefield's critics, including some historians who accuse him of starting the orphan house merely as an excuse for gadding about the countryside, do him an injustice.[30]

Even if he himself had not done the work at Bethesda, Whitefield had worked for Bethesda elsewhere and did not mind boasting about the improvements in a publication dated March 21, 1746: "We have lately begun to use the plough; and next year I hope to have many acres of good oats and barley." He would be gone by harvest time, but he liked to identify himself with Bethesda:

> We have near twenty sheep and lambs fifty head of cattle, and seven horses. We hope to kill a thousand weight of pork this season. Our garden is very beautiful, furnishes us with all sorts of greens, etc, etc. We have plenty of milk, eggs, poultry and make a good deal of butter weekly. A good quantity of wool and cotton have been given me, and we hope to have sufficient spun and wove for next winter's clothing. If the vines hit, we may expect two or three hogsheads of wine out of the vineyard.[31]

The tone is that of an English lord of the manor, and indeed, this son of a tavern-keeper regarded himself as a gentleman planter. In fact, the thought occurred to him even more frequently now that he was back in Georgia and on his land. What might he do with the help of slave labor! He weighed his abhorrence of the way slaves were treated in Virginia, North Carolina, and South Carolina against the profits that might be made for Bethesda by the cultivation of rice and indigo by slave labor. He decided that a heavenly reward would

---

[30] Whitefield to Robert Keen, February 13, 1765, *Select Collection*, 3:322; Gillies, *Memoirs*, 107.

[31] George Whitefield, "A Brief Account of the Rise, Progress, and Present Situation of the Orphan House in Georgia," in George White's *Historical Collections of Georgia*, 329–331.

compensate for an earthly bondage. His resolution to preach the gospel to his slaves allowed his mind to rest easy on the subject of slavery.

George Whitefield thoroughly concurred with the recent policy of accommodation with the Savannah folk. Within the week of his arrival, on November 1745 two of Whitefield's emissaries—Francis Harris and William Woodroofe—paid a courtesy call to William Stephens to beg permission for the "Great Itinerant" to preach in Savannah's public place of worship. Stephens, remembering the earlier confrontation, agreed somewhat reluctantly, provided that Whitefield not denounce the clergy appointed by the trustees. "Now we will see how well he complys [sic] with these Engagements," Stephens wrote to the trustees, who were always interested in Whitefield's activities. Whitefield preached to a packed congregation and, to Stephens's immense relief, avoided controversy. Stephens dutifully reported that Whitefield had pleased everyone, even to the wearing of a surplice, as a good minister of the Church of England should.[32]

Following up his advantage, Whitefield called upon Stephens with the idea he had contemplated for several years. He needed Stephens's help, along with the help of the more successful Savannahians, in opening Bethesda to young gentlemen for an education in the classics and sciences. Their tuition would help defray the cost of caring for needy children.[33] The decision on Whitefield's part to invite non-Methodists to Bethesda indicated clearly that the monastic, isolated era had ended. In December 1745, Whitefield's friend, the Reverend John Martin Bolzius of the German Lutheran town of Ebenezer, paid a social call to the Reverend and Mrs. Whitefield at Bethesda. The conversation soon turned to Whitefield's plan of saving Bethesda by introducing slavery to Georgia. Bolzius strongly objected, both in person and in a subsequent letter. His first argument was more practical than moral: Negro labor would drive out white labor, as it had done in South Carolina. He rejected Whitefield's "Providence of God" contention that God fashioned black people to work in hot climates, pointing out that parts of Germany were as hot as Georgia.

[32] Stephens, *Journal*, November 16–17, 1746, 251.
[33] Stephens, *Journal*, November 18, 1746, 252.

Workers could follow the example of those at Ebenezer who worked early or late during the hot months. Besides, the heat in Georgia was oppressive for only a relatively short time. Bolzius quoted Habersham, stating that Philadelphia's summer heat troubled him more than Georgia's.

As for Whitefield's argument that he could not continue to operate the orphan house without black workers, Bolzius said that the home should be given up rather than drive white laborers out of the colony. He pointed to Habersham as one who advanced his business without having slaves. Even if Whitefield brought the slaves to Christ, it would do no good unless white Georgians could be made to practice Christianity. If Whitefield wanted to work among slaves, there was work enough awaiting him in South Carolina. Bolzius closed with a Whitefield-like warning: if the Itinerant introduced slaves, he would no longer deserve God's blessing.[34]

In the end, Bolzius accepted the inevitability of slavery, even remained on good terms with the evangelist and continued to visit Bethesda. In a 1756 letter, Bolzius commented on the state of Bethesda. The orphan house itself, he said, "is a large, beautiful building like a rich and noble castle..." The inside walls were paneled and inside and outside surfaces were coated with oil paint. At the time, there were "forty or fifty" boys and a few girls at the institution. They ate boiled rice three times a day and, at least once a day, salted beef or pork. A treat was thickly boiled grits or ground Indian corn with syrup made from sugar cane. On occasion they had a weak beer or a concoction made from syrup and hops. "With that they are healthy and merry," observed Bolzius. In his opinion, the young people had exercise enough doing the necessary chores. Their summer uniforms consisted of a linen shirt, trousers to the ankles, shoes, and a cap. They donned warmer clothing in the winter. Bolzius concluded, "This orphanage is without a doubt a useful institution, in which the children are well

[34] Bolzius to Whitefield, December 24, 1745, *CRG*, 24:434–44.

instructed in reading, writing, and arithmetic and are led to the fear of the Lord and to good order."[35]

Not everyone approved of the improved relations between Bethesda and Savannah. John Dobell, who had originally come to Georgia as a disciple of Whitefield and who taught school in Savannah, did not like the attitudes of some of his former colleagues: "Pride and Poverty have a great while went hand in hand, but Pride has now, I think, gotten the start, and a Spirit of Gentility seems to be gone forth and seized the brains of the meanest whereby some are intoxicated to no small degree... as if they fancied themselves equal to the Children of Nobles." Even Whitefield himself had changed, said Dobell, "relishing only the Company of the greatest, which is the opposite extreme to that he was in when I first knew him." Dobell conceded that Whitefield's natural endowments made him "a great man," but as for his Christianity, "I have no notion of his having more than those who make less Noise." Though Lord Egmont had retired from the board of trustees, Dobell kept him informed of events. On June 11, 1746, he described the mood of Georgians quite generally: "My Lord, they are stark Mad after Negroes."[36]

The Rise of the Firm of Habersham and Harris

Because the leaders of Bethesda realized that the future of their house was connected hip and thigh with the prosperity of Savannah, and because Bethesda furnished some of Savannah's leaders, it is appropriate to notice what happened during the twilight years of trustees' rule.

In February 1746, William Stephens received orders from the trustees to examine the accounts of the trustees' storekeeper, Thomas

---

[35] George Fenwick Jones, ed., "A Letter by Pastor Johann Martin Boltzius about Bethesda and Marital Irregularities in Savannah," *The Georgia Historical Quarterly*, 84/2 (Summer 2000): 283–94. Professor Jones found the letter in the Prussian State Archives in Berlin and translated it into English.

[36] Dobell to Trustees, May 17, 1746; Dobell to Egmont, June 11, 1746, *CRG*, 24:50–51, 73.

Causton. This represented the second effort to audit Causton's books. As long ago as 1739, the trustees had instructed three magistrates—Stephens, Thomas Jones, and Henry Parker—to inspect the accounts. The obstacle to their progress seemed to be that they could not make heads or tails of Causton's ciphers. Causton went to London to appeal his case directly to the trustees, and those gentlemen tossed the ball back to a new commission formed of Habersham, his partner Harris, and William Spencer. They further ordered Causton to return to Georgia, presumably to answer any questions the examiners might have. Unfortunately, the *Judith* proved to be a death trap. Spotted fever broke out, killing the captain and twelve others, including Causton. The new commissioners decided that there was no point in going over the accounts with Causton dead. It is significant that the trustees recognized Habersham and Harris as two who knew how to do business and keep accounts. Privately, Habersham told William Spencer that he had so much work to do for Bethesda that he could not afford the now empty exercise of checking already old ledgers. Francis Harris admitted to Spencer that he himself did not know much about accounts; he left that to his partner Habersham.[37]

Habersham and Harris warehoused their goods in the trustees' store. Their policy of refusing credit, even to the trustees' employees, rankled many. In September 1746, Francis Harris went to London to set up direct trade with suppliers, circumventing the Charlestown middlemen. While in London, Harris made an appearance before the trustees, explaining that salaried Georgia officials usually ran up such large bills that their pay, when it eventually arrived from England, could not cover their debts. Harris humbly asked the trustees to assume responsibility for the debts owed to their store. In London, Harris arranged with John Nickleson for the lease of a vessel to ply trade between Savannah and London. Habersham and Harris would export rice, deerskins, and staves in exchange for goods. Harris obtained for the firm a renewable fourteen-year lease on the town

[37] William Spencer to Trustees, July 21, 1746, *CRG*, 24:86–87.

wharf. Habersham then tore down the rickety old structure and built one three times larger, the first decent landing facility in Georgia.[38]

The disbanding of Oglethorpe's regiment proved only a short setback for the two merchants because they obtained the contract to supply the Independent Companies stationed at Augusta, Frederica, and at Fort Barrington on the Altamaha. So many soldiers and their families chose to remain in Georgia that the breaking up of the regiment had the happy result of boosting Georgia's population.

Habersham and Harris supplied Indians who visited Savannah and charged the trustees for the cost. The merchants reaped a bonanza when the Reverend Thomas Bosomworth, garbed in his clerical gown, returned to town with his wife, her cousin Malatchi, and an escort of two hundred Creek Indians. Thomas Bosomworth argued forcefully for the payment of the colony's debts to Mary. Malatchi, as the most prestigious chief in the Creek Nation, said that Mary should have the lands reserved by the Creeks in Chigilli's treaty with Oglethorpe—namely, the islands of St. Catherine, Ossabaw, and Sapelo; as well as her settlement on Pipemaker Creek. If they did not get satisfaction, they would not allow any settlement above the tidewater. They had agreed to the establishment of Augusta, but not to further expansion. After some nervous moments, the Bosomworths and their Indian friends left without satisfaction. They would have to wait eight years until the capable Governor Henry Ellis could work out an amicable solution. Meanwhile, Habersham and Harris profited by supplying month-long encampment. They shrewdly took advantage of their opportunity to set up a direct trade in deerskins, thus by-passing the Augusta trading houses.[39]

The rise of James Habersham to prominence was recognized by the trustees who named him to the board of assistants in 1749, and in 1750 appointed him as secretary succeeding William Stephens.

[38] Stephens to Trustees, September 15, 1746; Habersham to Trustees, May 24, 1749, *CRG*, 24:112–16, 389–93.

[39] Stephens to Trustees, July 25, 1749; Habersham and Harris to Trustees, January 1, 1750, *CRG*, 24:408, 449–50; Coleman, *Colonial Georgia*, 85–86; Proceedings of President and Assistants, July 24, 1749, *CRG*, 6:252–53.

Habersham was surprised at the promotion because his letter to the Reverend Bolzius had been severely critical of the trustees' policies, and the letter had even found its way to the gentlemen in question. Yet the appointment came in spite of the criticism.[40] Habersham took advantage of his position on the board to engross more trade for his firm.

Savannah struggled for survival during the decade of the 40s, while Augusta flourished. Settled largely by South Carolina Indian traders who began crossing into Georgia in 1736, Augusta had monopolized the Indian trade. Various independent traders merged into one great company headed by John Rae, George Galphin, and Lachlan McGillivray. They imported their supplies through Charlestown and sent their skins to Charlestown for export. The traders, and the inhabitants of Augusta generally, paid little attention to the trustees' regulations and attributed their prosperity to that fact. Ironically, Oglethorpe thoroughly approved of the independent spirit of the Augusta people and the good work of his garrison there. By curtailing abuses in the Indian trade, Oglethorpe gained the good will of the powerful Cherokee and Creek Nations.

In 1750 Habersham, in his new position as secretary and his unofficial capacity as chief booster of Savannah, prompted a request to the trustees to put a stop to Augusta's monopoly and to guarantee to Savannah a share of the Indian trade and export. Lachlan McGillivray wrote a cogent appeal to the trustees, noting that his company maintained good relations with the Indians during the war with Spain and France and that the trustees ought not interfere with a good thing.[41] But his company prudently began to send some of their business to Savannah. As the trustees neared the end of their tenure,

---

[40] Habersham to Trustees, July 7, 1749, *CRG*, 24:393–94; Hugh M'Call, *The History of Georgia*, 2 vols. (Atlanta: Cherokee Publishing Company, 1969) 1:143.

[41] Brown, Rae, and Company to Trustees, February 13, 1751, *CRG*, 26:152–55; for the context of the dispute, see Edward J. Cashin, *Lachlan McGillivray, Indian Trader and the Shaping of the Southern Colonial Frontier* (Athens: University of Georgia Press, 1992) 119–21.

they decided to prepare Georgians for the same privileges enjoyed in other provinces, calling for an assembly of delegates elected from every town, village, and district having at least ten families. Savannah was allowed four delegates: Augusta, Ebenezer, and Frederica two each; one for the smaller settlements. Interestingly enough, Frederica, in drastic decline with the mustering out of the regiment, did not send delegates.

This first Georgia-elected assembly met on January 14, 1751, when the delegates elected Francis Harris as Speaker. The delegates asked not to be merged with South Carolina, also requesting improvements in river navigation, a court system, and the right to make by-laws and other sensible reforms. Perhaps heartened by this show of maturity, the trustees prepared to surrender their charter to the king in 1752, a year before the end of their mandate.[42]

Thus, the Bethesda family exerted leadership in insuring the prosperity of Savannah. An important friend and ally of Bethesda's, Jonathan Bryan moved from Carolina to Georgia in 1750. With friends like Habersham, Harris, and Bryan, Bethesda's future looked bright. Although no one could have anticipated the outcome or relate it to Bethesda, another event in this pivotal year of 1750 proved important to Bethesda's future. Coincidentally, Bethesda boys played an essential part. Peter Tondee and Richard Milledge, both alumni of the orphan house, joined with Benjamin Sheftall to organize the Union Society. The date is still celebrated every year by the society as founding day, April 23, the Feast of St. George. The founders of the society intended to lobby for the interests of the artisans of Savannah: the carpenters, blacksmiths, tailors, and bricklayers, among whom were many young men formerly of Bethesda. In anticipation of the admission of skilled black slave labor, they formed a lobby for the interest of white artisans. Later, after its members achieved a measure of security, the society turned to charitable works, the care of widows

[42] Coleman, *Colonial Georgia*, 174.

and orphans.[43] It is logical to suppose that the Bethesda tradition influenced the decision to care for orphans. And as such, it is entirely appropriate that the Bethesda boys should, in time, assume responsibility for maintaining Bethesda.

Working for Bethesda in England

George Whitefield kept Bethesda in mind during his four-year absence. For one thing, he had left his wife behind to manage the House. He cared for her in his own way, of course, and referred to her from time to time in his journal. As unfair as the comparison may be, though, he probably loved Bethesda more than his wife. At any rate, he went on another of his fundraising tours without her in January 1747. In South Carolina, Jonathan Bryan helped him purchase a rice plantation worked by slaves, to which he gave the name Providence.

Whitefield wore himself out preaching, soliciting funds, and traveling 1,100 miles by his own count. To recover his health, he stopped at Bermuda on his way to England, arriving there March 15, 1748. He never let poor health interfere with saving souls and raising money. In fact, he collected over £100 and wrote in his journal, "This will pay a little of Bethesda's debt, and enable me to make such a remittance to my dear yoke fellow, as may keep her from being embarrassed, or too much beholden in my absence."[44]

Whitefield's correspondence on the homeward voyage reveals his new, less antagonistic attitude:

> I have been too rash and hasty in giving characters both of places and persons. Being fond of scriptural language I have often used a style too apostolical, and at the same time I have been bitter in my zeal. Wild-fire has been mixed with it, and I

[43] Harold E. Davis, *The Fledgling Province Social and Cultural Life in Colonial Georgia 1733–1776* (Chapel Hill: University of North Carolina Press, 1976) 169–70.

[44] Gillies, *Memoirs*, 107, 116.

> find that I frequently wrote and spoke in my own spirit, when I thought I was writing and speaking by the assistance of the Spirit of God.[45]

Whitefield was no less convinced of his own special election, but he tempered his criticism of those not so blessed, especially the clergy.

As soon as he arrived in England in July 1748, he dispatched a letter to the trustees with a strong argument for the admission of slavery into the colony, contending that otherwise Georgia would never amount to much. He forwarded several other similar petitions entrusted to him by Georgians. The weight of Whitefield's prestige finally broke the trustees' resistance to allowing slavery in the colony. First, though, they sent instructions to Stephens to convoke a meeting of responsible citizens to suggest guidelines for the regulation of slavery. Twenty-three Georgians met to discuss the issue, but the final report was signed by five; including Habersham, Harris, and Bolzius. Whitefield's influence might be seen in the committee's resolution to "set an example of Humanity" for other provinces. They would not limit the number of slaves, but except for coopers and sawyers, they would not allow slaves to work in town. The intent was to protect white artisans, but there were not enough skilled whites to make the hundreds of barrels rice planters needed. Most suggestions focused on white Georgians' responsibilities toward slaves rather than slave behavior.[46]

Convinced that the ban on slavery would soon be removed, white Georgians began to cheat in ingenious ways. Some planters leased slaves from South Carolina for life, the leases amounting to the

---

[45] Gillies, *Memoirs*, 117. Whitefield's letter was written to the Reverend Birch, author of a pamphlet titled "The Enthusiasm of Methodists and Papists Compared" and found in the Birch Collection, Additional Manuscripts 4264, British Library, London.

[46] M'Call, *History of Georgia*, 145; Gillies, *Memoirs*, 121; President, Assistants, Counselmen to Trustees, January 10, 1749, *CRG*, 24:347–51; for a discussion of the adoption of the Georgia slave code, see Betty Wood, *Slavery in Colonial Georgia 1730–1775* (Athens: University of Georgia Press, 1984) 80–85.

purchase prices. Others openly flouted the law. James Habersham procured slaves for Bethesda, alleging that his people at the orphan house could not do the work necessary to sustain the home. Habersham, acting for Whitefield, applied for five hundred acres near the village of Hampstead, arguing that most of Bethesda's property consisted of unproductive pine land. When that petition was granted, he promptly filed for a second tract of five hundred acres. The trustees, generous as their tenure neared an end, granted that also.[47]

Meanwhile, Whitefield's latest adventure in England had a major but unforeseen implication for Bethesda's future. He met Selina Hastings, Countess of Huntingdon, and thus changed his own career as well as Bethesda's. His first biographer suggests that the invitation to Whitefield by the Countess came as a complete surprise: "And at this time [July 1748] a very unexpected thing happened to him."[48] The Countess had admired Whitefield's zeal since she first heard about his preaching ten years earlier. Selina Hastings, daughter of the Earl of Ferrars and widow of the Earl of Huntingdon, ranked so high on the social scale that no one dared criticize her conduct—at least, not to her face. She retained her eminent respectability when she espoused Methodism and began to wear clothing of muted, if not somber, colors. One of her gowns is displayed at the Costume Museum in the Assembly Rooms at Bath, a place she visited frequently during her lifetime. Her first biographer portrayed her as contemporaries saw her: "There was an attraction and an influence about her which were felt by many of the great in an extraordinary degree, and not only the courtly Chesterfield, the political Duchess of Malborough, the gay and frivolous [Beau] Nash, but the infidel Bolingbroke paid her marked and sincere homage." In short, this high-born and feisty lady was not the sort whose invitation could be taken lightly. George Whitefield went immediately to her house in the Chelsea section of London and, at her request, preached to some of her friends of high rank. Ten years earlier, Whitefield might have chastised the noble assemblage for their

---

[47] M'Call, *History of Georgia* 144; Proceedings of President and Assistants, December 20, 1949, April 4, 1750, *CRG*, 6:302–13.

[48] Gillies, *Memoirs*, 117.

unconverted way of life; now, however, he personified tact and diplomacy, making such a favorable impression that the Countess invited him back to preach to some of her acquaintances who stood most in need of repentance. Whitefield exuded deference in his reply: "When your ladyship styled me your friend, I was amazed at your condescension... As there seems to be a door opening for nobility to hear the gospel, I will defer my journey, and God willing, preach at your ladyship's. Oh that God may be with me, and make me humble!"[49]

Donnington Hall, Leiscestershire, England, the ancestral seat of the Hastings family, as it looks today. It is the headquarters of an airline company. (Photo by the author.)

Lord Chesterfield, rightly celebrated for his letters to his son on proper behavior, was moved by Whitefield's oratory. The preacher

[49] Aaron Crossley Hobart Seymour, *Selina, Countess of Huntingdon*, 2 vols. (London: William Edward Painter, 1844) 1:xvii; Gillies, *Memoirs*, 118.

painted a graphic scene of a blind beggar tottering on the brink of a precipice, then falling. Chesterfield jumped up and cried out, "Good God, he's gone!"[50] Like most of the British gentry, good manners constituted his closest approach to religion. His wife, however, fell under Whitefield's spell and began to wander about in clothing of subdued colors. When she appeared in court wearing her new restrained garb, King George II laughed and said, "I know who chose that gown for you—Mr. Whitefield."[51]

In token of her approval of Whitefield's influence upon the peerage, Lady Huntingdon named him one of her chaplains. Although this appointment might have distracted Whitefield's attention from Bethesda, in fact it had the opposite effect. It attracted Lady Huntingdon to Bethesda. The chaplaincy caused Whitefield to remain in England longer than he intended. His followers detained him by building a chapel or tabernacle at Moorfields, where Whitefield had first preached in the open. The erection of a chapel and the prospect of others (within a few years a larger tabernacle was built on Tottenham Court Road) caused John Wesley to inquire whether Whitefield intended to link his chapels with Wesley's Methodist churches. Wesley wondered about the possibility of a union. "I am afraid an external one is impracticable," Whitefield replied. "I find by your sermons that we differ in principles more than I thought and I believe we are upon two different plans." Then Whitefield added the principal reason he would not emulate Wesley and organize his own followers, one of the best statements of the priority Bethesda enjoyed among his values: "My attachment to America will not permit me to abide very long in England, consequently I shall but weave a Penelope's web if I formed societies."[52]

---

[50] Kirby, *The Elect Lady*, 11.

[51] Henry, 85.

[52] Gillies, *Memoirs*, 119; Noorah Al-Gailani, Curator of the Wesley House and Museum of Methodism, told this writer on June 30, 1999, that Whitefield's Moorfields Tabernacle is still extant, part of a school within a block of Wesley's house. The Tottenham Court Tabernacle was destroyed by a German bomb in World War II, but subsequently rebuilt. It still bears Whitefield's name.

Whitefield's attachment to Bethesda, in his own words, "brought me upon the carpet." The incident occurred in Scotland. The Synods of Glasgow and Perth met to decide whether Whitefield should be allowed the privilege of their pulpits. Among the objections voiced by his critics was the "Chimerical scheme of the Orphan-house" and the suspicion that the money he collected was not used for the orphan house. Other objections included his earlier denunciation of the unredeemed clergy and the suspension levied by Commissary Alexander Garden. One of Whitefield's defenders replied, "Whether Mr. Whitefield's scheme of the Orphan-house be prudent or not, it is demonstrable it was honestly meant." The comment was not exactly a vote of confidence in Bethesda. His defenders quoted the audit of Bethesda's accounts by the Savannah magistrates (actually by James Habersham) as evidence of Whitefield's integrity. His recent temperate sermons gained him favor: "And now he scarce preaches a sermon, without guarding his hearers against relying on impressions, telling them that faith, and a persuasion we are justified, are very different things, and that a holy life is the best evidence of a gracious state." The joint synods voted thirty-seven to thirteen to admit Whitefield to preach in their churches.[53]

The almost invisible Mrs. Whitefield left Bethesda for reasons of her own and joined her husband in England in 1749. That may have caused the Reverend to plan to return to Bethesda. At any rate, after a progress through Scotland and Ireland, he boarded a ship for America on August 29, 1751, taking several needy children with him to Bethesda. On board the *Antelope*, the issue of slavery weighed heavily on his mind. He wrote a friend that he had no doubt about the "lawfulness" of slavery because after all, Abraham owned slaves. However lame their biblical justification might seem, it sufficed for those who wanted profitable plantations, including the Itinerant himself. He continued, "It is plain to a demonstration that hot countries cannot be cultivated without negroes." In any case, he would rather not argue about slavery now that the trustees permitted

[53] Gillies, *Memoirs*, 120.

it: "Let us reason no more about it, but diligently improve the present opportunity for their instruction."[54]

On October 27, 1751, Whitefield arrived in Savannah only to learn—that is, if he did not know already—that Habersham and Harris had risen to the position of Savannah's leading businessmen, as well as prominence in local government. Habersham had acquired two tracts of 500 acres from the trustees for Bethesda, and Bethesda boys were occupied as artisans and mechanics. His friend and benefactor Jonathan Bryan had become a Georgian, an assembly had been held, and Bethesda's students had made strides in learning. No wonder he wrote to a friend that he found the orphan house "in as good a situation as could be expected." It is an interesting indication of Whitefield's changed attitude that he commented on the children's improved learning rather than their degree of piety. He believed that the foundation for a college had been well laid, even rededicating himself to the institution. "I intend," he wrote, "by God's assistance now to begin; for as yet alas! I have done nothing; it is a new year; God quicken my tardy pace, and help me to do much work in little time! This is my highest ambition."[55]

Whitefield remained at Bethesda, making short visits to Charlestown from November to April in preparation for the transition from orphan house to academy. He made no changes in the daily schedule, except to specify the most suitable texts for reading. Students were expected to furnish their own rooms and not to fall into arrears in payments over six months.

The trustees' policy permitting slavery went into effect on January 1, 1751, and incorporated the recommendations of Habersham's Georgia committee. A ratio of slaves to white laborers was imposed, black sawyers and coopers could work in towns, whites who mistreated slaves would be punished, and masters were required to attend to the spiritual welfare of their slaves. In his letters to the trustees, Whitefield had stressed the necessity of extending the benefits of religion to the slaves, and he had excoriated planters in other southern

---

[54] Whitefield to B., March 22, 1751, *Select Collection*, 2:404–405.

[55] Whitefield to J. T., November 20, 1751, *Select Collection*, 2:424.

provinces for not doing so. Therefore, he insisted that at Bethesda all Negro boys and girls be baptized, that boys be taught to read and that girls learn to do needlework.

The emphasis Whitefield placed on religious instruction and spiritual welfare of slaves was not shared by most planters. White Georgians regarded teaching slaves to read as particularly dangerous. The literate slave might read anti-slavery material and be led to thoughts of freedom. In 1755, Georgia adopted a slave code based on South Carolina's, one that said nothing about religious instruction. As Betty Wood observed in her history of colonial slavery in Georgia, "The Georgians preferred to rely not on religion but on the rigorous policing and harsh punishment of their slaves."[56]

Bethesda, of course, continued to set an example of humane treatment of slaves, including affording them religious instruction. So did Bethesda's friends and allies such as Habersham, Harris, and Bryan. Habersham later said, "I once thought it was unlawful and unjust to keep slaves, but am now inclined to think God may have a higher end in permitting them to be brought into a Christian country, than merely to support their masters." He looked forward to the day when "many thousands may embrace the gospel." Habersham and Harris followed the Charlestown route to social success; for them merchandizing made possible a country estate befitting aspiring English gentlemen. The partners turned the management of their company over to Thomas Rasberry, retained their investment in the firm, and retired to plantations. Habersham named his estate Silk Hope; Harris called his Wild Heron.[57]

Whitefield's new instructions spelled out the days of special observance—including Christmas and Easter, of course, and also his own birthday, December 27th, the anniversary of the laying of the first brick, and the celebration of the Glorious Revolution on November 5th. Whitefield's paternal concern for Bethesda included a strong

[56] Wood, *Slavery,* 83–85, 115.

[57] M'Call, *History of Georgia,* 118; Calvin Smith, "The Habershams," *Forty Years of Diversity, Essays on Colonial Georgia,* eds. Harvey H. Jackson and Phinizy Spalding (Athens: University of Georgia Press, 1984) 204.

commitment to Georgia. Particularly interesting was his stipulation that students at Bethesda must be taught "the history of Georgia and the constitution of England." Furthermore, one of the tactics he suggested for consideration on the special days was "The Rise and Progress of the Colony of Georgia."[58] Bethesda boys of his day as well as those of today can justly regard their founder as a Georgia patriot. George Whitefield loved Bethesda, not as a place apart, but as Bethesda in Georgia.

---

[58] Whitefield's Instructions, Bethesda Collection 1133, item 384, Georgia Historical Society.

CHAPTER FOUR

THE QUEST FOR A COLLEGE

The Georgia trustees surrendered control of the colony in 1752, just as the British ministers began to pay more attention to American affairs. The trustee era falls within the span of years that historians refer to as the period of "salutary neglect." During the administration of the first "prime" minister, Robert Walpole, the American colonies were left to shift for themselves. As a result, they grew accustomed to a large degree of independence. However, in 1748—at the conclusion of the war with France and Spain known in America as King George's War—British policy changed. In that year, a dynamic administrator in the person of George Montegu Dunk, the Earl of Halifax, became head of the Board of Trade, the agency responsible for formulating American policy. Halifax took bold initiatives, the first being colonization of Nova Scotia with English subjects. In 1752 Halifax secured the right on behalf of the board of trade to appoint colonial officials. That meant Georgia was handed from one set of parliamentary gentlemen to another, from the Board of Trustees to the Board of Trade.

The ambitious Halifax seized upon the opportunity to make Georgia a model colony with a clear set of regulations stipulating what a colony might do and what it might not do. He assumed that Georgia would be a better candidate for a model colony than Nova Scotia with its many French-speaking Acadians. In 1753 Parliament approved the Georgia model providing for a strong governor authorized to convoke an assembly, recommend legislation, erect courts, grant lands, and otherwise administer the province. The charter stipulated that the legislature consist of an assembly composed of two representatives from each county as soon as counties could be created. A council of appointed officials would serve as an upper house and a court of appeals, its members to be nominated by the Board of Trade and approved by the king in council. Lord Halifax hoped that Georgia would set an example of constitutional government for the older colonies, most of which had developed dangerously deviant attitudes. South Carolina, for example, assumed to its legislature the powers and prerogatives of Parliament itself.[1]

The machinery of Parliament moved slowly, so it was two years after the trustees handed Georgia over to the Board of Trade that Georgia's frame of government was approved and Halifax could appoint the first royal governor. He named John Reynolds, a captain in the royal navy, on August 6, 1754, and gave him ten days to get aboard ship for Georgia. The new governor landed without advance notice at Habersham's wharf on October 29, 1754, and as the news of his arrival spread, a crowd gathered to welcome him.[2]

George Whitefield preceded Reynolds, returning to Georgia in May 1754 and bringing twenty children with him, swelling Bethesda's population to a hundred, the largest number since 1742. The total included slaves who worked the plantation. Whitefield radiated optimism, his health had improved, and he was greeted warmly in Charlestown and Savannah. His friend James Habersham acted as governor until Governor John Reynolds arrived and then enjoyed leadership on the royal council, upon which Francis Harris and Jonathan Bryan also sat. Whitefield's love of Bethesda was matched only by his love of travel, and he soon set off on another "progress" through the northern provinces. His fundraising message emphasized the need for a college in Georgia similar to the college of New Jersey chartered in 1746, where dissenters would be welcome. He visited the college of New Jersey at Princeton and preached to the Presbyterian Synod there, receiving in return an honorary degree. He went on to

---

[1] For the role of Halifax in American affairs, see chap. 8, "The Halifax Initiatives,", in Edward J. Cashin's *Governor Henry Ellis and the Transformation of British North America* (Athens: University of Georgia Press, 1994) 109–30.

[2] Reynolds to Board of Trade, December 5, 1754, *CRG*, 27:32–34.

Boston and expressed pleasure that "souls fly to the gospel like doves to their window." While there, he heard that Governor Reynolds had brought a commission for James Habersham as president of the council and wrote his congratulations: "May the King of kings enable you to discharge your trust, as becomes a good patriot, subject, and Christian!" After a pleasant and successful journey southward, he was back at Bethesda in February 1755.[3]

Despite the helpful advice of Jonathan Bryan, Bethesda's plantations failed to produce the revenue the house required. Whitefield had to reduce the size of his family in successive years. Whitefield's hopes for Georgia's prosperity dimmed because of the first royal governor's incompetence. Whitefield's friends on the council were not without fault. Prior to the governor's arrival, the council angered settlers around Augusta and in the old Darien district by favoring Savannahians in the allocation of land grants. The Augusta merchants resented the efforts of Savannah to garner part of the Indian trade. Thus, in Georgia's first election to a royal assembly, factions developed. A charismatic backcountry newcomer named Edmund Gray organized Georgia's first political party by contacting individuals who had real or imagined reasons for opposing Savannah's control of government. When the assembly met in January 1755, Gray sat as a delegate from Augusta, claiming that two of his party had been defeated by fraudulent vote-counting. He and five of his friends refused to remain in what they believed to be an illegal body. The eleven other members branded Gray's dissenters as outlaws. Governor Reynolds put out a proclamation aimed at the Gray faction, forbidding demonstrations of any kind. Protesting that they did not mean to be insubordinate to the governor, Gray and an estimated 300 of his followers settled below the Altamaha, outside the bounds of Georgia.

For the moment, Reynolds was a hero to the council. However, he soon alienated those gentlemen who expected the benefits of royal appointments by giving his friend and former naval surgeon, William Little, all seven of the appointive positions at his disposal. The

---

[3] John Gillies, D.D., *Memoirs of Rev. George Whitefield* (Middletown CT: Hunt and Noyes, 1837) 162–63.

members of the council complained that Little neglected his many duties, and the governor, in an incredible display of poor judgement, ordered William Little to investigate the charges. Little offered to give up two of his sinecures before allying with the anti-Savannah faction and getting himself elected to the 1756 session of the assembly. After complaining about Little, the council members began to complain about Reynolds. The governor threatened to ignore the council and govern without them. After William Little became speaker of the 1756 assembly, the governor openly sided with the opponents of the Savannah Council. He complained that the council should have assisted him, yet failed to do so because "they were unwilling to part with that power that had so long arbitrarily exercised."[4]

Jonathan Bryan wrote to the Earl of Halifax about the sad state of affairs in what was supposed to be a model colony. Halifax agreed with Bryan and the council that the governor should have conferred with the council on important matters. After receiving other complaints, Halifax recalled Reynolds and named as his replacement his own friend and protégé—the explorer, sea captain, and member of the Royal Society—Henry Ellis. Historian Alan Gallay calls the council's victory over the first governor "the single most important political event to affect the structure of the Georgia political system" until the coming of the American Revolution.[5]

Jonathan Bryan went to Charlestown to greet the new governor personally and to escort him to Savannah. Habersham and Harris's colleague Thomas Rasberry reflected the attitude of the Savannah merchants. Henry Ellis's coming was "a Matter of Joy," he wrote in his journal. Ellis had the gift possessed by the most successful statesmen: he appealed to all segments of society, inspiring them to rise above factionalism for the sake of Georgia. The Union Society with its Bethesda alumni expressed satisfaction with Ellis's administration, citing the preservation of peace in the midst of an Indian war, the relief granted to debtors from provinces other than South Carolina,

---

[4] For Reynolds and his problems, see Cashin, *Henry Ellis*, 115.

[5] Alan Gallay, *The Formation of a Planter Elite: Jonathan Bryan and the Southern Colonial Frontier* (Athens: University of Georgia Press, 1989) 71.

and legislation that barred slaves from engaging in skilled crafts as reasons for their appreciation.[6]

Ellis displayed sympathy for the growing number of slaves: 1,066 in 1753; 1,899 in 1757; 2,100 in 1758; and 3,678 in 1760. He encouraged religious instruction to Savannah's slaves, also recommending that mulattos be freed to form a class in society between whites and blacks. He advocated freeing all slaves when they reached the age of thirty, "[s]omething of the sort I tried in Georgia... but could not accomplish."[7] White Georgians had such hopes of prospering by following the rigid South Carolina slave code that they rejected Ellis's more flexible approach. A more fluid racial system, akin to that in Latin America, might have been the result of Ellis's proposal.

Ellis was at his best in dealing with Indians. In October 1757 he entertained 150 Creek Indians with all the pageantry at his disposal. Captain John Milledge rode out with a new ranger unit to form an escort for the visitors, who were met outside the town by Jonathan Bryan at the head of the Savannah mounted militia. Colonel Noble Jones and the foot militia met the entourage at the Ogeechee gate and they all marched to the governor's house to be greeted by a salvo from seven cannons. Ships in the harbor also joined in the salute. A company of regulars even came over from Charlestown for the occasion, firing a volley and executing some impressive drills. Ellis gave a gracious speech and invited the head chiefs to supper at his house. The Wolf of Muccolossus said he had made many visits to Charlestown and Savannah, but was never received so well.[8]

The result of Ellis's diplomacy was the final settlement of the Bosomworth claims and the continued neutrality of the Creeks during the ongoing French and Indian War. The Creeks helped defend Augusta against an attack by the Cherokees during the winter war in 1760. Ellis returned to England in 1760 to act as advisor to the British ministry on American affairs. In that role, he advised extending

---

[6] Address of the Union Society, *South Carolina Gazette*, November 15–22: 1760.

[7] Cashin, *Henry Ellis*, 115.

[8] Council Minutes, October 29, 1757, *CRG*, 7:645–47.

Georgia's boundary to St. Mary's River. He actually drafted the king's proclamation of 1763 that forbade settlement west of the Appalachian Mountains, reserving the interior for Indians. He helped shape the terms of the treaty of 1763 that ended the Seven Years War with France and Spain. His successor, James Wright, presided over a major Indian conference in Augusta in 1763, at which the Creeks ceded the strip of land between the Savannah and Ogeechee Rivers.[9]

George Whitefield had been frustrated in his efforts to return to Bethesda from England during the Seven Years War. He could not obtain passage while enemy ships were on the prowl. He did not forget Bethesda, however. In September 1756, he had an interview in London with newly appointed Governor Henry Ellis, informing him about the general conditions in Georgia and affairs at Bethesda in particular.[10] He worried about Bethesda, but was relieved by reports that his family there were in no danger. By his preaching alone, he raised enough money in England to pay the obligations he had incurred on Bethesda's behalf. "Blessed be God," he wrote, "that I can send you word, a never failing Providence has put it in my power to pay off all Bethesda's arrears." He wanted to return to Georgia, "but how to do it in war time... I cannot, as yet, be clear in." So, he continued to preach across England, Scotland, and Ireland, never in one place for too long. A lady in Scotland offered to give him her entire estate, but he declined. She then proposed to give everything she had to Bethesda, but once again, he declined. We must suppose that he had sound reasons, but her £7,000 would certainly have made a difference in Bethesda's future, perhaps even assuring the success of the college Whitefield promoted.[11]

---

[9] Cashin's *Henry Ellis* treat Ellis's role in British diplomacy; for Governor Wright, see Edward J. Cashin, "Sowing the Wind: Governor Wright and the Georgia Backcountry on the Eve of the Revolution," *Forty Years of Diversity: Essays on Colonial Georgia,* eds. Harvey H. Jackson and Phinizy Spalding (Athens: University of Georgia Press, 1984) 234.

[10] Gillies, *Memoirs,* 172–73.

[11] Gillies, *Memoirs,* 172–73.

This Whitefield Tabernacle in London was built in 1868 to replace the 1752 tabernacle. It was closed in 1958 and is now used as the Central Foundation School for Boys, so like Bethesda it continues Whitefield's work. It borders on the street still called Tabernacle Street. (Courtesy Royal Commission on the Historical Monuments of England.)

By this time, Whitefield had achieved celebrity status, and fame brought both praise and ridicule. The poet William Cowper wrote in admiration, "He followed Paul; his zeal and kindred flame, His apostolic charity the same...." Fashionable society tended to ridicule rather than praise him. Alexander Pope called Whitefield "a braying ass." On the other hand, the great actor David Garrick once said, "I would give a hundred guineas if I could only say 'O!' like Mr. Whitefield." Another popular actor satirized Whitefield in a play called *The Minor*. The preacher was portrayed as "Dr. Squintum," a reference to Whitefield's slightly crossed eyes. The keeper of a bawdy house loved Dr. Squintum because he assured her of her salvation, despite the fact that she continued in her profession. Lady Huntingdon was so angered by the production that she called upon the Lord Chamberlain to have the play suppressed. Whitefield's biographer, however, believed the attack won more sympathizers for Whitefield than otherwise.[12]

Finally, the war—with its various names—ended. In Europe it was the Seven Years War, in America the French and Indian War, and more recently it has been called the Great War for the Empire. The Treaty of Peace in 1763 had important implications for Georgia. Besides the new southern boundary of the St. Mary's, Georgia had an undisputed western boundary, the Mississippi itself. Of course, the Indian nations occupied the region, but Georgians felt they could persuade the Indians to relinquish their claim by one means or another.

For Bethesda, the end of the war heralded the return of the founder. Whitefield embarked for America from Greenock, Scotland, on June 4, 1763, aboard the *Fanny*. Twelve weeks later he put ashore in Virginia. He wanted to go directly to Bethesda, but doctors strongly advised him against going south in the heat of the summer. So, he went north to Philadelphia and New York instead, stopping as often as he could at Princeton and renewing his resolution to establish a similar college at Bethesda, one in which dissenters from the Church of England would be welcome.

While at Princeton in March 1764, Whitefield met his old and dear friend James Habersham, who happened to be visiting his two sons, James and Joseph, then enrolled in the college. Habersham assured Whitefield that affairs at Bethesda were in good order. His family there longed to see him, but Habersham understood the necessity of the Itinerant's lingering in the North for reasons of health: "a cold climate seems to brace up his decayed Nerves." Habersham remarked with amazement on the crowds that continued to turn out for Whitefield's sermons.[13]

---

[12] Henry, 159–61, 165; Gillies, *Memoirs*, 174.

[13] Habersham to Messrs. Deberdt and Barket, March 31, 1764, GHS *Collections*, 6:20; Gillies, *Memoirs*, 180.

Whitefield studied the charter of the college at Philadelphia (later the University of Pennsylvania) as he prepared his proposal for a college in Georgia. He discussed the project with the Reverend William Smith, the college president and minister of the Church of England. Smith agreed with his visitor on the need for a college in the South, because there was none below William and Mary in Virginia. He questioned Whitefield about the religious affiliation of the institution. Would the college become a "nursery of Methodism"? Whitefield assured him that it would not be sectarian, but that a clergyman of the Church of England would be president. If the Bishop of London appointed an American commissary, Whitefield would name that prelate to the Board of Trustees. Smith wrote the Bishop of London, endorsing Whitefield's proposal.[14] Apparently, Whitefield changed his mind after speaking with President Smith regarding the religious affiliation of the future Bethesda College president.

Whitefield followed the cool weather south and was in Savannah by December 1764. Governor James Wright greeted him warmly and agreed to support the college in any way he could. One way, suggested Whitefield, would be to grant Bethesda 2,000 additional acres for more plantation land. With Habersham, Harris, and Bryan enthusiastically supporting the application, the council immediately agreed to the grant.[15]

Lord Adam Gordon happened by Savannah on his tour of the southern provinces, and on February 12, 1765, Governor Wright escorted him out to Bethesda to see the most handsome house in Georgia. Lord Adam commented favorably on the location and the impressive size of the building, listening attentively as Whitefield described his plans for a college. He wrote in his journal that over £12,000 had been spent on Bethesda—£3,000 of that Whitefield's own contribution and the rest from well-wishers. Gordon thought the college would tend very much to the advantage of Georgia and the other southern provinces. Whitefield expressed his delight at the visit

---

[14] William Smith to Bishop Terrick, June 25, 1765, *Fulham Papers*, Lambeth Palace Library.

[15] Whitefield to Mr. S.S., January 14, 1765, *Select Collection*, 3:30.

of Lord Adam, Governor Wright, and their entourage, describing how Gordon took him aside and congratulated him on his contributions to Bethesda, telling him that his plan for a college "was beautiful, rational, and practicable." The best part was Gordon's assurance that the king himself would look favorably on the project.[16]

Whitefield was pleased at the good work of his new superintendent, Ambrose Wright. Wright had made much needed repairs on the big house, also stocking it with provisions and putting all its accounts in good order. Everything seemed to be going well. Whitefield wrote, "What a blessed winter have I had! Peace and love, and harmony, and plenty, reign here!" The next logical step was the presentation to the king's council of his request for a college charter. He loved Bethesda better than any other place, but he never stayed there long. Again, as in the past, it was for Bethesda that he traveled back to England. "Now farewell, my beloved Bethesda," he wrote, "surely the most delightful place in all the southern parts of America."[17]

The Itinerant preached a farewell sermon in Savannah. As usual, the church was crowded, the attendees spilled out into the yard, and individuals climbed on ladders to see through the windows. One interested observer happened to be the famous Olaudah Equiano, a Nigerian-born slave who later wrote a narrative of his own life. Equiano had rarely seen a church so crowded, and one of the locals informed him that George Whitefield was speaking inside. The incident remained fresh in Equiano's memory when he penned his life story many years later: "I had often heard of this gentleman, and had wished to see and hear him; but I never before had an opportunity. I now therefore resolved to gratify myself with the sight and pressed in amidst the multitude. When I got into the church I saw this pious man exhorting the people with the greatest fervor and earnestness, and sweating as much as ever I did while in slavery on Montserrat

---

[16] Lord Gordon's account is in Newton D. Mereness's, *Travels in the American Colonies* (New York: Antiquarian Press, 1961) 396–97.

[17] Gillies, *Memoirs*, 182–83; Whitefield to Mr. S. S., 14 January 1765; Whitefield to Robert Keen, February 13, 1765, *Select Collection*, 3:329–22.

beach."[18] Equiano had never before witnessed clergymen exerting themselves so forcefully.

Negotiating for a Charter

James Habersham informed Georgia's agent William Knox about Whitefield's intentions regarding Bethesda. Knox, who had come to Georgia with Henry Ellis and served on the governor's council, now acted as one of the clerks on the king's council. Habersham asked Knox to enlist Lord Dartmouth's support in obtaining a charter for Bethesda College. Because Whitefield published the correspondence concerning the application of a charter, contemporaries and historians since then have assumed that published account contained the whole story. Whitefield's proposal, addressed to the king and presented to Granville Sharp, a clerk of the king's council, recited how important Bethesda had been in helping Georgia survive the difficult early years. The home had employed artisans who might otherwise have left the colony, and it had trained skilled workers who remained in Georgia. Whitefield expressed the opinion that Bethesda helped make Georgia "a very flourishing state." At the present time, young gentlemen had to travel to the north to get an education; how much better it would be to have them remain in Georgia for their education. The addition of the two Florida colonies by the Treaty of 1763 gave Georgia a central location in the deep South. Finally, Whitefield got to the point, writing in his application that he intended to transform Bethesda into a college after the model of the College of New Jersey at Princeton. He had in mind "the education of persons of superior rank."[19]

---

[18] Robert J. Allison, ed., *The Interesting Narrative of the Life of Olaudah Equiano Written by Himself* (Boston: Bedford Books, 1995) 116. The editor errs when he writes, "The evangelist was in town to close the orphanage he had opened with such high hopes thirty years earlier" (8). The evangelist was off to England to convert his academy into a college.

[19] Habersham to William Knox, July 17, 1765, GHS *Collections* 6:38–40; George Whitefield, *A Letter to His Excellency Governor Wright Giving an*

The men Whitefield proposed as wardens, or trustees, of the college represented Savannah's wealthiest gentlemen: Governor James Wright, Attorney-General Anthony Stokes, John Graham, Noble Jones, Noble W. Jones, John Smith, James Read, William Gibbons. Whitefield's Bethesda allies were represented by James Habersham, James Habersham Jr., Joseph Clay (Habersham's nephew), Francis Harris, and Jonathan Bryan. The Church of England clergymen Samuel Frink and Edward Ellington were included, probably to allay fears of "a seminary of Methodism." Henry Laurens, his brother James, and six other South Carolina gentlemen were also included. Others were from Boston, Philadelphia, New York, Edinburgh, Glasgow and London, Lord Dartmouth being among the latter nominees. The international character of the Board of Wardens was intended as more of a lobbying group than a functioning committee.[20] And, too, Whitefield hoped to impress the ministry with the number and importance of his friends.

The facts of the college negotiations, to the extent that Whitefield knew them, were straightforward. He gave a copy of the petition to Granville Sharp, the clerk of the king's council, who delivered it to the Lord President, the Earl of Northington, who in turn submitted it to the Archbishop of Canterbury, Thomas Secker. Whitefield gave a second copy to Lord Dartmouth, and Dartmouth referred it to the same archbishop, Thomas Secker. That dignitary wrote Whitefield to inquire, "Would the president of the college be a member of the Church of England? What endowment could be provided?" Whitefield answered candidly. He could not require the head of the college to be a minister or even a member of the Church of England. He said that the College of New York (Columbia) had been retarded in its progress by a similar provision. He preferred to build his college on a "broad bottom." The College of Philadelphia and the College of New Jersey had no such qualifications, yet they prospered nonetheless. Whitefield

---

Account of the Steps taken relative to the Converting The Georgia Orphan House into A College (London: 1768) 3.

[20] Draft of an Act for Founding a College, *Huntingdon Papers*, Cheshunt Collection A 3/1 (Westminster College: Cambridge, England).

had collected money from many persons not of the Church of England on the condition that the college be non-sectarian. He believed the president probably would be an Anglican, perhaps even a member of the clergy, but he did not want to stipulate the requirement in the charter. If the archbishop worried about his becoming president, he should worry no longer. Whitefield said he had no intention of becoming the chief administrator: "Alas! My shoulders are too weak for the support of such academic burden." In fact, he would not even nominate the first president himself. Rather, he would ask Lord Dartmouth to name the first head of the college.[21]

As for the endowment, Whitefield could guarantee an income of £500 a year. Besides that, Bethesda owned nearly 2,000 acres in the immediate vicinity, plus two thousand acres on the Altamaha. The Reverend Bartholomew Zouberbuhler willed another 1,000 acres on the condition that slaves there be taught religion. In 1767, Bethesda owned thirty slaves. Negro children belonging to the college would be instructed by one of the students in lieu of tuition. Whitefield intended to instruct Indian children also. "The whole [effort] will be a free gift to the colony of Georgia."[22]

The final response to Whitefield came from Lord Northington. Using strong language, he insisted on a guarantee that the head of the college be a member of the Church of England and that public prayers be taken from the Anglican prayer book. Whitefield then wrote a letter to the archbishop that deserves to be better known. He defended his decision to erect the college on a "broad bottom":

> This I judged was sufficiently warranted to do, from the known, long established, mild, and uncoersive genius of the British government; also from your grace's moderation toward Protestant dissenters; from the unconquerable attachment of the Americans to toleration principles, as well as from the

[21] Whitefield to Archbishop Secker, June 17, 1767, in *A Letter to Governor Wright*, 6–8.

[22] Whitefield to Archbishop Secker, July 4, 1767, in *A Letter to Governor Wright*, 11.

> avowed, habitual feelings of my own heart. This being the case, and as your grace, by your silence seems to be like minded with the lord president; and as your grace's and his lordship's influence will undoubtedly extend itself to others, I would beg leave, after returning all due acknowledgments to informs your grace that I intend troubling your grace and his lordship no more about this so long depending concern.[23]

Whitefield wrote the letter on October 16, 1767. On November 11, 1767, he asked the Archbishop to return all correspondence, without saying why. On February 12, 1768, he revealed that he intended to publish all the letters connected with Bethesda, claiming he owed it to Governor Wright, the Council and the Assembly of Georgia, and all who were interested in the matter.[24] Whitefield never knew that the archbishop did not hand over the entire correspondence. The complete record is housed in the Lambeth Palace Library in London, and a thorough reading reveals that Archbishop Secker was less than candid in his dealings with Whitefield.

In May 1767, when Lord Northington forwarded the proposal to the Archbishop of Canterbury, the archbishop asked the advice of Bishops Terrick and Greene. The two clerics made helpful recommendations, suggesting that Bethesda change the regulation stipulating that professors hold their office at the pleasure of the wardens. Professors would not accept such uncertain tenure. A similar statute in the original draft of the William and Mary charter had been changed at Bishop Terrick's suggestion. Terrick would prefer to state that prayers confirm to the Church of England rubric, as in the charter of the College of New York. However, he admitted that the requirement was not advisable in a college open to various denominations. If Whitefield would consent to these minor adjustments, "it would be... as much as we can expect in a scheme coming from such a

[23] Whitefield to Archbishop Secker, October 16, 1767, in *A Letter to Governor Wright*, 16–19.

[24] Whitefield to Archbishop Secker, February 12, 1768, in *A Letter to Governor Wright*, 21.

quarter." He had no other objections, except to suggest trimming the number of wardens. Clearly, Terrick, the Bishop of London, believed that there were no serious obstacles to the granting of a charter.[25]

Lord Northington had even fewer objections. In his letter to the archbishop on August 27, 1767, he seemed to assume that the charter would be approved. He observed that the charter did not require the head to be a Church of England member, but he thought this omission was entirely appropriate in a colony where few ministers had academic training. He wondered at the vagueness of the clause referring to public prayer, but deferred to the judgment of the Archbishop.[26] Whitefield never realized that two bishops had no serious objections to his college and that the minister who had the responsibility of granting the charter saw nothing wrong with allowing individuals other than Anglicans to head the institution.

The Archbishop of Canterbury reacted swiftly to Lord Northington's innocuous letter. On the day after it was written, the archbishop wrote a reply, saying that Lord Northington must reject the charter, but must not let Whitefield know about the archbishop's involvement. "Mr. Whitefield will think it is my fault if you do not yield to this scheme," he wrote, "whereas I want him to fear that your Lordship's consent to it cannot be obtained." The prelate than spelled out in specific detail what he wanted Lord Northington to say to Whitefield. He should insist on the head of the college being a member of the Church of England, also demanding that public prayer should not be extempore. Lord Northington must not add "the least civility," but must be quite definite in his response.[27]

Shortly afterwards and before Whitefield received Northington's decision, Whitefield wrote to ask if the Lord President had reached a conclusion. The archbishop scribbled a note to Northington that

---

[25] Remarks by Bishops Terrick and Greene on Whitefield's proposal for a college, May 1767, *Society for the Propagation of the Gospel* 9, 251–53, Lambeth Palace Library.

[26] Northington to Archbishop of Canterbury, August 27, 1767, *SPG*, 9, 254, Lambeth Palace Library.

[27] Archbishop Secker to Northington, August 28, 1767, *SPG*, 9, 255, Lambeth Palace Library.

Whitefield should be told to expect an answer any day. Clearly, the Archbishop of Canterbury was intimidated by the Great Itinerant and declined to reveal his own part in the refusal of the charter. Northington's answer to Whitefield conformed exactly to the archbishop's instructions, word for word.[28] Although Whitefield put on a brave public face, he was deeply disappointed in the rejection of the charter. He wrote a friend, "None but God knows what a concern is upon me now, in respect of Bethesda." He would not give up his dream of a college, but he lowered his immediate goal. He would first launch a public academy, then build it into a college.[29]

Bethesda boys, and indeed all Georgians, might wonder: "What if" a charter had been granted? Bethesda College would today rank with other eighteenth-century colleges, like Columbia, Princeton, and Pennsylvania. Whitefield came so close to getting his charter. He involved the highest ranking persons in the British government and the Church of England, as well as the governor and both houses of the Georgia legislature. Was he to blame for this failure to obtain a charter? He could have accepted the condition that the head should be a member of the Church of England; after all, he assumed that such would be the case. However, he had promised his donors a "broad bottom," and we cannot fault him for being a man of his word. Clearly, Archbishop Thomas Secker deserves criticism. His advisors had no real objections, nor did the king's councilors. He alone vetoed the charter and dissembled about the part he played.

Turning to Savannah

Once again, Whitefield had to call upon his friends in Savannah to come to Bethesda's assistance. He wrote Governor Wright to inform him of the rejection of the charter, but solicited his help in starting a public academy at Bethesda, "My beloved Bethesda will not only be

---

[28] The Archbishop's note is on the reverse of Whitefield's letter of September 1, 1767, *SPG*, 9, 256.

[29] Gillies, *Memoirs*, 189.

continued as a house of mercy for poor orphans, but be confirmed as a seat or nursery of sound learning and religious education." Whitefield's prediction set a goal for Bethesda and, in effect, challenged Georgians in general and Savannahians in particular to assist in achieving that goal. Two centuries later, the friends of Bethesda are still guided by that policy.[30]

Elizabeth Whitefield died of a fever on August 9, 1769. Stuart Clark Henry, Whitefield's biographer, has this to say about their marriage: "Mrs. Whitefield, though an unsuccessful wife, was a constant one, and her husband, though oblique, was faithful."[31]

Other than burying his wife, there were other duties for Whitefield to take care of before returning to America. Lady Huntingdon kept building chapels at her scattered houses to give employment to Methodist ministers. Whitefield dedicated the Huntingdon chapels at Bath, Bristol, and Tunbridge Wells, and he presided at the opening of Lady Huntingdon's college at Treveca in Breconshire, Wales. Declining health held him in England longer than he intended, but on August 8, 1769, he boarded the *Friendship* bound for America. He recruited a young man named Cornelius Winter to join his Bethesda family for the specific purpose of instructing the plantation slaves.[32]

Ambrose Wright, custodian of the orphan house, met Whitefield as his ship landed at Charlestown on November 30, 1769, and escorted the Itinerant to a joyful reception at Bethesda. Wright had hurried construction in anticipation of the Founder's arrival; the nearly finished wings were a pleasant surprise to Whitefield. The great house in its peaceful setting always had a curative effect, and Whitefield's letters from Bethesda have a buoyant, optimistic, and above all, happy tone. "Everything exceeds my most sanguine expectations," he wrote soon after arriving. The *Georgia Gazette* carried the news of the ceremony that attended dedication of the new additions. Habersham

---

[30] Whitefield, *A Letter to Governor Wright*, 20.

[31] Henry, 76.

[32] Gillies, *Memoirs*, 191–92; William Jay, *Memoirs of the Life and Character of the Late Rev. Cornelius Winter* (New York: Samuel Whiting, 1811) 59.

arranged for Governor Wright to do the honors on Bethesda's anniversary day, March 25, 1769. The Reverend Samuel Frink, rector of Christ Church in Savannah, delivered the sermon, and members of the council and house and "a great many others" attended.[33]

The orphan house had never been so well staffed as it was at the turn of 1770. Whitefield recruited the Reverend Edward Ellington to serve as chaplain as well as professor of English and Rhetoric. Ambrose Wright's two brothers, Thomas and Robert, joined him on the staff. Robert's wife, Ann, proved particularly helpful in managing the girls' department. James Crane served as steward. Benjamin Stirk, Peter Edwards, William Trigg, and Cornelius Winter helped in various ways. Winter, who had lived with the Whitefields before Elizabeth Whitefield's death, had the responsibility of tutoring the blacks on the plantation. Robert Smith acted as Whitefield's personal attendant; in another echelon of society, he would have been called "a gentleman's gentleman."

Early in January, Whitefield decided to demonstrate Bethesda's progress to his Savannah neighbors and to promote his plan of expanding the orphan house into an academy. There had never been a grander show before at Bethesda, and very few since. A participant described the event in detail in the *Georgia Gazette*. As the dignitaries reached Bethesda, they were met by Whitefield himself and escorted upstairs into the fifty-foot gallery. As more visitors arrived, two other rooms were opened: a drawing room and a library across the hall. The guests regaled themselves with what we today would call "heavy hors d'oeuvres," including ham and cold tongue and, of course, tea.

At noon the large bell sounded for chapel. Whitefield had prepared an impressive demonstration displaying the new "academical" function of Bethesda. A procession formed, consisting of the students in flat caps and black gowns. Then came the women on the staff and the male assistants, the stewards, and Superintendent Ambrose Wright—all carrying white wands. Next came the clerk of the chapel, followed by the Founder in his Oxford square cap and accompanied

[33] Gillies, *Memoirs*, 199; *Georgia Gazette*, March 29, 1769.

by the Reverend Ellington. The guests paraded in after the Bethesda family had entered.

Whitefield, basking in the moment, addressed the assemblage for forty-five minutes. He reflected upon the difficult early years and upon the criticism Bethesda endured. He told how he had been ridiculed for opening an orphanage in a desert, dwelling on what a marvelous contrast this day presented. Few speakers could move an audience the way George Whitefield could, and he played skillfully upon the emotions of his listeners. The reporter for the *Georgia Gazette* wrote that the "whole auditory was affected."[34]

One of the orphans then spoke in an eloquent old-style rhetoric that enhanced Bethesda's educational pretensions. He began by protesting his ignorance in language that made his protestation sound like burlesque: "For what am I, a poor unlettered orphan, unlearned, almost in the very rudiments of my mother tongue, and totally unskilled in the persuasive arts of speaking, that I should be called to speak before such a venerable, August assembly as is this day convened under Bethesda's roof?" The speaker went on in purple prose to rejoice over Bethesda's progress, to heap praise upon the Founder, to thank the governor for "laying the first brick of yonder wings," to recognize James Habersham for all his labors, and to say something appropriate to everyone present. All in all, this was quite a *tour de force* for a poor, unlettered orphan.[35]

After the speeches, the guests and family moved downstairs to the forty-foot dining room, with its eight tall sash windows and, on the end wall, a full-length portrait of the Founder. Abetted by "plenty of wine and punch" as well as "a handsome and plentiful dinner," all present "seemed most pleasingly surprised with their spiritual and bodily entertainment." The company dispersed with mellow opinions of Bethesda. The next day the Speaker of the House of Assembly entered into the minutes a resolution praising "the decency and

---

[34] *Georgia Gazette*, January 19, 1770.

[35] Gillies, *Memoirs*, 200–201.

propriety of behavior" of the Bethesda residents and Whitefield's "indefatigable zeal" for promoting the welfare of Georgia.[36]

We know much about Bethesda in 1770. The great house, its new wings, and outbuildings sat on the edge of a marsh. Its schooner could maneuver up the Vernon River and the Back River to its dock at high tide. Five hundred acres surrounded the house. Two nearby plantations, Nazareth and Ephrata, belonged to the house and were worked by forty-nine slaves. Five hundred acres near Bethesda and two thousand on the Altamaha remained uncultivated, but were considered part of the endowment, as were another thousand acres contributed by Reverend Zouberbuhler. Unfortunately, we do not know the names of the orphans or students.

One Bethesda boy, Daniel Stevens, wrote his memoirs many years later, his clear writing a credit to the education he received at Bethesda. Stevens narrated that he was born in Charlestown in 1749, and his father, Samuel, had died when he was very young. His mother, Abigail, the granddaughter of the famous Colton Nather, was consoled in her distress by George Whitefield. Whitefield offered to take Daniel to Bethesda and Mrs. Stevens agreed. Whitefield himself taught Latin while he was at Bethesda, and Nathaniel Polhill took over the Latin class during the Itinerant's frequent absences. Stevens recalled that two of his classmates achieved prominence in the Revolutionary War: Colonel John Barnwell and Major William Harold Wegg of Beaufort, South Carolina. Stevens's mother was taken into the care of Reverend John J. Zubly of Savannah's Independent Presbyterian Church.

While still at Bethesda and at the age of nineteen, Stevens married Patience Catherine Norton, originally from Rhode Island and presumably a resident of Bethesda herself. When their first son was born in 1768, the young couple left Bethesda to seek their fortune in Charlestown. After serving as an apprentice with John Champness, a "wharfholder" and factor, he became a partner in the firm. Stevens went on to a successful career as a merchant and performed distinguished service during the American Revolution. Daniel Stevens

[36] Resolution of the Commons House of Assembly, January 29, 1770, in Gillies, *Memoirs*, 199; *Georgia Gazette*, January 19, 1770.

attempted to repay his moral debt to George Whitefield by serving as Chairman of the Board of Commissioners for the Charleston Orphan House, founded in 1790. After thirty-seven years on the commission, he estimated that he had helped nearly two thousand children, placing them in useful occupations. We do not know the story of hundreds of Bethesda boys and girls, but if Daniel Stevens is a typical example, they were the stuff of which a new nation was fashioned.[37]

George Whitefield's letters from Bethesda reflect his state of mind. On February 10, 1770, he reported a conversation with Governor Wright about the establishment of a college. Wright vigorously supported the plan. At the time, two dissenting ministers solicited funds in Savannah for the College of New Jersey, so Whitefield postponed a collection for his own college. He contacted Henry Laurens and other Charlestown gentlemen and secured their consent to act as wardens. Wardens from Savannah and Charlestown would be active, while those from abroad and in the North would be corresponding.[38]

On February 27, Whitefield noted that "all things at Bethesda go on quite well... Mr. Wright is the main spring, with regard to the buildings; and all other wheels move orderly and well." On April 20, 1770, he wrote to a friend in England, "We enjoy a little heaven on earth here... O Bethesda, my Bethel, my Peniel! My happiness is inconceivable." He left Bethesda, not knowing it would be for the last time, on April 24, 1770. In a letter written that day, he complimented Robert Wright, "a quiet, ingenious, good creature"; and Ann Wright, "an excellent mistress of the family." He also praised the good work of his staff, saying they would go on improving Bethesda "while I take my gospel range to the northward." He planned to follow old habits, traveling in the North during the hot season and returning to Savannah in the cool weather.[39]

---

[37] Stevens's narrative is in the Daniel Stevens Papers, South Carolina Historical Society, Charleston.

[38] Gillies, *Memoirs*, 201–202.

[39] Whitefield to Robert Keen, April 20, 1770, *Select Collection*, 3:419; Gillies, *Memoirs*, 203–206.

From May through September, Whitefield circulated through New York and New England, everywhere preaching to the usual crowds. On September 29, 1770, he lodged at a house in Newburyport, Massachusetts, but when a severe asthma attack came on, he had increasing difficulty breathing. His attendant, Robert Smith, was with him at the last and related how Whitefield's mind remained clear even as he gasped for breath. He prayed for a blessing on Bethesda "and his dear family there," for his chapels in England, and for all those who had heard him preach. Early on the morning of the September 30, he said to Smith, "I am dying." Those were his last words.[40]

Eulogies in honor of Whitefield were voiced from pulpits all over America and England. John Wesley preached a funeral sermon for his old friend in London. One of the most remarkable tributes was a poem written by seventeen-year-old Phyllis Wheatley, a slave girl belonging to J. Wheatley of Boston and addressed to the Countess of Huntingdon. She wrote, in part:

> He prayed that grace in every heart might dwell,
> He longed to see America excel;
> He charg'd its youth to let grace divine
> Arise, and in their future actions shine."[41]

Needless to say, Savannah fell into mourning at the news of Whitefield's death. Cornelius Winter wrote to a friend, "You have no conception of the effect of Mr. Whitefield's death upon the inhabitants of Georgia. All the black cloth in the stores was bought up; the pulpit and desks of the church, the branches, the organ loft, the pews of the governor and council, were covered with black. The governor and council, in deep mourning, convened at the state house." The honorable gentlemen proceeded to the church to listen to the rector Reverend Samuel Frink give the eulogy. Bethesda's professor Edward

---

[40] Gillies, *Memoirs*, 212.
[41] Gillies, *Memoirs*, 225.

Ellington preached another sermon in the afternoon, while John J. Zubly did the same in the Independent Presbyterian Church.[42]

The Georgia Assembly voted to defray the expense of bringing the body of the Itinerant back to Georgia to be buried at Bethesda, the place he loved best. However, Georgians were thwarted by the Reverend Jonathan Parsons, in whose house Whitefield died. Parsons hastened to inter the famous preacher in his own church, the Presbyterian Church of Newburyport. Even in death, Whitefield would not rest at Bethesda.[43]

James Habersham, whose friendship with Whitefield was deep and lasting, published a letter in the *Georgia Gazette*, stressing his friend's "uncommonly warm, affectionate, and unabated regard" for Georgia. He called attention to the heavy burden Whitefield bore of constantly raising money for Bethesda. Habersham could not resist chiding those who accused Whitefield of profiting from Bethesda, even accusing him "with unrelenting virulence, as a cheat, an importer, and a public robber." Habersham felt a sense of vindication as all Savannah praised Whitefield's virtues.[44]

---

[42] Gillies, *Memoirs*, 229.

[43] Henry, 15.

[44] Habersham to Countess of Huntingdon, December 10, 1770, GHS *Collections*, 6:102–110.

CHAPTER FIVE

BETHESDA AND THE AMERICAN REVOLUTION

Whitefield willed Bethesda to the Countess of Huntingdon and charged her, in his gracious and circumspect way, with the task of completing the transformation of Bethesda into a major college. As executor of the will, James Habersham wrote to the countess on December 10, 1770, enclosing the testimonial he had written in the *Gazette*. He asked for the power of attorney to act on the countess's behalf for himself, Francis Harris, John Smith, Joseph Clay, Ambrose Wright, and James Habersham, Jr. They would promote legislation to create a college as Whitefield intended. Unfortunately, though, Whitefield's will was poorly drawn. A great deal of legal trouble would have been spared "had the good man known as much about the law as he did of the Gospel."[1]

Whitefield had indicated to Habersham his intention to increase the number of slaves to seventy or so, in the hope that their labor would help support the school. With the consent of the countess, Habersham procured the slaves, urging as an immediate priority the appointment of a president for Bethesda College, one who was both a clergyman of the Church of England and a gentleman. Work was still being done on the chapel and the two wings, but that work would soon be completed. Habersham thought Richard Smith should have returned to Georgia after Whitefield's death, but instead, Smith had taken the draft of the proposed college legislation to England to give the countess, thus wasting valuable time in Habersham's opinion.

Whitefield had engaged Edward Ellington to teach at Bethesda, but Habersham thought Ellington lacked credentials to head the school.

---

[1] Habersham to Countess, December 10, 1770, Georgia Historical Society Collections, 6:102–109.

Besides, Samuel Frink, the rector of Christ Church, disagreed with Ellington's views, and besides, Ellington intended to accept the offer of a church in Charlestown. Finally, Habersham explained that Cornelius Winter would deliver Whitefield's will to the countess in person. Winter intended to seek ordination and to return to continue preaching to slaves.[2]

Ambrose Wright, the acting superintendent, also informed Lady Huntingdon that he would proceed with construction unless she objected. More work had to be done on the new chapel behind the house. A new multi-purpose building one hundred feet long would be used not only for corn storage, but also as a stable, coach, and cart house. He intended to construct other outbuildings as well, all in preparation for the new college clientele. Needless to say, Bethesda was a busy place.

James Habersham reverted to his old role of thirty years ago in assuming control of the institution. He paid Ellington for six months service as Ellington left for Charlestown, and also hired Ambrose Wright's brother-in-law Edward Langworthy to replace Ellington. He did not mean that Langworthy should "supercede the necessity of a Gentleman," but should make a beginning in teaching the classics. He had the support of the wealthy planter-merchant John Graham and other Savannah gentlemen for a school aimed toward "academical learning," and believed that all "the better families" would send their sons to Bethesda. He would continue to take in orphans as charity cases and charge tuition for other students. The poor children would learn trades and the scholars, by implication, would become gentlemen.[3]

Habersham felt it important to continue Whitefield's efforts to cultivate support for Bethesda in Savannah, so he celebrated Anniversary Day on March 25, 1771, in much the same way

---

[2] Habersham to Countess, January 9, 1771, Huntingdon Collection, Cheshunt College Archives, Westminster College, Cambridge, England. All citations are from folder A 3/1, unless otherwise noted.

[3] Habersham to Countess, January 9, 1771, Huntingdon Collection.

Whitefield had done the previous year. Again Governor Wright attended with several members of the council and formally dedicated the new chapel. George Whitefield's nephew Peter Edwards, described as an orphan in the *Gazette*, reminded the assembly that Governor Wright had laid the first brick two years before. The new wings were "intended for the accommodation of young gentlemen intended to be educated in Academical Learning to enable them to move in a superior sphere of life." Edwards borrowed from Habersham's testimonial and repeated some of the points made by the student speaker the previous year, ending by assuring the guests that he and his fellow students had received a more than sound education.[4] Reverend Edward Ellington also came over from St. Bartholomew's parish in South Carolina to preach a suitable sermon. Then the students recited passages "from some of the most approved English authors." Their teacher, Edward Langworthy, managed to make the point that if he had had more time coaching them, they would have done an even better job. The entire performance celebrated the educational function of the new Bethesda, while afterwards the company retired to the great hall where they enjoyed good food and drink.[5]

Meanwhile, Habersham kept Robert Keen, Whitefield's London executor, apprised of events at Bethesda. On March 28, 1771, he wrote that Ambrose Wright had suffered the loss of two sisters and a brother. In spite of that, he had married and bought a townhouse in Savannah, thanks to a loan by Habersham. John Crane intended to marry and "end his days" at Bethesda. Four sons of Savannah's "first gentlemen" were enrolled at Bethesda. By May, Habersham could report to the countess that he had taken in four orphans, making a total of sixteen on charity and ten boarders.[6]

Not everyone liked the direction Bethesda was taking. In fact, Cornelius Winter took a jaundiced view of what he considered to be

---

[4] *Georgia Gazette*, March 27, 1771.

[5] *Georgia Gazette*, March 27, 1771.

[6] Habersham to Keen, January 3, 1771, Georgia Historical Society, Collections, 6:111–12.

the secularization of Bethesda. In the same month that Habersham assured the countess all was well at the home, Winter informed the good lady through an intermediary that she had reason to be concerned. There were only a few orphans, he said, "and no symptoms of grace in any." Gone were the days of weeping and gnashing of teeth, of letters about dry bones and hellfire. To make matters worse, Winter had no use for Whitefield's favorite manager, Ambrose Wright. He said that Wright lacked grace and had little zeal, "a mere cabinet maker, without godliness." The founder himself fell into disfavor with Winter over the "sumptuous feast" he served on January 28, 1770, "for all the better dressed people." Whitefield had intended to make the dinner an annual event, but "I hope you will put a stop to this guttling business." Winter added that he hoped "the Orphan-house may not become a mere Blue-coat Hospital and Grammar School."[7]

Winter comes across as a talebearer and something of a snob, especially for his criticism of Ambrose Wright, a man Whitefield admired and called "the main spring" moving the machinery of Bethesda. However, there was some retributive justice in the treatment Winter received when he applied to the Bishop of London for ordination. In his interview with Bishop Terrick, Winter presented testimonials from Governor Wright, James Habersham, and Reverend Samuel Frink.

> The Bishop began by asking, "You have been over to America as a preacher?"
> "No, as a catechist," Winter answered.
> "But you have preached," persisted the bishop.
> "I have attempted to explain the scriptures to the Negroes, and the curiosity of some people have excited them to hear;" Winter explained, sensing that he was in trouble.
> "It was illegal," snapped the bishop, "you had no right to do so."

---

[7] A. C. H. Seymour, *Selina Countess of Huntingdon*, 2 vols. (London: William Edward Ranter, 1844) 2:255–58.

The interview ended with the bishop sending the young man down to the headquarters of the Society for the Propagation of the Gospel to see if he could get their endorsement to be ordained as a missionary. The society had no intention of sponsoring Methodist missionaries and told Winter they could not recommend him. But Winter did not give up without a final struggle. He appealed to Benjamin Franklin, explaining that he was a disciple of Whitefield, and asked for a recommendation. Franklin obliged him, as did the Countess of Huntingdon. Still, the new testimonials failed to impress the Bishop of London. "Now Mr. Whitefield is dead, you want to throw yourself under our wing," accused the prelate. On that rude note, the interview ended.[8]

On the basis of Winter's information, Lady Huntingdon lectured James Habersham, reminding him that the aim of the institution should be the propagation of the gospel and that he must beware of an "unconverted" minister. After all, such a person was considered a "dangerous Enemy to the Cross of Christ." Habersham's letters took on a different, slightly discouraged tone. Langworthy had proven a disappointment as a classics instructor. "He appears to be of a fickle and unsettled disposition, and seems to have accepted of his present employment rather from convenience than choice." Ambrose Wright believed Langworthy's problem stemmed from "a Defect in the Brain." Also, Langworthy's religious life left much to be desired. Indeed, Langworthy left Bethesda, and rumors immediately began to spread that the grand plans for a college had gone awry.

Only two scholars remained by May 1772: the sons of John Graham and of Joseph Clay. Clay happened to be a nephew of James Habersham, and a new friend of Bethesda. Habersham had sunk almost three hundred pounds of his own money into Bethesda and could see no way for it to become a self-sustaining proposition. At the time, James Habersham shouldered the laborious duties of acting governor while Governor James Wright lobbied in England for permission to deal

[8] A. C. H. Seymour, *Selina Countess of Huntingdon*, 252–53.

with the Indians for a cession of land. The times were increasingly troubled. Habersham worried that Georgia's future was uncertain; so was Bethesda's.[9]

Lady Huntingdon and Bethesda

For Habersham and Bethesda, help was on the way. Selina, Countess of Huntingdon, took to heart Whitefield's commission to her to make the college a reality. She has been mentioned earlier in this narrative, but other details of her life should be added. Few women in England were more distinguished by birth and marriage than Selina Shirley, born on August 24, 1707, the second of the three daughters of Washington Shirley, Earl Ferrers, whose lineage traced back to the eleventh century. One of the family ancestors came over with William the Conqueror. When she was nine years old, the death of a child her age made a profound impression. Thereafter she thought often of heaven and of religious matters. On June 3, 1728, she married Theophilus Hastings, Earl of Huntingdon, her senior by ten years, and went to live with him in his ancestral estate in Leicestershire. He respected her piety and they enjoyed eighteen years of a loving relationship; she outlived him by forty years. During many of those years she enjoyed the close friendship of Lord Hastings's sisters, Lady Anne and Lady Margaret, the wife of Benjamin Ingham. Influenced by Ingham, she placed her faith in God and recovered from an illness she believed to be fatal. George Whitefield explained that her experience amounted to a conversion. Thereafter Lady Huntingdon thought of Whitefield as God's messenger and believed that, through him, she had been called to do wonderful things in America. Ingham's stories about his missionary work among the Indians in Savannah

---

[9] Habersham to Governor Wright, May 30, 1772; Habersham to Countess, May 15, 1771, Georgia Historical Society Collections, 6:180–81, 126–31; Habersham to Countess, June 5, 1771, Bethesda College Collection, Georgia Historical Society, Savannah.

stirred her romantic imagination, and visions of Bethesda as a seminary for missionaries who would go forth into the wilderness and bring the gospel to heathen Indians excited her. At times, she imagined herself going to America as a missionary. Though it may seem surprising that George Whitefield bequeathed Bethesda to the countess instead of to his friend Habersham, Whitefield had good reasons for doing so. The countess shared his spiritual values; she had proven her ability as an organizer and manager, and not least of all, she had enough money to support a college in America, just as she supported a college at Treveca in Wales.

The countess's first inspiration was typically bold and daring. She had more students than were needed at Treveca. Bethesda had too few, so she would ask for volunteers to go to Bethesda. There they would prepare to become missionaries. "It looks as if we are to have our way through the whole continent," said the countess in a Whitefieldian moment. The countess convoked a meeting of her friends and followers at Treveca and told them that she considered the opportunity to do good work in America as the most important in her life. She named ordained ministers to be in charge in the persons of the Reverend William Piercy as President and the Reverend John Cosse as "master and chaplain of the orphans." Another clergyman, C. S. Eccles, would go as schoolmaster. Seven students were selected from the volunteers: John Cosson, William White, Joseph Cooke, Daniel Roberts, Thomas Jones, Thomas Hill, and Lewis Richards. Elizabeth Hughes, housekeeper at Treveca, also volunteered to go to Georgia.[10]On October 20, 1772, the countess posed for her portrait. The artist, John Russell, declined payment, stating that he intended to offer the painting to Bethesda in honor of George Whitefield.[11]

The countess's biographer wrote that thousands prayed for the success of the "glorious undertaking." Multitudes accompanied the

[10] Edwin Welch, *Spiritual Pilgrim: A Reassessment of the Life of the Countess of Huntingdon* (Cardiff: University of Wales Press, 1995) 136.

[11] George Williamson, D.Lit., *John Russell* (London: George Bell and Sons, 1893) 45.

heroic volunteers to the dockside where they boarded the *Georgia Packet* on October 27, 1772. The housekeeper, Betty Hughes, resented the fact that the men got all the glory. "I was so cast down in London," she wrote the countess, "having so many prayers given up for the Students and not one grone [*sic*] for me." None of the plans of the countess worked out as she would have liked. The winds proved contrary and the missionaries grew tired of waiting in the port of Deal. Some, including William Piercy, disembarked to do some preaching. The wind changed and left them on shore; only Cosson, Cooke and the housekeeper sailed as planned and arrived in Georgia before the others.[12]

John Cosson wrote the countess from Georgia that, in his opinion, four of the volunteers never intended to go to Georgia. Thomas Hill merely wanted to qualify for ordination. Daniel Roberts signed on to please the countess; the two of them and Cooke "had been extravagant" at Deal, powdering their hair and buying gold rings. The countess had to spend more money booking passage for those left behind and also for William Piercy's brother Richard, Piercy's servant, and Piercy's horse.[13]

James Habersham met the first three—Cosson, Cooke, and Hughes—when they arrived on December 28, 1772, and might have been surprised that Cosson and Hughes, the housekeeper, asked to be married at once. The marriage helps explain at least one reason Betty Hughes wanted to come to America. The ceremony took place in Habersham's parlor, then the newcomers went out to their new home. Bethesda is not at its best in the winter, and the new buildings lacked furniture. Cosson, who was supposed to catechize the slaves, could not understand them, nor they him. As to be expected, the newcomers felt discouraged.[14]

Piercy's party reached Charlestown on January 31, 1773. Piercy thought of himself as another George Whitefield whose base might be

---

[12] George Williamson, D.Lit., *John Russell*, 137; Seymour, *Selina*, 259.
[13] Welch, *Spiritual Pilgrim*, 137–38.
[14] Welch, *Spiritual Pilgrim*, 138.

at Bethesda, but America awaited his coming. It did not bode well for Bethesda that he lingered at Charlestown most of the winter. William Tennent, who had been a friend of Whitefield, invited Piercy to preach, which Piercy did—"to immense congregations," as he told the countess. He finally arrived at Bethesda on March 13, 1773. James Habersham agreed to stay a few days at Bethesda to explain the accounts. Governor Wright offered to come out any time and give advice on planting. Meanwhile, Piercy planned a grand opening for the college and expected a crowd to attend.[15]

Piercy expressed surprise when John Cosson asked for a family apartment at Bethesda. Piercy said no, he would not sacrifice the one available room on the ground floor "to satisfy the whim and folly of dear Cossons." He confided to the countess that "marrying, I fear, has much heart his soul." Piercy expressed satisfaction at the turnout for the grand opening of Bethesda College on April 4, 1773. Governor Wright, his council members, and many of the lower house of the Assembly came out to the home, much as they had done the two previous years. Samuel Frink, the rector of Christ Church, did not come. Piercy was too much a Methodist for him. In fact, Piercy told the countess that the "Minister in Savannah looks upon us with an evil eye."[16]

Two days after the public celebration, Betty Hughes Cosson, who had been married under James Habersham's roof only three months before, surprised everyone by giving birth to a baby boy. Mr. Eccles assured the countess that no one had the slightest suspicion of the imminent arrival "until after the poor Babe proclaim'd his mother's shame by loud cries." William Piercy reprimanded the Cossons severely for their "harden'd spirit," their "Hypocrisy," and their "committing fresh sins daily." He suspected that they hoped the child would be stillborn, because they took no precautions for the birth. The unfortunate Cosson tried to explain that they had really been married

---

[15] Piercy to Countess, February 20 & March 17, 1773, Cheshunt Collection.

[16] Piercy to Countess, March 22 & April 5, 1773, Cheshunt Collection.

at Treveca, and that is why they wanted to come together to America. Piercy dismissed that excuse because the ceremony had been performed by a lay person. After consulting James Habersham, Piercy sent Cosson back to England; his wife was in no condition to travel, so she was put up with a family in Savannah.[17]

Though his opinion is not recorded, Piercy must have been surprised that Lady Huntingdon arranged to have John Cosson ordained in spite of his matrimonial problems and then paid his return voyage to Bethesda. So the Reverend and Mrs. Cosson and their child occupied a family room at Bethesda after all. They remained at the home until the summer of 1776. Piercy advised against their leaving, and in fact, Mrs. Cosson did not want to leave, but her husband had been offered a church in Carolina. So, with mixed feelings they departed from Bethesda. Within ten days of their leaving, Betty Cosson contracted a fever and died. Piercy attended her funeral.[18]

After expressing disappointment with the Cossons, Piercy evaluated the other members of his staff soon after arriving. Ambrose Wright had been misrepresented by Cornelius Winter; he acted "with honesty and simplicity." John Cooke managed the domestic business matters and "dear Roberts" took care of external business. However, "dear Eccles" showed a childishness of behavior and had lost all authority over the orphans. Piercy dismissed Eccles and sent him back to England while Richard Piercy took his place as housemaster. Daniel Roberts and Lewis Richards chafed at not being allowed to go about preaching as Piercy did.[19]

Two months after the surprise delivery of the baby Cosson, a greater calamity visited Bethesda. Lightning struck the great house, igniting a fire and sending the whole building burning to the ground. Fortunately, the two new wings were spared. Bethesda's friends in

---

[17] Seymour, *Selina*, 140–41; Piercy to Countess, April 15, 1773, Cheshunt Collection.

[18] Piercy to Countess, April 19, 1775, Cheshunt Collection; Richard Piercy to Countess, June 10, 1777, Cheshunt Collection, A 4/2.

[19] Piercy to Countess, May 26 & 27, 1773, Cheshunt Collection.

Savannah were determined to rebuild it. Habersham contributed three hundred pounds himself, and two other gentlemen donated two hundred pounds.

The caption under this portrait of the Rev. William Piercy (misspelled "Percey" on the painting) reads "Chaplain to the Right Hon. The Countess of Huntingdon, president of the Georgia College, North America." (From the Collection of the Museum of Early Southern Decorative Arts, Winston Salem, North Carolina, Courtesy Old Salem, Inc., Winston Salem, North Carolina.)

Revolutionary Rumblings

If Bethesda had been semi-sheltered from the events of the decade ending in 1773, it could not continue to be so. Events outside the control of Piercy, Lady Huntingdon, and James Habersham reached out to engulf Bethesda and to change the course of its history. It was on December 16, 1773—if we need to be reminded—that some citizens of Boston, dressed like Indians, threw a shipload of tea into Boston Harbor. Revolutionary agitation came late to Georgia. Indian cessions in 1763 and 1773 opened a vast expanse of fertile land to the thousands of new settlers. Georgians ignored the modest quitrent they were supposed to pay for free grants of land. The colony continued to be subsidized by Parliament. Governor James Wright, in office since 1760, was generally popular, even with those like Jonathan Bryan who opposed Parliament's efforts to tax Americans.

Oddly, the man who experienced the most problems as a result of the assertion of American rights was Bethesda's guardian and Savannah's pioneer merchant, James Habersham. Governor Wright objected to the election of Noble Wimberly Jones as Speaker of the 1771 House of Assembly. The House declared the rejection a "high Breach of the Privilege of the House." Wright failed to persuade the lower house to rescind the resolution so he dissolved the session after only its third day. He then left for London on a two-year leave of absence. James Habersham, as president of the council, became acting governor. When the assembly met in 1772, the House promptly elected Noble W. Jones again. Habersham objected to Jones and ordered another election. The defiant House reelected Jones. Another disapproval followed with another election of Jones. Even though Jones resigned for the sake of peace, the House refused to delete his name as the elected Speaker, so Habersham dissolved the assembly again. When the assembly met in December 1772, Jones withdrew his name from consideration. So this session was able to enact legislation for the first time since 1769.[20] Perhaps the best evidence of James Habersham's love

---

[20] Coleman, *Colonial Georgia*, 260–61.

of Bethesda is that he devoted so much attention to the home even as he wrestled with the legislature over matters of prerogative.

Governor Wright returned to Georgia in mid-February 1773 with permission to negotiate for a new land cession in Georgia's backcountry. The impetus for the cession stemmed from the fact that the Cherokees had acquired a huge debt since their failed 1760 war. Their suppliers suggested that they exchange land for debts. The Indians would cede the land above the 1763 cession to the king, and in the meantime, the government would sell the land and, with the proceeds, pay off the debts the Indians owed.

The Indian Congress began in Augusta in May 1773 with the compliant Cherokees and the reluctant Creeks present. The Creeks, whose debts were far less than the Cherokees', refused to give up the strip between the Ogeechee and Oconee Rivers. They finally agreed to cede land they claimed east of the Ogeechee and above the old 1763 line. A minor land rush began in the late summer 1773. Many of the new settlers were products of the Great Awakening. Daniel Marshall and Shubal Stearns founded the first Baptist Church in Georgia on Kiokee Creek in 1772. Wait Palmer, a wandering preacher from Connecticut, started a Baptist Church for George Galphin's slaves at Silver Bluff on the Carolina side of the Savannah River below Augusta around 1773.

In 1773 Governor Wright sent a surveying team to map the new cession. Colonel Edward Barnard headed the small army of surveyors, Indians, and gentlemen speculators. One of their number was the Philadelphia botanist William Bartram, commissioned by Dr. John Fothergill of London to roam about the countryside collecting rare plants. In the process, he gathered notes for his classic journal of his travels. Barnard completed his tour of the backcountry and returned to Savannah to take his seat in the Assembly in July. As a vestryman at St. Paul's Church in Augusta, Barnard had attempted to prevent the Baptist pioneer Daniel Marshall from preaching without a license. An old tradition maintains that Barnard was so impressed by Marshall's piety that he not only released the preacher, but he also he became a convert. Barnard did not abandon the Church of England, but

William Piercy is the best witness to his religious zeal. Barnard met Piercy in August during the session of the Assembly. He told Piercy about the rapid settlement of the backcountry and about the need for preachers in that region. When Piercy expressed interest in this kind of "Whitefieldian" activity, Barnard offered to introduce him to some important individuals in Augusta and in the outlying region. Piercy referred to Barnard as a "John the Baptist" sent by God to prepare the way. He praised Barnard's zeal and piety and his "truly methodistical spirit." Piercy wrote the countess that he even planned to preach to the Cherokees. He knew that the idea of converting the Indians had a special appeal to Lady Huntingdon.[21]

Piercy's circuit through St. Paul's Parish lasted eight weeks, but he got no nearer the Cherokee country than the old boundary, the Little River, some twenty-five miles above Augusta. He met some of Daniel Marshall's Baptists around Kiokee Creek. They were not his sort of people; in fact, he called them "ignorant men of Baptist persuasion." He discovered that "none could give a rational account of the nature of the Gospel." On the other hand, Reverend James Seymour, rector of St. Paul's Church in Augusta, complained about Piercy's unlicensed preaching to dissenters in Seymour's parish.[22]

While Piercy visited settlements as far as the Little River, Governor Wright and his entourage traveled through the Ceded Lands about the Little River in the hope of chasing off squatters and advertising the cession to those Governor Wright called "the better sort." In late December, with both Piercy and Wright safely back in the lowcountry, Indian raiders attacked Wrightsborough and other isolated settlements. Some of the young warriors resented their leaders' giving up land in the 1773 treaty. When two Cherokee youths from the village of Tugaloo were murdered in July by savage white squatters on the Ceded Lands, some Tugaloo warriors joined a maverick band of Creeks to carry out the raids and terrify the trespassers on the Ceded Lands. People flocked in to Augusta and residents who could

[21] Piercy to Countess, August 12, 1773, Cheshunt Collection.
[22] Piercy to Countess, December 10, 1773, Cheshunt Collection.

afford to do so put up stockades around their houses. The raiders struck again in January and panic spread from Charlestown to Pensacola. The zealous students at Bethesda who had been pleading for a chance to preach to Indians decided to wait a bit.

Governor Wright secured the cooperation of the other southern governors in imposing a ban on Indian trade. He stationed a company of rangers under Piercy's new friend Edward Barnard in a new fort in the Ceded Lands and charged them with enforcing the ban. This bold action won for Wright the approval of backcountry settlers who resented traders selling guns and powder to the Indians, guns that might be used on them. For the time being (most of 1774), revolutionary sentiment ebbed in Georgia.

William Piercy decided that if he could not preach to the Indians, he would preach elsewhere. Following Whitefield's example, he set out by land for the northern provinces. In June he preached in Pennsylvania, and in August, New York, although he did not go as far as Boston. In the aftermath of the tea dumping episode of December 16, 1773, the British imposed a series of punitive acts—termed "Intolerable" by American radicals—and New England seethed with resentment.[23]

Even before he returned to Bethesda, Piercy became involved in two curious historic events. The first concerned George Whitefield's great friend and patron, the pious entrepreneur, Jonathan Bryan. Bryan had an insatiable appetite for land, as his biographer Alan Gallay details in *The Formation of a Planter Elite: Jonathan Bryan and the Southern Colonial Frontier*. Bryan had cultivated friends among the Lower Creeks ever since he welcomed Oglethorpe to Georgia. In February 1774, with the Indian scare still causing alarm, Bryan confided to Piercy that he intended to acquire a vast tract in Florida from his good friends in the Creek Nation, even though they were under a trade embargo. He explained to Piercy that when he had obtained the title to the territory, he would be glad to open a college or

[23] Piercy to Countess, March 21, June (no date given), August 7, November 28, 1774, Cheshunt Collection.

several colleges for the instruction of the Indians. Piercy informed the countess that he himself had participated in Bryan's discussion with certain chieftains. Piercy seemed not concerned that this exciting idea happened to be illegal. Private acquisitions of land from Indians were forbidden by British policy and colonial legislation. John Stuart, the Indian Superintendent, kept the ministry informed of attempted land grabs such as Bryan's.[24]

Bryan's scheme reached a climax when Governor Wright hosted a peace conference in Savannah in October 1774 and signed a treaty by which trade would be resumed in return for the punishment of the guilty Indian raiders. Backcountry Georgians had hoped for another land cession as a condition of peace, but the great trading companies opposed that measure, as did John Stuart. The land-hungry settlers began to turn against the governor, whom they regarded as too friendly to Indians, and aligned themselves with the radicals of St. John's Parish in coastal Georgia.

Jonathan Bryan invited some of the Indians who were at Governor Wright's conference to visit him at his plantation outside Savannah. He persuaded them to sign a treaty giving him an enormous but vaguely delineated tract in northern Florida. The fact that the Indians repudiated the treaty as soon as Governor Wright and John Stuart denounced the transaction did not dissuade Bryan from continuing his efforts. On the contrary, he called upon the help of his friends at Bethesda. William Piercy did not seem to regard Bryan's request to be as bizarre as it really was. Bryan asked Piercy to ask the pious Lord Dartmouth to persuade Lord North, the head of the King's Council, to recognize Bryan's claim to the Florida lands. Bryan, in fact, suggested that the countess join him in the petition and share some of the land.[25] There was plenty to go around. Bryan's attempt to use Piercy in order to bypass the Governors of Georgia and Florida and go over the head of John Stuart was an amazing example of effrontery—not to

[24] Alan Gallay, *Planter Elite,* 127–52; Piercy to Countess, February 25, 1774, Cheshunt Collection.

[25] Piercy to Countess, May 6, 1775, Cheshunt Collection, A 4/2.

mention, the ultimate in attempted land grabs. The American Revolution, not the opposition of the British government, dashed his dreams.

At the same time that William Piercy and his colleagues at Bethesda were being titillated with the notion of colleges in the Indian country, another unusual situation caused a minor crisis. This one involved Bethesda with Charlestown, a hotbed of revolutionary sentiment in 1775. The news of the skirmishes at Lexington and Concord reached Charlestown on May 8, 1775, about the same time Henry Laurens received a letter from Arthur Lee in London that the British intended to enlist slaves and Indians in a war against Americans. Though false, the rumor spread like wildfire. One result was the arrest and execution of a free black harbor pilot, Thomas Jeremiah, on the basis of dubious testimony of other slaves that he intended some kind of rebellion.

The Countess of Huntingdon could not have chosen a more ill-advised time to send to Bethesda an African seminarian named David Margate to replace John Cosson as an instructor to the slaves. John Cosson, once dismissed by Piercy and now restored by the countess, returned to Georgia on the same vessel. William Piercy attempted to explain to Lady Huntingdon why it was not a good idea for David to come just then. Shortly after Margate arrived at Bethesda, "the devil put it into his head" that he should act as a second Moses who would deliver his people from slavery. Margate explained to Richard Piercy that God told him lead slaves to freedom and had appointed a time for the deliverance.[26]

House managers John and Betty Cosson cautioned David that he should not preach such a message. Piercy admonished him also. Not long afterward, Margate told Piercy he had received another message from God saying he should marry a certain black woman of the plantation. Piercy said David must be mistaken, for the woman was already married. Margate then said that he had been wrong about that particular woman; God clearly meant another. David's certainty that

[26] Piercy to Countess, May 6, 1775, Cheshunt Collection, A 4/2.

God ruled his emotions may have stemmed from the Whitefield theology that "feeling" called means "being" called and that feeling represents inspiration. This kind of thinking almost cost him his life.

Richard Piercy described to the countess how Margate went with John Cosson to Charlestown to speak at the house of a Quaker gentleman. Cosson warned David about the penalty for instigating slave uprisings and strongly advised against saying anything at all on the subject of slavery. Cosson preached a general sermon about the need for repentance. Then David stood up to speak. There was something heroic in his audacity, ill-advised though it was. He denounced the harsh South Carolina slave code, then condemned the institution of slavery itself. The slaves were like the children of Israel: now in bondage, he warned, but soon to be set free by the hand of God.[27]

Cosson knew Margate had gone too far and he hurried him out of Charlestown before a bench warrant could be issued. William Piercy wrote the countess that "had he not instantly retired to Georgia privately, he would have been taken up and hanged by the Negro laws of this province." Piercy appealed to James Habersham to arrange for David's immediate departure. Habersham explained to the countess's agent, "The Gentlemen of this town are so possessed with an opinion that his Designs are bad that they are determined to pursue and hang him if they can by hold of him." Habersham called Margate "very proud, very superficial, and conceited." He blamed people in England for spoiling the Africans among them "through a mistaken kind of compassion because they are black." Habersham arranged with Captain Inglis to take David Margate away as a steerage passenger on the *Georgia Planter*. Margate departed as a prophet without honor among white Georgians.[28]

---

[27] Richard Piercy to Countess, October 10, 1777, Cheshunt Collection, A 1/3.

[28] Piercy to Countess, May 6, 1775, Cheshunt Collection, A4/2; Habersham to Countess, April 19, 1775, same to Robert Keen, May 11, 1775, Georgia Historical Society Collections, 6:238–44.

The extradition of the black seminarian would be the last favor James Habersham could do for the countess and for Bethesda. His health had declined so badly that he could not even write his last letter dated May 11, 1775. Instead, his youngest son, John, acted as his clerk. Even as his own health failed, he worried about the critical situation of the province of Georgia. His words to the countess proved prophetic: "If conciliating Measures do not soon take Place, I expect no less than an open breach amongst us, Father against Son and Son against Father, and the dearest connections broke through by the Violent Hands of Faction and Party." He planned to go northward in the hope of recovering his health.[29]

Bethesda and the Revolution

The news of the fighting at Lexington and Concord reached Georgia on May 10, 1775, and on the next day several individuals broke into the powder magazine and, as tradition has it, sent some to the patriots in Boston. On June 2, a larger number of radicals spiked the twenty-one cannon on the battery, hoping to prevent the celebration of King George's birthday on June 4, 1775. Governor Wright's friends managed to repair some of the guns and fired them in a defiant kind of celebration.

The public storehouse was raided several times during June and July as people armed themselves. The *Georgia Gazette* of June 21 contained a summons to a meeting at Mrs. Cuyler's lodging house on June 26. The presence of moderate Whigs, and the chairmanship of Lachlan McGillivray who remained loyal to the king, resulted in only a mild protest against Parliament's efforts to raise a revenue in America However the radical Whigs felt that they had delayed long enough. They dominated the Provincial Congress that met in Savannah on July 4, 1775, and adopted the Continental Association

---

[29] Habersham to John Edwards, May 25, 1775, Georgia Historical Society Collections, 6:245.

banning trade with England, elected a permanent executive body called a Council of Safety, and authorized local committees to enforce the ban on commerce with Britain. Thus, political power devolved from the royal government to local "Sons of Liberty."[30]

On July 7 the Congress elected five delegates to the Continental Congress. On the following day the Savannah Sons of Liberty, flying a flag emblazoned with the words "American Liberty," boarded a vessel carrying ammunition intended for the Indian trade and confiscated it by order of the Provincial Congress. Joseph Habersham, second son of James Habersham, acted as spokesman for the liberty men. On June 10, 1775, the elder James Habersham left Savannah accompanied by his youngest son John. His health continued its decline and he died in Brunswick, New Jersey, on the August 28. The *Georgia Gazette* paid him a gracious tribute: "As he was possessed of many valuable and amiable qualities, both in publick and private life, his death is much and sincerely lamented. In the first, where he conducted himself with abilities, honour, and integrity which gained him the general love and esteem of his fellow citizens; nor was he less distinguished in private life by a conscientious discharge of the social duties as a tender and affectionate parent, a sincere and warm friend, and a kind and indulgent master."[31]

For Bethesda, Habersham's death marked the end of the founding era. Whitefield and Habersham were giants in Bethesda's history; they set standards for every future Bethesda administrator and Bethesda boy to strive to reach. Few institutions are so fortunate in having founders of almost mythic stature of Whitefield and Habersham, whose abilities complemented each other so well.

Peter Tondee, one of the original Bethesda boys, died on October 21.[32] Many former students like Tondee welcomed the revolutionary movement. They realized that change meant opportunity to better themselves—both politically and financially. Tondee's tavern became

---

[30] *Georgia Gazette*, June 21 & 28, 1775.
[31] Cited in Weeks, *Peter Tondee*, 209.
[32] Cited in Weeks, *Peter Tondee*, 211.

famous as the gathering place for the Sons of Liberty. On November 1, 1775, a long-time neighbor of Bethesda, Noble Jones, died at Wormsloe. His son, Noble Wimberly Jones, became a leader of the revolutionary faction, one of Georgia's delegates to Congress, and President of the Union Society.

On August 16, 1775, Attorney-General Anthony Stokes acknowledged that "the Powers of Government have been in a great measure, wrested out of the Hands of his Majesty's Officers by several Bodies of Men, unlawfully convened."[33] Stokes was thoroughly disgusted that the rector of Christ Church in Savannah had been displaced by the authority of the Provincial Congress and a layman put in the pulpit. By one of those quirks of chance that make history interesting, Edward Langworthy, the former Bethesda teacher, was the layman now preaching at Christ Church. The teacher of the classics had joined the radical Whigs and devoted his talents to writing propaganda for the Liberty Party. He would be rewarded by election to the Continental Congress in 1778.

The activities of the Reverend Piercy at this critical moment in history are more interesting than those of the upwardly mobile Langworthy. Complaints about Piercy's arbitrary management of Bethesda by some of Lady Huntingdon's students, along with the school's mounting expenses, caused that Lady to put a stop to the erection of new buildings at Bethesda. More intriguing were reports from the students that Piercy had gone over to the rebel side.[34]

In his frequent visits to Charlestown, William Piercy met a lady of about thirty years of age and asked her to become Mrs. Piercy. She agreed and brought £2,000 dowry to the marriage. She was the sister of one of Charlestown's most radical liberty men, Barnard Elliott. In July 1775 Governor James Wright referred to Elliott as one of the most brash revolutionaries; at that time Elliott had crossed into Georgia some sixty miles above Savannah and had begun recruiting Georgians

---

[33] Anthony Stokes's charge to Grand Jury, August 14, 1775, *CRG*, 12:428–33.

[34] Robert Keen to Countess, March 15, 1777, Cheshunt Collection, A 1/13.

for enlistment in the South Carolina militia companies. Barnard Elliott drove Piercy around Charlestown in his carriage until Piercy married and could afford his own carriage as well as his own plantation in Carolina. After March 1776, Piercy stopped preaching except on infrequent visits to Bethesda.[35]

Whitefield's nephew Peter Edwards informed the countess, through her attorney Robert Keen, that Piercy had joined the rebels and had been invited to preach at Christ Church. The invitation was symbolic of the way the Church of England yielded to the American denominations of the Great Awakening. Edwards claimed that Richard Piercy, who remained at Bethesda through 1777, held the rank of major in the Georgia militia. Edwards described Ambrose Wright, the talented manager at Bethesda, as "a great man amongst them and is lately admitted to one of their provincial congress(es)."[36]

The *Revolutionary Records of Georgia* confirm the fact that Piercy received an invitation from the revolutionary Council of Safety to preach at the opening of the January 22, 1776, session of Georgia's Provincial Congress. The best evidence that Piercy had cast his lot with the patriot faction is that he was listed on the Georgia Treason Act passed in 1780 when royal government was restored in Georgia.[37]

A visitor to Bethesda during the Revolution provides a rare glimpse of the Piercys at home. Elkanah Watson set out from Rhode Island with letters to the leaders of Georgia's revolutionary government. In Savannah he delivered dispatches to George Walton, Commodore Oliver Bowen, and others of importance in the new government. Watson had heard so much about George Whitefield and his favorite project, the orphan house, that he decided to see the place for himself. He rode out "through a succession of fine plantations" and was hospitably received by Mr. Piercy. If Piercy had lingering loyalty to the king, he did not indicate anything of the sort to his visitor. Watson

---

[35] Keen to Countess, January 10, 1778, Cheshunt Collection, A 1/13.

[36] Keen to Countess, January 10, 1778, Cheshunt Collection, A 1/13.

[37] Allen Candler, ed., *Revolutionary Records of Georgia*, 3 vols. (Atlanta: 1908) 1:19, 340–63.

said that he "found the family of Mr. Piercy highly refined and intelligent, and enjoyed their kind hospitality with much interest." He expressed surprise at finding such refined persons in "this remote and solitary abode." He commented on the destruction of the central portion, leaving only the wings standing (ironically that part of Bethesda's history repeated itself when the 1870 central portion was torn down in 1952, leaving only the two wings). Piercy showed his visitor the grand portrait of Selina, Countess of Huntingdon, a gift from the countess to Bethesda College worthy of the great expectations she had for its future.[38]

Ambrose Wright's name was fourth on the list of members of Georgia's First Provincial Congress; Peter Tondee's name came next. Wright joined the radical Liberty Society and signed a petition to remove General Lachlan McIntosh from Georgia, blaming him for the fact that some of his relatives remained loyal to the king. Wright later participated in an invasion of Florida, as did Edward Langworthy, and received an officer's pay of £1000.[39]

The war came early to Georgia. Four British warships anchored off Tybee Island in mid-January 1776. They had come to Savannah for provisions, but the Georgians believed they planned to attack Savannah. The Council of Safety ordered Governor Wright, the members of the council, and other royal officials to be held under house arrest. When two hundred British troops in transports joined the warships, Georgians felt certain that an invasion impended. Archibald Bulloch, head of the Council of Safety, called upon all Savannahians to defend the town and placed Lachlan McIntosh in charge of the militia. The Charlestown Council of Safety, headed by Henry Laurens, sent two hundred men under Stephen Bull to bolster

---

[38] William Bogart called attention to Watson's publication *Men and Times of the Revolution* in a letter to William Wadley, April 22, 1887, Bethesda Archives. Watson's mention of the portrait of the countess is important in establishing the provenance of the painting, restored at considerable expense in the 1990s.

[39] Robert Scott Davis, *Georgia Citizens and Soldiers of the American Revolution* (Easly SC: Southern Historical Press, 1979) 25, 38.

the nerves of the anxious Georgians. Governor Wright, a prisoner in his own house, believed that Savannah had been invaded and captured, not by the British, but by the Carolinians. He escaped out his back door and took refuge aboard the warship *Scarborough*. For many of the slaves around Savannah, the arrival of the British ships signaled deliverance from bondage. Over two hundred blacks gathered on Tybee Island, hoping to be taken away by the British. Among them were several runaways from Bethesda.

The presence of a band of Creek warriors at Jonathan Bryan's plantation (Bryan had not given up his dream of a Florida land cession) gave Stephen Bull an idea. He would set the Indians upon the black refugees on Tybee; the real Indians would be accompanied by Georgians dressed like Indians. The tactic, to his mind, had a double advantage: the runaways would not join the British, and similarly, a lasting animosity between Indians and blacks would prevent the two races from joining together. To the discredit of Henry Laurens and the South Carolina Council, Bull's reprehensible scheme was approved. Laurens argued that the slaves would be used against the Americans if they were not killed. Archibald Bulloch, thoroughly intimidated by the overbearing Stephen Bull, acquiesced and actually led the raid on Tybee.[40]

Fortunately for the honor of the new Georgia government, the slaves had already been taken aboard the British ships. William Piercy communicated with Captain Stanhope, the official in charge of the transports, and asked for the return of Bethesda's slaves, arguing that they belonged to Lady Huntingdon, a British subject. History is filled with coincidences; in this example, Captain Stanhope happened to be a relative of the countess. However, he declined the request to deliver over the slaves. The British warships captured most of the rice vessels anchored at Savannah and sailed away. The last vestige of royal authority disappeared with the departure of Governor Wright. The

---

[40] Stephen Bull to Council of Safety, March 14, 1776, in David R. Chesnutt, *The Papers of Henry Laurens*, 14 vols. (Columbia: University of South Carolina Press, 1968–1994) 11:162–64.

historic episode is known in Georgia history as the "Battle of the Rice Boats."[41]

In the absence of any other government, the Provincial Congress met in Augusta and adopted a rudimentary constitution on April 15, 1776. The delegates elected Archibald Bulloch governor. The Continental Congress created the Southern Military Department in February 1776. Georgia's congressional delegates George Walton, Button Gwinnett, and Lyman Hall secured the appointment of Lachlan McIntosh as Brigadier General of Georgia's Continental Brigade.

In 1777 Bethesda enjoyed a tranquil period while the rest of Georgia went through turmoil. On June 10, 1777, Richard Piercy wrote the countess that they lived "undisturbed" at Bethesda, that the plantations produced good crops, and that William Piercy had engaged a Mr. Dupont from South Carolina to manage the plantations. William Piercy also had good news. His wife bore their first child. Neither of the Piercys, however, mentioned that they had joined the rebels.[42]

Bethesda enjoyed the protection of its friends and alumni. General Lachlan McIntosh himself was a Bethesda boy, and as such, deserves to be remembered as another role model for future generations of Bethesda boys. Most of the Bethesda boys who took up arms against the British are not known. General Daniel Stevens tells us in his memoirs that he was a Bethesda boy, as were his schoolmates General John Barnwell and Major William H. Wegg. Many friends and associates of Bethesda joined the Revolution. Jonathan Bryan, the oldest friend, enjoyed enormous prestige in the new government. He went with General McIntosh and John Houstoun to visit General Charles Lee in 1776 to persuade the general to send troops to pacify the Florida

[41] James M. Johnson, *Militiamen, Rangers and Redcoats: The Military in Georgia 1754–1776* (Macon GA: Mercer University Press, 1992) 138–51; Piercy to Countess, October 3, 1777, Cheshunt Collection, A 4/2.

[42] Richard Piercy to Countess, June 10, 1777; William Piercy to Countess, October 3, 1777, Cheshunt Collection, A 4/2.

borderlands. The three patriot sons of James Habersham had grown up with the awareness that Bethesda was beloved by their father. The same was true of Frankie Harris, whose father, James Habersham's partner in business, died in 1771. Joseph Clay, James Habersham's nephew, occupied important positions in the state government and showed a continuing concern for Bethesda. So did Henry Laurens, whom Whitefield had listed as a warden of his college. Laurens loomed large in revolutionary America; he served as president of the Continental Congress and acted as an American peace negotiator along with Benjamin Franklin and John Adams. We have referred to Ambrose Wright and Edward Langworthy's involvement in the American cause. And, of course, William Piercy seemed to have chosen the winning side in casting his lot with the Americans.

The problem with Georgia politics during 1776–1778 was that having expelled the representatives of the king, the Georgians started to quarrel with each other. Radicals who wanted a democratic constitution that opened government to those who had not participated previously took sides against conservatives who preferred to restrict government to the better educated and wealthier class. Bethesda had friends in both factions. A climax of contention occurred following the failed Georgia invasion of Florida in 1777. Button Gwinnett, as chief executive of the civil government and therefore commander of the state militia, refused to communicate with Lachlan McIntosh, commander of the Continentals. The world, or that part of it that happened to notice, was treated to the spectacle of an attempted invasion of Florida by the Georgia state troops and the Georgia continental brigade, with the two armies ignorant of the other's intentions.[43]

After the inevitable failure of the invasion, Button Gwinnett and Lachlan McIntosh fought a duel at deliberately close range. Both men hit their marks; Gwinnett died three days later from infection of his wound. McIntosh recovered but was hounded out of Georgia by the radical faction controlling the government. Ambrose Wright and

---

[43] Davis, *Georgia Citizens and Soldiers*, 25.

Edward Langworthy signed the petition to Congress to remove McIntosh from command of the Georgia Continentals, as did James Papot, the aging architect of Bethesda.

In 1778, while Bethesda continued to enjoy tranquility, Georgia tried again to invade Florida with the same lack of success. Later in the year, the war caught up with Bethesda. With the British effort stalled in the North, Lord George Germain, the king's war minister, decided to shift the initiative to the South. The exiled governors of South Carolina and Georgia had pleaded for two years for a southern strategy, arguing that there were thousands of loyal people just waiting for the sight of the king's colors to declare their allegiance.

Coincidental with the invasion of Georgia, the British ministry sent a peace delegation to welcome the rebellious colonies back into the kingdom without having to pay the obnoxious taxes. As it turned out, only in Georgia was royal government restored. The capable and gentlemanly Lt. Colonel Archibald Campbell commanded the invasion force consisting of his own regiment of Highlanders (the 71st), a regiment of New York Volunteers and a Hessian Regiment, about three thousand in all. Thirty-seven ships of the line anchored off Tybee Island on December 24th. The story is well known in Savannah about a black man, Quamino Dolly, who showed the British a lightly guarded approach to the town by way of Brewton Hill, two miles south of Savannah.[44]

The Georgians later insisted on a court martial for the American commanding officer, General Robert Howe, for a poorly planned defense of Savannah. The invaders overwhelmed the militia at the south end of town. The continentals, facing eastward toward the coast, broke and fled across the river when taken in the flank. Those who could not swim were taken prisoner. Mordecai Sheftall, one of the prisoners, described a colorful moment when amidst the

[44] Colin Campbell, ed., *Journal of An Expedition Against the Rebels of Georgia in North American Under the Orders of Archibald Campbell, Esquire, Lieut Colol of His Majesty's 71st Regiment, 1778* (Darien GA: Ashantilly Press, 1981).

confusion, Sir James Baird, a Highland chief, mounted a stepladder and blew his brass horn. The Highlanders immediately gathered around and he gave them orders in Gaelic. They dispersed and plundered the houses of known rebels.[45]

General Augustine Prevost marched up from Florida at the head of his regiment of Royal Americans led by Lt. Col. Thomas Brown and his King's Rangers. Brown had been nearly killed by the Augusta liberty boys for his refusal to take an oath to abide by the continental association. In January he led Archibald Campbell's army to Augusta, hoping to meet friendly Indians there and subdue the backcountry. Campbell held Augusta for the first two weeks of February, but instead of British-allied Indians, an army of North Carolinians appeared on the Carolina side of the Savannah River across from Augusta. Campbell retreated precipitously, abandoning those who had recently declared loyalty to the king. Loyalists on their way to join Campbell were defeated by Georgians and Carolinians at Kettle Creek near present-day Washington, Georgia. However, the British retreated only as far as Briar Creek where they defeated the pursuing Americans on March 3, 1779. The result of this marching and counter-marching was that the British occupied all of Georgia below Briar Creek and James Wright and the other royal officials returned to resume government.

The commotion of war ended the four decades of undisturbed tranquility at Bethesda. William Piercy felt it necessary to dissemble in his report to the countess. He did not want her to know that he had been consorting with the king's rebellious subjects. He informed her that he had left Bethesda in December 1779 (actually 1778) "to avoid that immediate scene of war." He left two honest and trusty men in charge of the House. He blamed General Prevost for confiscating bed linens and kitchenware for his own use, in spite of Piercy's written protest. He consulted Habersham's nephew, Joseph Clay, and decided to sell some of Bethesda's slaves and invest the proceeds at interest. He

[45] Edward J. Cashin, ed., "Narrative of Mordecai Sheftall," *Setting Out to Begin a New World* (Savannah GA: Beehive Press, 1995) 183.

estimated the value of the countess's property at £70,000. For a clergyman, Piercy's ethics were unusually lax. His brother Richard conveyed forty-one slaves to Boston and sold them, but the countess received none of those funds or any of the £70,000 Piercy offered her. Piercy implied that he had delivered a protest to General Prevost for taking Bethesda's property. Apparently, though, that was not quite true.[46]

We know what actually happened at Bethesda, thanks to a remarkably complete report written to the countess by Margaret Floyd, wife of the caretaker and an unsung heroine in Bethesda's history. She related how Piercy and his family left Bethesda a month before the British invasion, leaving her and her husband in charge. She confirmed the fact that the British plundered the place. She remonstrated in Piercy's name, but the officers told her that Piercy was a rebel and if he had been there, they would have put him to death. As far as they were concerned, Piercy had forfeited his property by siding with the enemy. In February the Hessians came out and appropriated all the poultry and the foodstuff in the pantry. On February 13, a Hessian guard of twenty-five men bivouacked in the great house. Then on February 28, General Prevost sent out wagons and loaded them with furniture, sheets, table linen, pillowcases, and everything else of value. Meanwhile, the Hessians killed off the cattle for food.[47]

When Lewis Johnston, an old friend of Whitefield and Habersham, was named commissioner of police in the restored royal government, he gave the Floyds approval to live in the schoolhouse. They obtained permission from William Telfair, commissioner of claims, to take what was left of the plantation corn for their use. George Baillie, another of the commissioners of claims, came out with his family to live in the house on May 13, 1779, and the Hessian guard left the premises. Baillie put his own slaves on the plantation and made pine tar for sale, as well as other timber products. On April 13, 1779,

[46] Piercy to Countess, January 15, 1781, Cheshunt Collection, A 4/2.

[47] Margaret Floyd to Countess (no date given) Cheshunt Collection, A 3/1.

George Baillie wrote to the countess notifying her that he had been appointed caretaker of Bethesda and that he was willing to be employed permanently in her service. He wrote again when better acquainted with the place, explaining that Floyd told him that General Prevost's men had carried off the contents of the house and that Richard Piercy had taken away the plantation slaves. He was doing his best and had planted fifty-five acres of rice and corn.[48]

Baillie was not one of Margaret Floyd's favorite persons, but he did at least one important service for Bethesda. On September 3, 1779, an astonishing sight greeted the loyal Georgians at Tybee. Twenty-two French men of war, fourteen frigates, and a number of transports carrying an army of over five thousand anchored off the Georgia coast. Their landing craft came up the Vernon River and the troops disembarked unopposed at Beaulieu, once the plantation of William Stephens, less than three miles from Bethesda. Count Casimer Pulaski and his troops in the American service joined D'Estaing at Beaulieu. Today's Whitefield Road marks the route they took; Bethesda lay on their way. French soldiers camped at Bethesda, carried off 39 hogs, 13 steers, 10 cows, 5 sheep, 50 fowl, and the newly harvested grain; and would have burned the houses, except that George Baillie could speak French. He pretended to be an ally of the French and obtained the written protection of the commander Count Henri d'Estaing. Though every other valuable property was lost, the buildings, at least, survived.[49]

The noble d'Estaing himself deigned to call at the great house. He commented in his journal on the painting of the countess, which he took to be a representation of the lady "liberty" and therefore approved. But when the Baillie children told him that it had been put up only the night before, presumably for his benefit, the Count suspected that the Baillies were really loyalists trying to fool him into thinking they stood for the American cause. He felt justified in carting

---

[48] Baillie to Countess, April 13, 1779, Cheshunt Collection, A 3/7.

[49] Baillie to Countess, November 5, 1779, Cheshunt Collection, A 3/7.

off everything his men could carry, even carrying off Bethesda's best horse for himself.[50]

The siege of Savannah climaxed by the "Grand Assault" of October 9, 1779—when the combined French and American forces attacked the British fortifications—was Savannah's moment of fame; England, France, and America waited and wondered at the outcome. The gallant Pulaski died, as did the Carolina hero of Fort Moultrie, William Jasper, along with hundreds of others. The British line held and the allies fell back. Attorney-General Anthony Stokes in Savannah witnessed the battle and wrote, "With the assistance of God, British valor surmounted every difficulty, and the siege has rendered famous a sickly hole which was in woods and had only one white man in it at the time General Oglethorpe landed. But insignificant as some may think it, this place is the key of the southern provinces, the Gibralter of the Gulf passage; for to the south of this province there is not a port on the continent that will receive a sloop of war."[51] On October 19, the dejected and defeated French marched past Bethesda to Beaulieu to re-embark on their waiting vessels. Anthony Stokes heard that they lost 2,500 men in the siege. Benjamin Lincoln's Americans retired to Carolina. Bethesda, stripped of everything but the land itself and the buildings, was once more left to the caretakers.

The successful British defense of Savannah caused the British high command to dispatch a larger force under Sir Henry Clinton to subdue Carolina. The British besieged General Lincoln in Charleston and accepted the surrender of the city on May 12, 1780. It seemed that the war was over and the British had won. One of the most famous moments in the history of the Union Society occurred during the British occupation of Georgia. Members of the society, all prisoners of war at Sunbury, determined not to let the war prevent their holding

[50] Alexander A. Lawrence, *Storm Over Savannah: The Story of Count d'Estaing and the Siege of Savannah in 1779* (Athens: University of Georgia Press, 1951) 33–35.

[51] Anthony Stokes to his wife, November 9, 1779, in Cashin, *Setting Out*, 201.

their annual meeting. They stressed their desire "to continue so laudable an institution" and elected officers: Josiah Powell, president; Mordecai Sheftall, Vice-President; John Martin, Secretary; Matthew Roach and Levi Sheftall, constables. Because four were present and five were elected, it might have been that Mordecai Sheftall nominated Levi.[52]

William Piercy, in British-occupied Charleston, resumed his interrupted allegiance to the crown. On August 5, 1780, he wrote to the Floyds, who had taken refuge in a hut a mile away from the orphan house, informing them that he had dismissed Baillie and put them in charge of Bethesda. He turned over power of attorney to three Savannah loyalists: John Glen, Josiah Tattnall, and Nathaniel Hall. Then Piercy obtained a British permit dated September 13, 1780, to return to England. His ship, the *Mary and Charlotte*, sailed October 5, 1780, and after a difficult voyage of two months landed at Cork, Ireland. Piercy made his way to Bath where he met the countess. The reception was a frosty one. Lady Huntingdon wanted to know why he had sold the slaves belonging to Bethesda and how he could explain reports that he had sided with the rebels. Piercy managed to reassure the countess that he had been loyal to her all along. Piercy was fortunate that Lady Huntingdon happened to be a friend of Lord George Germain, the Secretary for America in the British government. Although his name appeared on the treason list in royal Georgia, Piercy escaped prosecution in England.[53]

Piercy proceeded to write to Glen, Tattnall, and Hall, imploring them to sell all slaves at Bethesda and send the money to the countess; they should also send the proceeds from the sale of the 1778–1780 harvests. Piercy accused George Baillie of stealing household

---

[52] Thomas Gamble Jr., *Bethesda: An Historical Sketch of Whitefield's House of Mercy in Georgia and of the Union Society* (Savannah GA: Morning News Print, 1902) 95–96.

[53] Charlestown became Charleston at the time of the adoption of the first state constitution in 1776; for Piercy's return, see Seymour, *Selina*, 267–69; Piercy's permit to leave is dated September 13, 1780, Cheshunt Collection, A 4/5.

possessions. Of all Piercy's questionable activities, this charade for the benefit of the countess was the boldest. His brother had already sold off Bethesda's slaves. The British and then the French took everything from Bethesda, crops and all, before Piercy left America. Lady Huntingdon did not know what to believe. "Indeed, I have every reason to apprehend the worst from Mr. Piercy's conduct," she told her niece. "My poor heart is sadly perplexed in this affair."[54]

Josiah Tattnall went out to Bethesda to tell Baillie he was fired and that Piercy had reinstated the Floyds. Baillie refused to leave for a time; not trusting Piercy, he wanted to hear from the countess. Finally on November 29, 1781, he left the house and the Floyds moved in. Margaret Floyd accused the Baillies of taking away everything they could. However, with all the previous plundering, one wonders how much was left of value. The Baillies insisted that the French and rebels had ransacked the place, leaving them no money to send the countess. "Poor old Floyd and his wife are much pleased and very thankful to you for your particular attention to them," Tattnall informed Piercy.[55]

The war would not leave Bethesda alone. Augusta fell to Nathanael Greene's troops on June 5, 1781, and Greene sent his best officer, "Mad Anthony" Wayne, to put pressure on Savannah. Loyal refugees from the backcountry overflowed Savannah and occupied Bethesda. Margaret Floyd reported that they had letter after letter from Tattnall, ordering them to take in loyalists until there were a hundred and fifty persons at Bethesda and not enough to eat for anyone. "We could do nothing for a living now," she wrote, "only take care of the poor remains of the Orphan House and [see] that they did not burn the building." Her husband died on June 13, 1782, after an eleven-week illness. Savannah surrendered to Anthony Wayne's Americans on July 12, 1782, and Bethesda's refugees finally left Georgia along with the

---

[54] Seymour, *Selina*, 270.

[55] Josiah Tatnall to Piercy, December 24, 1781, Cheshunt Collection, A 3/7.

other loyalists.[56] At last, peace settled upon the broken ruins of Bethesda. For a while Whitefield's dream languished. That it did not die is the remarkable fact. The love that Whitefield and Habersham had for a succession of Bethesda boys proved contagious. Savannahians felt obligated to maintain Bethesda and to continue to care for its children.

When the British and the American loyalists left Savannah during the summer of 1782, Margaret Floyd struggled to maintain a token presence at Bethesda. Some plantation slaves who had hidden in the woods returned. Margaret set them to work in the garden. She had to manage them and care for her own blind sister for several weeks. When her son came out to help, she sent him into town to look for Joseph Clay and beg him to take charge of the house until orders came from the countess. To Clay's credit, he did what he could. He advanced funds on his own credit and that of James Habersham, Jr. He secured power of attorney from John Glen before Glen left Savannah with the loyal exodus. He hired an overseer to take care of planting, expecting that the twenty hands on the plantation would produce fifty barrels of rice. However, neither he nor James Habersham had time to give Bethesda the attention it needed.[57]

Clay was surprised to get a letter from the countess dated October 19, 1783, asking about the £70,000 William Piercy had said was forthcoming from the sale of slaves and from various harvests. Clay could account for only 142 barrels of rice sold by Piercy before the British invasion. He did not know where those funds were. He heard that some of the slaves had gone off to Florida; some had been hired out by Josiah Tattnall. He and James Habersham had advanced £200 to Bethesda, and Clay hoped to be reimbursed by the countess. He called attention to the loyalty of Margaret Floyd in caring for

---

[56] Margaret Floyd to the Countess (no date given) Cheshunt Collection, A 3/1.

[57] Margaret Floyd to the Countess (no date given) Cheshunt Collection, A 3/1; Joseph Clay to Joachim Noel Fanning, April 22, 1783, Georgia Historical Society Collections, 8:1990–94.

Bethesda as best she could and to her urgent need for a salary. Clay then wrote to Piercy, asking for an explanation of Lady Huntingdon's letter. He declared that "she observes that you... have left me so large a debtor to her, that she wishes to know the various particulars." He ended by saying, "To me this is all darkness."[58]

Back in England a tempest brewed between the strong-willed Lady Huntingdon and the artful Mr. Piercy. Lady Huntingdon had good reason to believe Piercy had deceived her. By accident, she met Henry Laurens's daughter in London in 1783 and learned that Laurens had been taken prisoner while on his way to join the peace negotiators in Paris and had been locked in the Tower of London where his health suffered. The countess knew of Whitefield's acquaintance with Laurens and remembered that Whitefield named Laurens to his Board of Wardens for Bethesda College. The countess realized that Laurens could be trusted to tell her what was going on at Bethesda. She attempted to visit him in the tower but was not allowed to. She then wrote Laurens on June 30, 1783, and asked him to look into the situation at Bethesda when he could.[59] After his release from the tower, Laurens went to Bath to recover from the ill effects of imprisonment. He enjoyed the amenities of that old and famous resort and referred to "rambles" with the ladies at the Crescent. He called upon Lady Huntingdon and learned about Piercy's duplicity. She repeated her comments in writing, referring to Piercy as "that poor unworthy man you have to deal with."

When Piercy first realized he had lost Lady Huntingdon's confidence, he tried humility, accusing her of "cruel and unjust attacks on the character and reputation of an innocent man." When he discovered that the countess had gone to court to put a lien on his property in England, he threatened her with a counter-lawsuit, claiming that she owed him £500 in back pay. He complained that he had been forced to spend a great deal of his wife's money, indicating

[58] Clay to Piercy, February 16, 1784, Georgia Historical Society, Collections, 196–99.

[59] Countess to Laurens, June 30, 1783, Cheshunt Collection, A 3/10.

that he was willing to accept some of the American properties of the countess by way of compensation. He even chided the lady for bringing "a matter in which religion and the cause of God were considered before the Tribunals of the Men of the World." He said that he could not account for her "unkind conduct" towards him and he supposed she had forgotten the promise she had made him that he could draw his salary from Bethesda instead of from her. He threatened to publish her letters, which he contended gave Bethesda to him. Piercy's effrontery amazed Henry Laurens, even as it angered the countess. Two years earlier Piercy had assured her that she had £70,000 coming. Now, however, he argued that what belonged to Bethesda also belonged to him.[60]

Lady Huntingdon informed Henry Laurens of Piercy's "insolent" demand for £500. She accused Piercy of threatening to put her in prison if she did not agree to pay large sums. However, she absolutely refused to pay him anything and, in fact, would no longer correspond with him. Laurens replied, referring sardonically to Piercy as "the Saint," and advised that "his impudent menaces merit equal disregard." In the end, Lady Huntingdon received nothing from Piercy and had to pay the bills charged to her by Josiah Tattnall, John Glen, Nathaniel Hall, Joseph Clay, and James Habersham. Presumably, she also remembered faithful Margaret Floyd. Unfortunately, Bethesda had not heard the last of the schemes of William Piercy.[61]

The Countess Tries Again

Despite her disappointments, Lady Huntingdon did not give up her determination to carry out George Whitefield's plans for Bethesda or

---

[60] Piercy to Countess, January 21, 1784, Henry Laurens Papers (microfilm), Caroliniana Library, University of South Carolina; Countess to Laurens, January 21, 1784, Cheshunt Collection, A 3/10.

[61] Countess to Laurens, January 21, 1784, Cheshunt Collection, A 3/10; Piercy to Tatnall, Glen, and Hall, March 39, 1784, cited in Seymour, *Selina*, 268–70.

her own vision of using Bethesda as a base of venturing out among the American Indians. In 1784 she actually wrote to George Washington and asked for his support for her idea of sending forth missionaries. She still had hopes of going to America herself, even "if only to make coats and garments for all the poor Indians."[62]

Selina, Countess of Huntingdon is buried in the Hastings Chapel of St. Helen's Church. The church was built by William Lord Hastings in 1474 and is situated near the castle ruins in Ashby de la Zouch, Leicestershire, England. (Photo by the author.)

Before she could reopen Bethesda, Lady Huntingdon needed a clear title to the property from the virtually independent State of Georgia. She turned to her friends in Savannah for assistance, and Savannah responded, as they so often had in the past. Joseph Clay and John Habersham introduced a bill in the Georgia legislature vesting the "very considerable property" known as "Bethesda College or Orphan House" in Selina, Countess of Huntingdon. An endowment of land not exceeding five thousand acres was granted to the school in addition to a thousand pounds from the sale of confiscated property in

[62] Countess to George Washington, April 8, 1784, cited in Seymour, *Selina*, 274.

Chatham County. The bill named the trustees: Joseph Clay, John Habersham, former governor John Houstoun, his brother James Houstoun, William Gibbons, General and Governor Samuel Elbert, Seth John Cuthbert, William Stephens, and Richard Wylly. All of them were men of prominence in post-war Georgia. The state legislature, sitting in Augusta, enacted the bill into law on February 1, 1788, exactly one month after Georgia ratified the federal Constitution.[63]

Hastings' Memorial in the chapel of St. Helen's Church, Ashby de la Zouch, Leicestershire, England. (Photo by the author.)

John Habersham volunteered to serve as chief executive of Bethesda College until Lady Huntingdon's appointee arrived. The Reverend Benjamin Lindsay, rector of Christ Church in Savannah, agreed to teach Latin and Greek. The countess selected Reverend David Phillips

[63] W. P. A. Writers' Project, "History of Bethesda," 10, Georgia Historical Society Collections, 1355.

to head the institution. On June 13, 1788, Phillips advertised the reopening of Bethesda College on the 24th of the same month. The vision of a gentlemen's academy had not dimmed. Phillips solicited the attention of young men desirous of "instruction in every branch of useful and polite literature, comprehending English grammatically, Writing, and the use of Figures, and every branch of the Mathematics, the use of the Globes, Latin, Greek and French." Tuition, room, and board cost thirty guineas payable in four installments. John Habersham added a practical note. Students must bring their own bedding.

In the meantime, orphans were not forgotten. When the estate became productive enough to support them, orphans would be accepted "on the original benevolent plan." The announcement had all the promise of George Whitefield's plans of 1770 and William Piercy's grand opening of 1773. Unfortunately, reality did not match the pronouncement. Young gentlemen did not answer the call, expenses ran up, and to make matters worse, Mr. Phillips quarreled with the trustees. For a start, he dismissed Robert Boyd, the overseer Clay had hired for Bethesda, and sent him to Clay to be paid. A merchant named James Ding had to be paid for supplies, and a Doctor William Parker was engaged for medical services. Finally, Mr. Phillips became discouraged and returned to England in May 1790. Joseph Clay sent a bill for £277 for Phillips to give to the countess.[64]

Lady Huntingdon never gave up on Bethesda. In January 1791 she sent out yet another superintendent in Reverend John Johnson. It proved to be her last benefaction. The great lady died on June 17, 1791. Her biographer wrote that Bethesda was her biggest problem and her worst failure. Bethesda College never materialized, Treveca College closed, her followers joined Wesley's Methodists or drifted into Congregational churches. But in Georgia, and particularly at Bethesda, Lady Huntingdon occupied an important place in history.

---

[64] *Georgia Gazette*, June 3, 1788; Joseph Clay to Countess, May 10, 1790, Georgia Historical Society Collections, 8:229–30.

Georgians respected her in her lifetime and have honored her memory ever since.[65]

After the death of the countess, the transition of Bethesda from British to American possession corresponded to the war of revolution on a minor scale. The leader on the American side, fittingly enough, was the hero of Savannah, General James Jackson. Jackson commanded the Georgia continentals at the end of the war and General Anthony Wayne gave him the privilege of accepting the surrender of the city of Savannah on July 12, 1782. In 1788 Jackson was honored by election to the first US House of Representatives. Jackson had strong convictions on most issues and a habit of expressing them strongly. He admired Whitefield's work at Bethesda, noting the many "respectable characters" he knew who attended Bethesda. However, he faulted Lady Huntingdon who either "could not (or did not)" pay proper attention to the institution. In his opinion, Bethesda had begun to decline before the Revolution and had not recovered since. More recently, profits from Bethesda's rice plantations had been diverted to "the maintenance of several lazy, dronish Parsons, most of whom have been too supine to perform the common duties of Clergymen, and some of them have actually spent their time in Racing and Hunting with the overseers of the estate." The house no longer served the purpose for which it was established; that is, it housed no orphans. On hearing of the death of the countess, Jackson prepared legislation to transfer possession of Bethesda to Chatham County.[66]

The fact that the legislative had "vested" the estate to Selina, Countess of Huntingdon, in 1788, caused Jackson to entitle his bill "An act to explain an act entitled An Act to establish an academy in the county of Chatham." The explanation consisted in the questionable assumption that the countess did not actually own the Bethesda property and that her death terminated the trust. The bill

---

[65] W. P. A., "History of Bethesda," 20; Seymour, *Selina,* 135.

[66] The act is in Horatio Marbury and William H. Crawford, eds., *Digest of the Laws of the State of Georgia* (Savannah GA: 1802) 565–66.

stated that the heirs of the countess were not eligible to inherit because they were "British subjects and nonresidents." The unstated assumption of the legislation was that the State of Georgia now owned Bethesda and, as such, had the right to vest control in a corporate body of trustees. Several friends of Bethesda were named to the board, including Joseph Habersham, Joseph Clay, Jr., John Milledge Jr., and Josiah Tattnall Jr. George Whitefield's nephew James Whitefield, George Houstoun, William Stephens, William Gibbons, John Morel, George Jones, Jacob Waldburger, and James Jackson completed the membership of the new body. The legislature enacted the bill into law on December 20, 1791.[67]

The legislation represented the actuality that Bethesda's fate was linked to Savannah. George Whitefield realized that fact in 1745 when he stopped feuding with Savannahians and began a policy of cooperation. Savannah was not ready to assume proprietorship in 1770 when Whitefield left the estate to the countess, but in 1791 Savannah recognized the importance of Whitefield's vision and accepted responsibility for maintaining Bethesda. The fact that all thirteen trustees were Savannahians meant that the State of Georgia ratified Savannah's stewardship. The members of the board held their first meeting on Friday, January 6, 1792, electing Sir George Houstoun president and James Whitefield secretary. The first order of business was the notification of the Reverend John Johnson that the trustees intended to take possession of Bethesda on the following Tuesday. Then the trouble started.[68]

The Reverend John Johnson had arrived in Georgia in January 1791 as the last appointee of the countess. He must have been one of the "dronish" clergymen that James Jackson complained about, because only David Phillips and Johnson were post-war appointees.

---

[67] Marbury and Crawford, eds., *Digest of the Laws*, 565–66; Lilla M. Hawes, ed., "Miscellaneous Papers of James Jackson," 37/2, *Georgia Historical Quarterly*, 147–49.

[68] "Bethesda College (Orphan House) Trustees' Minutes, 1792–1809," typescript, Georgia Department of Archives and History.

However, he had a reputation for apostolic zeal in Lancashire, England. In fact, one of his more enthusiastic sermons had recently led to a disturbance. Yet Lady Huntingdon admired him enough to send him to America. The Georgia trustees seemed willing to allow him to remain as custodian of Bethesda if he were willing to recognize their authority. This last part, though, Johnson absolutely refused to do. He had observed the progress of Jackson's legislation with mounting alarm, seeking legal advice from William Gibbons, the brother of Thomas, the mayor. Johnson considered both men his friends. It did not help his cause that James Jackson accused Thomas Gibbons of fraud in the elections of 1791 in which Anthony Wayne defeated Jackson. The irascible Jackson challenged Gibbons to a duel. Johnson could not bring court action because he had not received power of attorney from Lord Dartmouth, one of the executors of Lady Huntingdon's estate. Johnson had no intention of recognizing Georgia's right to ignore the claims of the heirs of the countess. He wrote to George Houstoun on January 9, 1792, stating his case. How could the trustees think they were carrying out Whitefield's intentions when Whitefield intended the countess to inherit? Bethesda received money from England and from all parts of America; it should not become the possession of a single county. If the trustees tried to take possession by force, Johnson warned, "I would much rather open my breast to your fatal steel than act unworthy of my present trust." His letter to Houstoun might not have made a difference to the trustees in any case, but it was written too late. The day after he wrote it, a delegation of trustees arrived at his door.[69]

Rumors that Johnson had instigated the Bethesda slaves to resist the trustees' takeover circulated in Savannah for several weeks previous to the appointed day. In his own journal, Johnson confirmed the fact that the blacks on the plantation intended to arm themselves. He noted that one of the men went about brandishing a hoe, declaring that it

---

[69] John Johnson to George Houstoun, January 9, 1792, cited in William Harden, ed., "Bethesda's Crisis in 1791," 1/2, *Georgia Historical Quarterly*, 113.

was "war time." Johnson confiscated a musket and a sword from the slaves, but he made a mistake in judgement when he greeted the gentlemen of the trust, all of whom were unarmed, carrying the musket and wearing the sword. Johnson refused to allow the trustees to enter the buildings. The trustees sent for the sheriff. Two constables arrived around 8:00 P.M. on January 10, 1792. Johnson scuffled with one of them and received a wound. The deputies then broke down the door and the trustees took possession of the building. The next day Johnson and his wife were literally dragged out of the house and held prisoners in Savannah. The sheriff told the plantation hands that they must obey the new manager or else the militia would be sent out to arrest them as well. Most of the slaves ran off into the woods.[70]

Johnson had friends in Savannah who posted handbills, criticizing the trustees in general and James Jackson in particular for not giving Johnson a fair trial. Johnson himself tried to enlist the help of Anthony Wayne who defeated Jackson in the disputed congressional election. Johnson alienated potential supporters by writing to Sir George Houstoun, who had just lost his daughter, that God had taken his daughter as a punishment. James Jackson, forgetting for the moment that he himself was born and raised in the English county of Devon, was furious with Johnson who, "although an alien," determined to resist "the whole community." Jackson said if an American in England acted that way, he "would have his ears nailed to a pillory." Johnson was released from house imprisonment on January 24 and lingered in Georgia until March, vainly hoping for legal redress. He expressed his frustration and disappointment in a poem published in Charleston titled "The Rape of Bethesda." In part it read:

[70] "Trustees' Minutes," 1.

Ah Poor Bethesda! what of thee we once
Admired, how blasted now! destructive fire!
She's fallen! and all the orphans' hope is gone
But hush—lest we awake
The sleeping dust of Whitefield from the grave
There is no eye to pity, nor a hand
To rescue, now Selina is no more.
The unwelcome news has reach'd the negroes ears
Their hearts—their honor'd Mistress is no more![71]

The unlucky Johnson and his wife returned to England only to be imprisoned for debts he had incurred in erecting a chapel in Lancashire. He died at Manchester in 1804.[72]

The struggle between Savannah and England, personified by James Jackson and John Johnson, represented a local version of the American Revolution. Like colonial Georgia, Bethesda had looked to England for direction and support. Now, its fate rested with the gentlemen of Savannah. The poignant note sounded by John Johnson was echoed a year later by Bishop Francis Asbury. John Wesley, the great organizer, had succeeded in identifying free-will theology with Methodism. He sent Asbury to America to institutionalize Methodism and thereby completed the work he had begun in Georgia six decades earlier. Asbury built upon the foundations of the Great Awakening, as tireless as Whitefield and as saintly as Wesley. Asbury wished to pay tribute to Whitefield's memory and rode out to Bethesda on January 29, 1793. "We found the place," he wrote in his journal, "and having seen the copperplate which I recognized, I felt very awful; the wings are yet standing, though much injured, and the schoolhouse still more."[73]

---

[71] John Johnson, *The Rape of Bethesda or The Georgia Orphan House Destroyed: A Poem* (Charleston: Markland and McIver, 1792) in Emory University Library.

[72] Harden, "Bethesda's Crisis," 109.

[73] Ezra Squier Tipple, *The Heart of Asbury's Journal* (New York: Eaton and Mains, 1904) 356–57.

Bethesda's Trustees as the State's Founding Fathers

The same men charged with rebuilding Bethesda were engaged in building the new state of Georgia. During the Revolution, the country faction had driven events in a democratic direction. The Constitution of 1777, fashioned by a coalition of low-country and backcountry delegates, was one of the most democratic in the nation. After the war, the seat of government moved to Augusta until a new capital could be built at Louisville on the Ogeechee. Savannahians felt that political power had gotten into the wrong hands, as Joseph Clay once remarked. They struggled to regain leadership during the decade that followed the Revolution, succeeding in replacing the Constitution of 1777 with a more conservative document in 1788.

The focus of attention during the 1790s was the vast western frontier. By the terms of the 1783 peace treaty, Georgia extended westwardly to the Mississippi River. The fact that the area was occupied by the Creek Indians, among others, and that the head of the Creek Nation—the clever Alexander McGillivray—refused to allow the Georgians to cross the Ogeechee River caused Georgians at the constitutional convention to agree to establish a stronger central government and the Georgians at home to ratify the constitution almost without debate. Georgia expected George Washington to dislodge the Indians from the promised land. President Washington invited Alexander McGillivray to New York, wined and dined McGillivray and his chiefs, and signed the Treaty of New York. Georgians reacted angrily when they learned that Washington had obtained only the narrow strip between the Ogeechee and the next river to the west, the Oconee. Washington visited Savannah in April 1791 and was entertained by some of the same gentlemen who took control of Bethesda later that year. Washington also visited Augusta, the seat of government, before making his way back to New York.

Georgia's western lands tempted the politicians in various ways. During the 1790s, judges sold thousands of acres of non-existent land to gullible speculators. In 1795 the Georgia legislature committed a monumental fraud known as the Yazoo Act. Millions of acres amounting to most of the area comprised by the present states of Alabama and Mississippi were sold by the legislature to four companies, in which the legislators themselves held stock.

James Jackson resigned his United States Senate seat in 1795 to lead a reform movement against the perpetrators of the land swindle. Jackson allied his Savannah supporters with the recently arrived Virginians in the backcountry to form the political party that dominated Georgia politics for years. After he won the governorship in 1796, Jackson took the lead in nullifying the Yazoo Act. Stockholders took their case to the Supreme Court. In the landmark Fletcher versus Peck case, John Marshall and his colleagues declared that the Yazoo Act was a valid contract and the stockholders had to be compensated. In 1796 Jackson's house on his Bonaventure plantation burned and he moved his residence to his Cedar Hill estate. He was elected governor in 1798 and then to the United States Senate for a second time in 1801. He died in 1806 before his term expired. During the entire time of his continuous public service, he maintained an interest in Bethesda and remained an active member of the board of trustees until his death.

Other trustees also played important roles in state and national life. William Gibbons served in the state legislature from 1785–1789 and again from 1791–1793, then became an Associate Justice of Chatham County. Josiah Tattnall Jr., son of the loyalist supervisor of Bethesda during the British occupation, served several terms in the Georgia legislature as an ally of James Jackson, even succeeding Jackson as United States Senator in 1796. In 1801, he was elected Governor of Georgia, although ill health forced him to resign in 1802. John Milledge, son of the John Milledge who took his brother and sister out of Whitefield's custody, was another staunch ally of James Jackson and an anti-Yazooist. He moved to Augusta in 1790, served a term in the United States House of Representatives in 1792–1794, then went to the Georgia Senate, and from 1802–1806 was Governor of Georgia. He was elected to James Jackson's unexpired Senate seat in 1806. Joseph Clay Jr., though not nearly as prominent as his father, maintained his father's interest in Bethesda. "Old" Joseph Clay put a lien on Bethesda's land holdings until he was repaid for his loans during the post-war period. Joseph Habersham enjoyed national distinction, serving as President Washington's Postmaster General from 1796–1801.

If the Bethesda trustees had not been so involved in state and national politics, they might have been more successful in restoring Bethesda. During their seventeen-year tenure, they accomplished no more and perhaps less than Lady Huntingdon did during the twenty-one years of her administration. The trustees followed the lead of Whitefield and the countess in attempting to make Bethesda self-supporting. They decided they had to develop the rice fields before they could open the school. The task of operating the plantations proved more difficult than they expected. First, they had to gain the trust of the black workers on the two plantations. Their overseer Phillip Densler complained that Reverend John Johnson had caused some of the slaves to run away. The trustees appealed to the White Bluff militia to hunt down the fugitives and return them to Bethesda. They had to sell the flatboat belonging to the house to pay the militia for finding the runaways, and they even continued to have problems with discontented workers. One, Esther became "a great expense to the trust by frequently paying money for apprehending of her." An elderly slave named Leicester who left Bethesda with John Johnson returned in 1796. By 1800 there were seventeen men, seventeen women, and nineteen children in Bethesda's slave population. During most of the decade Colonel Joseph Habersham, Sir George Houstoun, and William Stephens served on the "planting committee" and supervised the operation of the rice fields.[74]

On April 1, 1793, the trustees agreed to support six poor children with the income of the estate. The plantations produced 132 barrels of rice, 100 bushels of corn, 150 bushels of potatoes, and 400 baskets of peas. By 1795 the estate was able to invest £450 in bank stocks. In the following year the trustees appropriated $150 to employ a school-

[74] "Trustees' Minutes," 3, 7, 20.

master "to be employed at Bethesda." A Mr. Ellerbee was hired as teacher, but he had to operate out of a small house on the main road; the buildings at Bethesda were not yet in good enough repair to be used.[75]

On May 4, 1797, a committee of trustees visited Ellerbee's school and awarded prizes to the students. Ann Whitefield received a sash and a book for best reader; Henry Harbock a hat and a book for best speller; Ben Alter, Ann Norton, Mary Whitefield, Elizabeth Whitefield, Charles Boyd, James Harbock, Elizabeth Harbock, and Benjamin Smith all received books. So, most of the seventeen children were rewarded. A lame boy named William Walker had a private tutor at the expense of the trustees. Walker posed a problem for the trustees. In two years time he had learned all Mr. Port could teach him. He had to go about on crutches, so could not do the usual forms of manual labor. The trustees discussed the boy's future in 1799 when he was sixteen, deciding they should find better instructors and prepare Walker to become a teacher at Bethesda himself. In 1801 his new mentors, identified as Mackay and Ball, reported that Walker was a genius. The happy result of the education provided by the trustees was that Mr. Mackay was hired as principal teacher at Bethesda with William Walker as his assistant. Walker was paid $50 per year in addition to room and board.[76]

The trustees made a point of visiting Bethesda on May 4 of each year, their anniversary. They inspected the buildings and met with the black workers. The trustees considered themselves generous by declaring the day a holiday for the slaves, meaning that the slaves could work for themselves that day. The minutes for August 4, 1798, indicate that the annual examination of the children was conducted at Bethesda instead of Mr. Ellerbee's house on the main road, but they did not yet reside at Bethesda. During the year 1799 Ellerbee taught forty-eight children, the largest number for a single year during the trustees' tenure. In 1799 and 1800 the examination took place in Ellerbee's

---

[75] "Trustees' Minutes," 3, 13.
[76] "Trustees' Minutes," 11, 21.

schoolhouse. By the annual meeting in 1800, the trustees had accumulated and invested $5,850 at eight percent interest. At last they felt ready to repair the north and south wings at Bethesda and invited proposals for the construction work. In May 1801 the board appropriated $2,000 for the restoration of the north wing and resolved to move the school to Bethesda as soon as rooms were available. At the same time, the board approved a salary of $500 for a tutor. Children of poor parents would be educated free of charge, whereas other children would pay tuition of three dollars per quarter for reading and spelling, four dollars for writing, and five dollars for ciphering. When accommodations for lodging at Bethesda were ready, terms for boarding would be set.[77]

As soon as work on the north wing was finished, the board planned to hire professors of Latin, Greek and French, Mathematics, Natural Philosophy, and the other sciences "usually taught in the respective colleges of the United States." Scientific equipment and a library would be provided. With all this accomplished, repairs on the south wing would begin. After ten years of slow progress, the trustees seemed to be on the verge of realizing Whitefield's vision. By February 1802 trustee John Morel had engaged a contractor. By May costs exceeded the $2,000 budget; naturally, this caused consternation among the trustees. Should they spend more money finishing the north wing? After all, the south wing desperately needed repairs. They made the decision to postpone the opening of the school at Bethesda until the construction work had progressed further.[78]

Mr. Mackay of Savannah began his duties as tutor in October, apparently using his own residence as a school. The trustees paid for their charges as Mackay took in additional paying students. The only poor students listed as of May 7, 1803, were William Walker, now twenty-one, James Collins, and John Harbock. Mackay taught nine other paying students. Three other poor children were admitted in the course of the year following.

---

[77] "Trustees' Minutes," 14, 17, 19.

[78] "Trustees' Minutes," 22, 25.

The long anticipated move to Bethesda took place before February 1804, but the exact date was not mentioned in the minutes. The minutes for February 4, 1804, state simply "the following orphans were at Bethesda on the bounty of this institution, viz. William Walker, John Harbock, James Collins, Howell Cobb, John Whitefield, Thomas Bryan, and Robert Dews."

The trustees ordered the pasture to be fenced in, a kitchen built, a cook and waiter hired, and cows purchased for the farm. At the same meeting, the board promoted William Walker to assistant tutor at the salary of $50 per year. Later that year the board resolved to sell Bethesda's lands on the Altamaha. The sale, they hoped, would pay for the work on the south wing.[79]

As the year 1805 began, the trustees had every reason to be optimistic. Bethesda had come to life again. The voices of young people sounded in the halls. The principal Mr. Mackay earned over $800 a year and gave general satisfaction. The two farms showed a profit. The trustees could not have guessed the disaster the year would bring. The first ominous sign was the reappearance in Savannah of Mr. William Piercy, come to collect as much money as possible now that Bethesda possessed money. Mr. Piercy's bill was read to the astonished trustees at their meeting of January 26, 1805. He claimed payment for the nine years he served as president of the institution, a sum amounting to £1800, and in addition, he also asked for £1000 for the furniture lost during the war, including the £500 Lady Huntingdon owed him. The total amount came to £3300. It will be recalled that the same Mr. Piercy had once assured Lady Huntingdon that her properties were worth £70,000, and that Lady Huntingdon accused Piercy of depriving her of any and all proceeds.[80]

The board president, Judge William Stephens, Judge George Jones, and Mr. William Bulloch formed a committee that looked into the claim. After conferring with Mr. Piercy, the committee reported that their board was not responsible for any obligations to the claimant. It

---

[79] "Trustees' Minutes," 29-31.
[80] "Trustees' Minutes," 31.

must have surprised the members present when Colonel Joseph Habersham said that he agreed with Piercy that the board should pay him for "his long and Disinterested Services." Lady Huntingdon and Henry Laurens would have questioned whether the services were disinterested. The fact that Joseph Habersham sided with Piercy may have had more to do with nostalgia than justice. Joseph Habersham was a firebrand of the Revolution at the time William Piercy identified himself with the radical cause. Piercy had the good sense to hire Joseph Habersham as his attorney. Habersham resigned from the board in 1806 and, acting for Piercy, brought a lawsuit against the board in federal court. The case dragged on until 1809 when the court awarded Piercy £500—"much to his dissatisfaction," according to President William Stephens.[81]

Piercy's appearance in 1805 was a harbinger of a worse fate. On July 2, 1805, a devastating hurricane swept across Bethesda, inundating rice fields, ruining the crops, and leveling trees. A fire broke out in the new north wing and the wind fanned the flames into a conflagration. The calamity was worse than Piercy's fire of 1773, worse than anything imaginable. The trustees gave the principal, Mr. Mackay, notice that they could not continue the school under the present circumstances. Mackay presented the board with a bill for $1390.14. President Stephens expressed embarrassment that he did not have that amount available. Apparently, there were only five children at Bethesda and after the storm they were boarded by the trust in Savannah.

The year 1806 was marked by the death of James Jackson: general, governor and senator, and a real leader among the trustees. The resignation of Joseph Habersham and the legal battle with Mr. Piercy added to the general discouragement. The slaves at Bethesda, twenty-one men, twenty-one women, ten boys and seven girls, had only two weeks provision of corn as of May 2, 1807. Several of them were ill; at least three died in that month. With the rice fields ruined, the trustees debated whether to plant cotton. They considered hiring out the slaves

---

[81] "Trustees' Minutes," 32, 39.

and renting the land. In the end, they had to face the fact that they were beaten. They could not do as much as George Whitefield did; he almost single-handedly kept the institution going for thirty years. With all her bad luck, the countess maintained it for twenty-one years. The trustees asked the legislature to dissolve the trust after seventeen years. By an act of December 22, 1808, the legislature authorized the president of the trustees of Bethesda College, the president of the Union Society, the president of the board of the Savannah poor house, the chairman of the commissioners of Chatham Academy, and the mayor of the City of Savannah to dispose of the property of the Bethesda estate. After all debts were paid, one-fifth of the remaining sums must be allocated to the Savannah poor house. Then the four-fifths would be equally divided between the Union Society and Chatham Academy. Chatham Academy was obligated to support and educate at least five orphan children. It was probably not a coincidence that Bethesda had responsibility for five orphans at the time. The proceeds from the sale of land amounted from $26,900, and from the sale of slaves $8,370.66.[82]

The trustees held their farewell meeting at Bethesda on March 13, 1809. They met in the barn, the only shelter available. Only six men attended: President William Stephens, George Jones, Peter Deveaux, William Parker, William Bulloch, and John G. Williamson, the mayor of Savannah. They approved the settlement of £500 to Reverend William Piercy and even rescued the portrait of Lady Huntingdon from the decrepit south wing. They also discovered a handsome clock donated by James Habersham Sr. to Bethesda in 1770, and they resolved to heal their differences with Joseph Habersham as a result of the Piercy litigation by presenting the clock to him.

President Stephens's letter to Colonel Habersham contained a note of regret that the board had disappointed public expectations. He stressed the important role that the senior James Habersham had played in Bethesda's earlier history, and hoped that the clock would

[82] "Trustees' Minutes," 33, 37–38.

help them remember "with no little emotion older times." Habersham returned a gracious thanks.[83]

William Stephens transmitted the accumulated minutes of the trustees meetings to Governor Jared Irwin at Milledgeville on December 6, 1809. His last sentence was almost an apology, "after our best exertions for the benefit of this ancient institution; and to promote its benevolent object, [we] have the mortification to find the result short of our wishes and of the end proposed."[84]

Several friends of Bethesda purchased sections of the estate: Charles Odingsell, 459 acres, Bryan Morel 853 acres; Peter Deveaux 173 acres; Joseph Stultz and Robert Gibson 525 acres; and Jonathan Norton (former overseer) 86 acres.[85] These tracts were later subdivided. Within just a few short years, hardly a trace of Bethesda remained except in the memory of those who loved the place.

[83] "Trustees' Minutes," 38–39.

[84] William Stephens to Jared Irwin, October 16, 1809, "Trustees' Minutes," 40–41.

[85] Gamble, *Bethesda: An Historical Sketch*, 91.

CHAPTER SIX

THE UNION SOCIETY AND WHITEFIELD'S LEGACY

The dissolution of Bethesda caused, or at least coincided with, an outburst of humanitarian effort in Savannah. "We have failed Whitefield and Habersham," Savannah seemed to say, "but we cannot abandon our children in need." Chatham Academy had no tangible existence when it inherited the responsibility to care for five orphans. Incorporated in 1788, the trustees of the academy placed their charges with private tutors. Spurred by their new responsibility, the trustees built their academy on South Broad Street between Bull and Drayton in 1813. Schoolmasters rented rooms in the academy and specialized in various subjects. The Union Society occupied the west wing of the building.[1]

The Savannah Female Orphan Asylum, established in 1801, acquired a home in 1810. Oral tradition maintains that boys and girls were separated in 1801. In fact, the records show that the Bethesda Trustees continued to be responsible for some girls until 1810 when the new asylum was ready. Judith Gromet, age thirteen, was admitted in 1807; her sister Mary Magdalen Gromet, age seven, in the same year; Harriet Mulryne, age thirteen, in 1808; and Marie Masolle, age eleven, in 1810.[2] The Savannah Poor House and Hospital profited from Bethesda's legacy and began operations in 1811. The Hibernian Society and the Irish Union Society, both organized in 1812, took care

---

[1] Joseph Frederick Waring, *Cerveau's Savannah* (Savannah: Georgia Historical Society, 1973) 63.

[2] Record of the Beneficiaries of the Union Society as far as could be ascertained, in *Minutes of the Union Society being an Abstract of Existing Records from 1750 to 1858* (Savannah: John M. Cooper and Company, 1860) 206+.

of needy Irish immigrants. The 1790 St. Andrews Society helped Scots. The Savannah Widows Society began in 1822. The Savannah Free School, supported by private donations, opened its doors in 1817. Only destitute parents sent their children there. Emily Burke, who taught at the female asylum, wrote, "Through these institutions prove a great blessing to many, still the odium attached to them prevents many more from availing themselves of the privileges they afford. Even teachers often shrink from incurring the stigma of teaching in these institutions."[3]

All these and other organizations vied with one another to help the poor and needy, of whom there were always more than could be helped. Of them all, the Union Society came closest to inheriting the original mission of Whitefield and Habersham, namely the care of orphans. The Union Society had been concerned with helping the needy since its foundation in 1750 by Peter Tondee, Richard Milledge, and Benjamin Shefthall. A professed society of "mechanics," it became a fraternity for many former Bethesda boys. The society advertised itself in the *South Carolina Gazette* in 1760 when it published a letter of appreciation to departing Governor Henry Ellis for the preservation of peace during the French and Indian War, for his legislation granting relief to debtors from provinces other than South Carolina, and for an ordinance barring slaves from competing with white artisans in certain crafts. The best remembered incident in the society's history, mentioned earlier in this narrative, occurred in 1780 when members Mordecai Sheftall, John Martin, John Stirk, Josiah Powell, and possibly Levi Sheftall, all prisoners of war at Sunbury, held their annual meeting under an oak tree.[4]

---

[3] Emily Burke, *Pleasure and Pain Reminiscences of Georgia in the 1840s* (Savannah: The Beehive Press, 1978) 72.

[4] *South Carolina Gazette*, November 15–22, 1760; Union Society, *Minutes*, 113. Gamble, *Bethesda*, 95-96.

The records of the society date from 1791 under the presidency of Noble W. Jones. Joseph Clay served as vice president and David Montaigut secretary. The members elected John Habersham, William H. Spencer, and George Millen to supervise the schooling of the poor children who were supported by the society. It is worth noting that this meeting occurred on April 23, 1791, before the state created a new board of trustees for Bethesda on December 20, 1791. Joseph Clay and John Habersham were still closely associated with the last effort of the Countess to maintain Bethesda. It does not require a stretch of the imagination to conclude that they and the other members of the Union Society intended to continue Bethesda's original mission. When the Bethesda trustees failed in 1809, Union stood ready to assume the care for the orphaned and poor children. Chatham Academy inherited Bethesda's second and never realized purpose of providing a classical education.

Among the society's sparse records of the 1790s is a regulation requiring parents or guardians of Union's charges to sign a contract honoring the apprenticeships arranged by the society. As at Bethesda, the Union Society Board considered the placement of children in trades or crafts a necessary component of its responsibility.

In 1797 members attended the funeral of Mordecai Sheftall, the Society's oldest member. The only surviving pre-revolutionary member was Mordecai's son, Levi Sheftall. In 1808, the Society members pledged that the society would continue as long as three members still lived and could meet together. Three had begun, and as long as there were at least three, the Society would last. Then, in 1809 the society accepted Bethesda's responsibility of caring for poor and orphaned children.[5]

The society boarded the children with reputable caretakers; Mrs. Christie seems to have been the first, followed by her son Robert. The

[5] Union Society, *Minutes*, 28, 49, 58.

boys attended Chatham Academy, and a committee of the Society visited the school once a week. The members of the Society debated whether to place the students at a new school at White Bluff, in the neighborhood of old Bethesda, but decided in favor of a wing of Chatham Academy. In 1817 the Society contracted with John Carr to board and teach the boys for an annual charge of $167 per boy.[6]

The records do not tell much about stories of human interest. However, Mr. Carr's problem with a student in 1817 *was* recorded. He had permitted young William Bollinger to visit his mother. The mother took the boy with her to Milledgeville, then the state capital. She met and married a man there and the couple returned to Savannah, abandoning William. Somehow, the boy made his way back to Savannah and asked Mr. Carr to take him in. The society board readily granted permission.[7]

In 1818 the board felt it necessary to set standards for the lodging of the boys. They resolved that not more than two boys should sleep in a bed and each should have a pillow, with a pair of clean sheets weekly, a coverlet in summer, and two blankets in winter.[8] The first ten years of the society's new trust were happy ones for Savannah. There were anxious moments during the War of 1812, with British warships off the coast and Georgia volunteers engaged in Indian fighting in the west. Andrew Jackson's troops routed the Creek warriors at Horseshoe Bend in 1813 and won his famous, post-war victory at New Orleans in 1815. A wave of national pride swept across the country. Militia promotions multiplied and generals, colonels, captains, and even majors wore their titles proudly.

The handsome Independent Presbyterian Church designed by John Holden Greene after the noble St. Martin in the Fields in London set

---

[6] Union Society, *Minutes*, 73.
[7] Union Society, *Minutes*, 74–75.
[8] Union Society, *Minutes*, 77–78.

the architectural tone for the city when completed in 1819. William Jay arrived from Bath, England, in 1818 and proceeded to adorn the city with elegant regency-style mansions: the Owens-Thomas House, the Scarborough House, and the Telfair Academy, prominent among them. Savannah looked its best for the visit of President James Monroe in May 1819. The officers of the society invited him to visit their boys at the academy. Ironically, the board had resolved just two years before that the printing business was "not of sufficient importance to bind any of the boys of this institution to." The board preferred "respectable" skills such as carpentry, bricklaying, or the mechanic arts. In his address to the boys, the president stated proudly that he had been apprenticed as a boy—to a printer! It is not recorded whether the board changed its policy regarding placing boys with printers.[9]

William Scarborough, whose mansion William Jay designed, headed a group of Savannah merchants who constructed the steamboat *S. S. Savannah*. On May 22, 1819, two weeks after the presidential visit, she set out for Liverpool. Preston Russell and Barbara Hines report in their history of Savannah that the British ship *Kite* chased the *Savannah* all day trying to rescue her, thinking she was aflame.[10] The *Savannah* made the crossing in twenty-nine days and eleven hours, the first steamship to cross the Atlantic. However, it could not claim to be the first vessel that bore the proud name "Savannah." That distinction belonged to Bethesda's first sloop.

During the year of the president's visit, the board's supervisory committee reported complaints about the boys "strolling about" and loitering on street corners. The board resolved that boys should be "confined" to the academy, except for a reasonable time for relaxation in the afternoon and after school. Presumably, "relaxing"

---

[9] Union Society, *Minutes*, 70, 86.

[10] Preston Russell and Barbara Hines, *Savannah: A History of Her People Since 1733* (Savannah: Frederic C. Beil, 1992) 85.

was more acceptable than "strolling about." The Union Society guardians must have worried about the moral perils of city life.[11]

On January 11, 1820, a terrible fire very nearly destroyed Savannah. Mayor Thomas U. P. Charlton reported 463 buildings lost to the flames. Later in the year, an epidemic of fever took a frightful toll of 666 out of a population just over a thousand. The twin disasters stalled Savannah's growth; the 1830 census showed an increase of only 200 persons. Chatham Academy and its Union Society wing escaped the flames. The society adopted a simple mission statement in 1821: "Its object shall be to support and educate Orphan Boys." The constitution of which the statement was a part simply confirmed a long-standing practice.[12]

The visit of the famous French general and American Revolutionary hero, the Marquis de Lafayette on March 19, 1825, revived Savannah's spirits. The general was wined and dined to the point that he had to leave the hall before the innumerable toasts were finished. The next morning the Union Society boys were among the 500 school children who gathered at Johnson Square to watch Lafayette lay the cornerstone of the Nathanael Greene monument designed by the Philadelphia architect William Strickland.[13]

The society cared for six or seven boys during the 1820s. In 1828 a Mrs. Cooper boarded the boys instead of Mr. Carr. The 1830s were a better decade for Savannah. The population grew from 7,723 to 11,214. The city posed for its portrait in 1837 by the ingenious Joseph Louis Firman Cerveau, who came to this country from Smyrna in Asia Minor in 1821 at the age of nine. He took up residence in Savannah around 1830. The painting is his most memorable accomplish-

---

[11] Union Society, *Minutes*, 87–88.

[12] Union Society, *Minutes*, 96–97.

[13] Russell and Hines, *Savannah: A History*, 91–92.

ment. In the background to the left of Bull Street, the cupola of Chatham Academy is clearly visible.[14]

Good things happened to the Union Society during this decade. In 1833, the wealthy bachelor Thomas Young left the society $5,000 in his will. In the same year, a former student presented a gift of $1,500 to the society. The president's report in 1834 noted that Anthony A. Suares, then living in Louisiana, donated the money while visiting Savannah. "In his property he has not forgotten the Institution from which he received the education which was the basis of his fortune." Anthony Suares asked to be admitted to the society, and the board gladly made him an honorary lifetime member. We know little else about the generous Suares, but he thus served as the prototype of later Bethesda boys who became benefactors of the institution.[15]

The board continued to wrestle with the question of whether the conveniences of boarding the boys in Savannah outweighed the disadvantages of city life, the lack of recreational facilities, the summer fevers, the questionable sanitation, the instances of crime, and general bad examples of immoral people. The officers took the bold step of removing their twelve boys to Springfield in Effingham County in April 1831. After six years, the board decided that Springfield was really too far away for close supervision, and the boys returned to Savannah. Mr. and Mrs. John Haupt agreed to board the boys for $125 each per year. One of the incentives to return to Savannah, at least as far as guardians were concerned, was that the boys would have the advantage of attending Mr. George White's school. White had made a name for himself for his high standards and strict disciplinary practice as principal of Chatham Academy, going on to open his own school. According to Joseph F. Waring, "White's Academy eclipsed the Chatham for the next fourteen years and was in its way famous." White

[14] Union Society, *Minutes*, 102; Waring, *Cerveau's Savannah*, 63

[15] Union Society, *Minutes*, 104–105.

was ordained as an Episcopal priest in 1843, then retired from teaching soon after that and devoted his time to his massive history compilations *Statistics of Georgia* and *Historical Collection of Georgia*.[16]

Though the men of the Union Society approved George White's methods, some of the students had a different opinion. Joseph Waring quoted one of White's former students at some length: "He had lost an eye and had contracted a habit of holding his head a little to one side to look at small objects," recalled William Starr Basinger. "Cock-eyed White, the boys used to call him...He used to give us terrible whippings and with little or no consideration whether they were deserved...He undertook to whip me one day, holding my head between his legs so as to get fairer blows at my nether parts—the blows hurt—I bit him sharply." That proved a bad idea; the whipping continued.[17]

In order to attract more members to the society, President Solomon Cohen recommended lowering dues from $6.00 to $5.00. Finances were in good shape, he reported, but he hoped for more members. On Anniversary Day, April 25, 1850, Mrs. Perla Sheftall Solomons, daughter of Dr. Moses Sheftall, presented the society with a beautiful box made from the wood of the live oak under which Mordecai Sheftall and his friends assembled at Sunbury while prisoners of war. Actually, two boxes were fashioned from the venerable oak. The second is in possession of Marion Abrahams Levy Mendell, a descendent of Mordecai Sheftall.

After acquiring a precious artifact of the past, the board surrendered one. John Russell's 1772 painting of the countess of Huntingdon, salvaged from the wreck of the orphan house in 1805 and housed unappreciated at Chatham Academy, was presented to the Georgia Historical Society in 1852. The trustees of Chatham Acade-

---

[16] Union Society, *Minutes*, 103, 108; Waring, *Cerveau's Savannah*, 65.
[17] Waring, *Cerveau's Savannah*, 66.

my, in the belief that the painting was done by Joshua Reynolds, paid $221.25 to have the canvas repaired by a New York restorer. The letter accompanying the donation stressed the need to protect and display the painting "as a relic connected with the early history of the state."[18]

The Board of Managers of the society approved of the good care John Haupt and his wife provided the boys, but after the departure of Reverend George White, they worried that the boys made little intellectual progress. The cost of board and tuition gradually increased. By 1854 the society expended $2,200 a year caring for fifteen boys. The year 1854 proved to be one of the deadliest since the fever epidemic of 1820; 560 people died during the year. The terrible

A rare photograph shows antebellum Bethesda as it looked after relocating from Savannah to its original site. (Courtesy Bethesda Museum.)

---

[18] The letter of transmittal, dated November 7, 1852, is in Georgia Historical Society Minutes, Book 1, 188; Union Society, *Minutes*, 110–12; Communication from Marion Mendel to the author, Historical Activities Committee, National Society of the Colonial Dames in the State of Georgia, *Early Georgia Portraits 1715–1870* (Athens: University of Georgia Press, 1971) 94.

visitation caused the fathers of the society to return to the ideal of a healthier retreat, a place where boys might be housed and taught, away from perils to their souls as well as to their bodies.

President Joseph S. Fay made an historic suggestion on June 21, 1854. The society could build its own home for twice the current yearly cost of sustaining the boys, but thereafter the cost would be half that. He proposed returning to the roots by the purchase of the old orphan house tract and building thereon a school, a dormitory, and a refectory. The board of managers agreed to the imaginative but bold proposal and named Robert D. Walker, Allen R. Wright, and John R. Johnson to act as a committee with President Fay to get the job done. Everyone agreed that the old name, Bethesda, should be retained.[19]

Although the costs exceeded estimates, as they usually do on such projects, the work was done in a remarkably short time. By January 22, 1855, eleven boys moved into their new home. The tract of 125 acres cost $2,500; the buildings $2,700; and other costs including that for two black servants, came to about $2,000. The genial husband and wife team, the Haupts, acted as house parents. President Fay made a special arrangement with the seller of the Bethesda tract. Simeon Z. Murphy would stay on as superintendent of the school. President Fay hired a northern man, R. C. Tasker, as teacher, but Tasker's health soon failed and William H. Shepard replaced him.[20]

The move to Bethesda proved to be an immediate success. Eleven boys formed the initial student body. A lad named Owen Brittle ran away, but eight others joined the original ten before the end of the first year. By Anniversary Day 1856, the number had risen to twenty-five boys, ages seven to thirteen. On that Anniversary Day, the boys

---

[19] Union Society, *Minutes*, 134.

[20] Union Society, *Minutes*, 140–43.

delighted the officers of the society with their singing, setting a precedent for festivities on future anniversary days.[21]

Two years later, Superintendent Murphy gave the first comprehensive report on progress at the Home. Fifty acres were under cultivation, growing corn, peas, potatoes, oats, beans, sugar cane, turnips, and melons. In addition, a garden produced other vegetables. The boys worked "cheerfully" in the fields after their school hours. They also helped with washing, ironing, scouring the buildings, and milking. The entire "family" attended morning and evening prayers and went to the Isle of Hope Church on Sundays. Each boy had a plot of ground in the cornfield. At harvest each would be paid double the market price for the corn produced on his plot.

William H. Shepard submitted a teacher's report on the same occasion. School lasted from 7:00 A.M. till noon during the summer; the schedule was moved back an hour in the winter. The boys had a morning recess, but they worked in the afternoon and studied for two to three hours in the evening. The student population had risen from twenty-five in 1856 to forty in 1858. Mr. Shepard praised them, insisting that "a more intelligent class of boys' cannot be found." Several of the older boys acted as tutors for the younger ones. Shepard had organized a debating society and singing classes. Thanks to donations, the library contained 380 volumes.[22]

In view of the long static period prior to Joseph Fay's presidency, Bethesda's resurrection was remarkable and exciting. Several presidents of the Union Society have been major benefactors to Bethesda. Fay must be numbered among them. At the 1859 anniversary, Fay announced his donation of eighty-five acres adjoining the property on the north, and other members of the society pooled their money to purchase 180 acres on the northwest side. Thus,

---

[21] Union Society, *Minutes*, 140, 154–55, 160.

[22] Union Society, *Minutes*, 175–78.

Bethesda reclaimed a total of 390 acres of Whitefield's original tract. Most surprising and novel, the farm had begun to show a profit. The usually staid and sober minutes of the society broke out in a statement very much like a cheer: "The restoration of Bethesda had awakened a local pride, it had appealed to the best sentiment of Savannahians and they rallied to its support as never before."[23] The founders of the Union Society might have imagined that Whitefield smiled in approval. His beloved Bethesda lived again.

Unfortunately, with prospects so brought, Bethesda was caught up in the cataclysmic struggle known by Georgians in general and Savannahians in particular as the War between the States.

Bethesda and the Civil War

By 1860 many southerners had begun to think of themselves as different from northerners—not just economically, but ethnically as well. Charles C. Jones, Jr., who joined the Union Society in 1859, expressed the opinion of most members of the society and probably of most southerners:

> I have long since believed that in this country have arisen two races which, although claiming a common parentage, have been so entirely separated by climate, by morals, by religion, and by estimates so totally opposite of all that constitutes honor, truth and manliness, that they cannot longer coexist under the same government. Oil and water will not

[23] WPA Savannah Writers Project, Bethesda Collection 1355, item 1894, 15–16, Georgia Historical Society.

commingle. We are the land of rulers; fanaticism has no home here. The sooner we separate, the better.[24]

The attitude had something to do with the supposition that the South was Celtic, whereas the North was Anglo-Saxon. It had more to do with American origins. Southerners modeled themselves after Virginians, who in turn imitated English country gentlemen. Northerners derived attitudes and values from the New England Puritans who came to America on a mission to form a godly society. Many northerners had decided that slavery, upon which the society plantation South was built, was immoral and must not be extended. The issue of the extension of slavery into territories was put to a vote in 1860. The Republican Party opposed further extension and garnered the most electoral votes; thereupon, South Carolina seceded on December 20, 1860.

The Savannahian who led the agitation for Georgia's secession was Union Society member Frances S. Bartow. Bartow became Savannah's greatest Civil War hero by giving his life at the first battle of Manassas, really before he had an opportunity to test his military ability. Confederate President Jefferson Davis appointed Union Society member Alexander R. Lawton Brigadier General in charge of the Savannah defenses. Lawton came in for a great deal of criticism, chiefly for permitting the unopposed Union landing on Tybee Island on November 23, 1861. Lawton believed that Fort Pulaski's thick walls provided adequate protection against the troops on Tybee. In this belief, he relied on the opinion of no less an expert than Robert E. Lee himself, sent by Jefferson Davis to supervise coastal defenses.

---

[24] Charles C. Jones, Jr. to Rev. C. C. Jones, January 28, 1861, in Robert Manson Myers, ed., *The Children of Pride: A True Story of Georgia and the Civil War* (New Haven: Yale University Press, 1872) 648.

Savannah had other defense works. Fort McAllister guarded the mouth of the Ogeechee, the back door to Savannah. In between Savannah and Fort McAllister, the most important Confederate position was an artillery battery of over a hundred men on the Isle of Hope, called Camp Claghorn after its Commander Captain Joseph Samuel Claghorn. Union Society member Charles C. Jones, Jr. served as mayor of Savannah from 1860–1861 at the height of the first warlike fervor, then took to the field as a lieutenant in Captain Claghorn's Chatham Artillery. Lieutenant Jones, second in command at Camp Claghorn, viewed the preparations for battle from relatively the same vantagepoint of those at Bethesda. Jones described his camp in a letter of October 18, 1861, as neat rows of white tents upon a bluff, overshadowed by noble live oaks, with the sun gleaming from the burnished barrels of the cannon, and the flag of the Confederacy waving in the breeze. Jones had a gift for expressive language: "The stillness is unbroken, save by the lazy flap of the tent curtains, the soft ripple of the tide as it gently chafes with the shore, and the occasional note of some waking songbird among the overshadowing branches. All else is hushed."[25]

Bethesda gleaned its intelligence from Confederate defenders on the Isle of Hope. On November 5, 1861, Union gunboats appeared in Ossabaw Sound. A few days later they heard the news that Union troops had landed on Hilton Head. On November 24, the enemy occupied Tybee Island without opposition. "What General Lawton is doing I cannot divine," Charles C. Jones Jr. wrote. On December 25, Christmas Day, five enemy vessels exchanged shots with a battery of seven guns on Skidaway Island, and the residents of Bethesda wondered if they would be attacked. For the following month, Union gunboats hovered off the coast and Confederate guns on Skidaway

---

[25] Charles C. Jones, Jr. to Rev. and Mrs. C. C.Jones, October 26, 1861; Myers, *Children of Pride*, 777–78.

fired sporadically. On January 29, 1862, Charles C. Jones wrote that his battery bivouacked at the western terminus of the Skidaway Bridge just across from Bethesda. He and his men expected an imminent invasion. General Lawton came out from Savannah to assume command. He ordered the Confederate guns on Skidaway to be removed lest they be captured. They were remounted at Beaulieu and Thunderbolt. Charles Jones noted that the removal of the guns disheartened the men who resented giving up Skidaway without a fight.[26]

General Hugh Mercer replaced Lawton. He massed 3,500 troops at Beaulieu on the Vernon River where the French had landed during the American Revolution. Captain Cornelius R. Hanleiter, stationed at the Beaulieu post, became acquainted with the Murphy family in nearby Bethesda, and on occasion his wife stayed at Bethesda as a guest of the home. Apparently, General Mercer had a solicitude for Bethesda that would be matched by his grandson, George A. Mercer, President of the Union Society. He placed several posts in the area. Captain Hanleiter's 8th Battalion Georgia Volunteer Infantry together with the 31st regiment of Georgia Volunteer Infantry were at Camp Beaulieu, the handsome plantation of Sheriff David Cole of Chatham County. Nearby was Camp Philips and the 7th Battalion Georgia Volunteer Infantry. In March 1862 the 7th Battalion was removed from Beaulieu to Bethesda itself. So, Bethesda became a military encampment, just as it had during the American Revolution.[27]

---

[26] Charles C. Jones, Jr. to Rev. and Mrs. C. C.Jones, November 27, 1861; January 29, 1862; March 14, 1862; Myers, *Children of Pride*, 803–804, 835–37, 857–58.

[27] For an account of Savannah during the Civil War, see Derek Smith, *Civil War Savannah* (Savannah: Frederic C. Beil, 1997) and James David Griffin, "Savannah, Georgia, During the Civil War" (Ph.D. dissertation, University of Georgia, 1963). For Hanleiter, see Elma S. Kurtz, "War Diary

On March 29, 1862, the Union troops landed as expected on Skidaway, burned the abandoned Confederate defenses. To the annoyance of Lieutenant Charles C. Jones and the relief of the residents of Bethesda, the enemy returned to their vessels. The long expected offensive would not take place on Bethesda's doorstep. Instead, to the astonishment of almost everyone on the Confederate side, Colonel Charles Olmstead raised the flag of surrender over the supposedly impregnable citadel of Fort Pulaski. Charles C. Jones expressed a general opinion that Olmstead should have fought to the last man. He thought it would have been better for Olmstead's reputation if he had preferred death to surrender.[28] Jones tended to view events as though they were scripted by Sir Walter Scott, whose novels were favorite reading for young men in the antebellum South. In the real world, Colonel Olmstead had no choice. The rifled cannon of the Union battery on Tybee had penetrated the stout masonry of the fort; continued bombardment would have exploded the powder magazine inside the fort.

The surrender of Pulaski caused panic in Savannah. The *Savannah News* reported that citizens began leaving the city for safer havens in the interior. Charles Jones lamented that General Mercer withdrew his brigade from the Isle of Hope, leaving Jones's battery alone to face a potential invasion. He had been disgusted at Lawton, then Olmstead, and now he vented his displeasure upon Hugh Mercer. On April 23, 1862, his battery was ordered to relocate on Ferguson's old lot, only a mile from Bethesda. Jones hated to leave his well-appointed Camp Cleghorn on the Isle of Hope for the desolate open field remarkable

---

of Cornelius R. Hanleiter," *The Atlanta Historical Bulletin,* no. 14 (September 1969) 12; for the location of the camps around Savannah, see William S. Smedlund, *Camp Fires of Georgia's Troops 1861–1865* (Lithonia: published by the author, 1995) 63, 66, 145, 225.

[28] Charles C. Jones, Jr. to Mrs. Mary Jones, April 14, 1862; Myers, *Children of Pride,* 876–77.

only for its innumerable fleas and, as he said in his postwar memoir, by its proximity to the famous Bethesda home. They called the place Camp Hardee.[29]

On May 26, 1862, the 7th Battalion abandoned Bethesda. In the same month, the encampments at Beaulieu were evacuated. On June 8 the Chatham Artillery at Ferguson's was ordered back to the environs of Savannah. Bethesda now had no military defense from a possible Union landing on Skidaway. According to tradition, the reason that the boys left Bethesda during the war was that the Home was needed as a hospital. It is not likely that it was so used while the boys were there, and a good reason for Superintendent Murphy to remove the boys was the same reason General Mercer removed the troops. A Union landing on Skidaway seemed imminent. Thomas Gamble noted that the Pavilion Hotel in Savannah, the property of the Union Society, was used as a wayside home for traveling soldiers. Perhaps that fact is the source of the tradition that Bethesda itself was used as a hospital.[30]

As one member of the Union Society withdrew his protection in the person of Lieutenant (later Lieutenant Colonel) Charles C. Jones, another offered to help remove the Bethesda family out of harm's way. William M. Wadley could identify with Bethesda boys. He came to Savannah from New Hampshire in 1833 at the age of twenty and began his career as a blacksmith's apprentice. He worked at the construction of Fort Pulaski, rising to superintendent of works after six years. He then built bridges for the Central of Georgia Railroad. In 1848 he joined the Union Society and in 1849 became general superintendent of the Central. When the war began, Jefferson Davis appointed him superintendent of Confederate transportation. In that capacity, he could offer help to his friend Simeon Z. Murphy and the

---

[29] Charles C. Jones, Jr. to Rev. C. C. Jones, April 22, 1862; Myers, *Children of Pride*, 883; Charles C. Jones, Jr., Sketch of the Chatham Artillery, 92.

[30] Thomas Gamble, *Bethesda: An Historical Sketch* (Savannah: Morning News Print, 1902) 129.

thirty-five boys at Bethesda. Wadley owned a plantation of 175 acres with a mansion and outbuilding a hundred miles up the line of the Central Railroad. Wadley indicated to Union President John M. Cooper that he would be willing to sell the plantation at a bargain price of 5000 Confederate dollars. Cooper, a printer and former publisher of the *Savannah News*, conferred with Superintendent Murphy and agreed to buy the property.[31]

The plantation lay just outside a railroad village called Bethany (now Wadley) and eight miles from the old Georgia capital of Louisville in Jefferson County. Mr. Mallon, who replaced William Shepard as teacher at Bethesda when the war began, opened a school in Bethany for the benefit of the Bethesda boys and a few villagers. William Wadley arranged transportation for the Bethesda people in November 1862. The train ride was exciting through the sand and swamps of Effingham County, the gradually rising pine lands of Screven County, the rich cotton fields of Burke, and finally, the rolling hills of Jefferson County. The great house, with its twelve rooms and columned porch commanded an open field of seventy acres. A creek ran by to the east furnishing a water supply. The creek flowed out of a pond, hidden from the rear of the house by a rise of ground. The pond meant good fishing for the boys, good watering for the cattle. The boys thought they were on vacation; the war seemed far away. Until the mansion could be furnished properly for the boys, they occupied a rented carriage factory in Bethany. Superintendent Murphy hired workers to construct a school building so that early in 1863 the boys lived and attended classes at the plantation.[32]

---

[31] Robert C. McMath, "William Morrill Wadley," in Kenneth Coleman and C. Stephen Gurr, eds., *Dictionary of Georgia Biography*, 2 vols. (Athens: University of Georgia Press, 1983) 2:1024–25.

[32] WPA, Bethesda Collection, 16. Remarkably, the house is still standing and is known as Bethany Farms, though the name of the town of Bethany was

For over a year, the Bethesda people enjoyed their bucolic tranquility. Then, in May 1864 ominous news reached Bethany: General Sherman's army penetrated the mountains on the Georgia–Tennessee line. On June 27, the Confederate army under General Joseph Johnston checked the advance of the Union forces at Kennesaw Mountain, but the setback proved only temporary. By July Sherman reached Marietta, and on the 17th his army crossed the Chattahoochee. Jefferson Davis replaced General Johnston with General John B. Hood, who attacked Sherman at Peachtree Creek in a savage hand-to-hand combat. It was brave but futile. Sherman gradually surrounded the city, cutting off the escape routes below Atlanta. The Confederates withdrew and the Union troops marched in unopposed on September 1, 1864. Many people then and later believed that the fall of Atlanta insured the reelection of President Lincoln.

On November 9, 1864, Sherman issued orders to his troops to move to the southeast, away from Atlanta and deeper into Georgia. "The army will forage liberally on the country during the march," he announced. Although he forbade soldiers from "entering the dwellings of the inhabitants," they did so, wreaking havoc along their line of march, following and destroying the railroads as they went. On November 23, Sherman entered Milledgeville, the state capital. Some of his soldiers held a mock session in the vacant hall and repealed the ordinance of session. Sherman noted that he "enjoyed the joke." On the next day he renewed the march accompanying General Henry Slocum's Twentieth Corp. At Sandersville Union troops deployed to drive back Confederate Joe Wheeler's cavalry.[33]

---

changed after the Civil War to its present name, Wadley, honoring the railroad magnate.

[33] William T. Sherman, *"War Is Hell": William T. Sherman's Personal Narrative of His March Through Georgia* (Savannah: The Beehive Press, 1974) 145, 155.

On November 28, Sherman camped at Spier's Turnout (today's Bartow). The tension at nearby Bethany must have been acute. A woman identified only as Nora H. lived on a neighboring plantation and gave vent to her fears in her diary: "For several days squads of cavalry—Wheeler's command—would pass and tell us where Sherman's army were and of the depredations they were committing, and warn us to prepare for the worst, as they were showing no mercy; and on Sunday the 28th of November, we heard that the destroyers were encamped just above our upper plantation, about four miles from our home."[34]

The 20th Corps entered Bethany the next day. One of the major officers occupied the orphan house. Local tradition has it that Mrs. Murphy nursed some of the wounded Union soldiers. If so, that good service protected the house and boys but did not prevent the "bummers" from confiscating the cattle, horses, and stores of corn. Mr. Murphy had to purchase 500 bushels of grain on credit after the visitation by Sherman. The occupation of Bethany lasted only one day. The irony is that Bethesda had hoped to escape the war by moving into the interior. Instead, the war found Bethesda.

Nora H. on the neighboring plantation suffered worse treatment. Union soldiers nearly killed her husband for not revealing where he had hidden his gold and other valuables. They took what they could and destroyed everything else, even the slave quarters. "Gin houses, packing screws, granary—all lay in ashes," Nora wrote; "not a fence to be seen for miles... Burning cotton and grain filled the air with smoke, and even the sun seemed to hide its face from so gloomy a picture."[35]

---

[34] Richard Wheeler, *Sherman's March* (New York: Thomas Y. Crowell, Publishers, 1978) 109.

[35] Wheeler, *Sherman's March,* 118.

Mary S. Mallard, sister to Charles C. Jones, Jr., recorded how it felt to have Sherman's "bummers" ransack the family home. "It is impossible to imagine the horrible uproar and stampede through the house, every room of which was occupied by them, all yelling, cursing, quarreling, and running from room to room in wild confusion. Such was their blasphemous language, their horrible countenances and appearance, that we realized what must be the association of the lost in the world of eternal woe."[36] The men belonged to Judson Kilpatrick's cavalry, acting as an advance patrol for Sherman's infantry.

Confederate cavalry under Joseph Wheeler skirmished with Kilpatrick near Waynesboro and fell back to guard Augusta, expecting Sherman to attack that town. Sherman continued his march to the sea unopposed. By December 3 he reached Millen. Realizing that Confederate General William Hardee had fortified the land approached to Savannah, Sherman moved southward to attack Fort McAllister on the Ogeechee. On December 13, Sherman watched from a platform atop Cheeves Mill as his troops overwhelmed the 250 gallant defenders of McAllister.

General Hardee evacuated Savannah on December 21 and Sherman marched in, triumphant. He sent his famous message to President Lincoln on the following day: "I beg to present you as a Christmas gift the city of Savannah, with one hundred and fifty heavy guns and plenty of ammunition, also about twenty-five thousand bales of cotton."[37]

A story told by Lillian Chaplin Bragg, who was born at Bethesda as the daughter of the superintendent and his wife, has it that a troop of Judson Kilpatrick's cavalry rode out to Bethesda intent on plunder.

---

[36] WPA, Bethesda Collection, 16; A. L. Archer to William Wadley, March 14, 1867, Bethesda Archives; Mary S. Mallard's Journal, December 13, 1864, in Myers, *Children of Pride*, 1220–27.

[37] Sherman, "*War Is Hell,*" 181.

The officer encountered "Bynuh," an elderly black man, probably left by Superintendent Murphy as caretaker. "Whose home is this, old man?" asked the officer. "It belongs to the Union Society," replied the old man. The officer assumed that the property belonged to the Union, the federal government, and he and his men galloped away.[38] Evidence that the elderly caretaker really existed is that one of Bethesda's fields for many years after the war was known as "Binah's Field."

Another tradition at Bethesda difficult to document is that newly freed men and women occupied the Home in 1965 and 1966. There is a basis for the tradition. In January 1865 General Sherman offered all "abandoned land" between Charleston and St. Marys and thirty miles inland to the freed people. President Johnson's amnesty in 1865 allowed many plantation owners to reclaim their property. Some freedmen in the Ogeechee area refused to relinquish the land they had occupied and armed themselves, only to be forced to yield by the United States Army.[39]

The building in Bethany, now Wadley, where the Bethesda boys sought refuge during the Civil War. The building still stands and the estate is known as Bethany Farms. (Courtesy Bethesda Museum.)

---

[38] Lillian Chaplin Bragg, "Stories of Old Savannah," Lillian Chaplin Bragg Papers, Georgia Historical Society.

[39] Karen B. Bell, "'The Ogeechee Troubles': Federal Land Restoration and the Lived Realities of Temporary Proprietors, 1865–1868," paper delivered at the Georgia Association of Historians Conference, April 17, 1999.

Finding a Superintendent

Superintendent Murphy and his wife liked Bethany, and they decided to remain in the town when the boys returned to Bethesda in February 1867. William Wadley, now Union Society president, suggested that Murphy purchase the plantation from the society. In a letter of March 20, 1867, Murphy explained that the house had suffered from unavoidable neglect during the war. The roof leaked; some plaster had fallen from the ceilings. The land proved poorer quality than they thought when the society bought the place. Murphy settled with Wadley on a price of $3000. A year later, Murphy asked for an extension of payment, citing the low price of cotton.[40]

Marvelous to relate, the grand plantation house is still there, and its town is called Wadley, not Bethany. There are problems of maintenance and repair, but the building appears to be in better condition than when the Bethesda boys romped through the high-ceilinged rooms of the mansion. Simeon Z. Murphy became a principal citizen of the town; in fact, one of its main streets is "Murphy Street," and we can also speculate that he had something to do with the renaming of Bethany in honor of his friend William Wadley.[41]

Mr. Murphy probably recommended the man who succeeded him as superintendent. Murphy became acquainted with Captain Cornelius Redding Hanleiter when the latter commanded the artillery battery at Beaulieu, less than three miles from the home. The Murphys on occasion offered accommodations to Anna Shaw Hanleiter, the captain's wife. At age fifty-two, Hanleiter had an interesting career behind him. His grandfather belonged to the first settlers of Ebenezer, and his first job was as a printer's apprentice at a Savannah

---

[40] Simeon Z. Murphy to William Wadley, March 16, 1868, Bethesda Archives.

[41] This writer visited the house and toured the grounds on April 4, 1999.

newspaper. He then went on to work at printing shops at Augusta, Madison, and Atlanta. In Atlanta he founded the Franklin Printing House, served on the city council, and was appointed judge of the inferior court. When the war began, he raised a volunteer company and was stationed in Savannah and commanded the gun battery at Beaulieu, as mentioned earlier in this narrative. In addition to his acquaintance with the Murphys at Bethesda, Hanleiter became good friends with Lieutenant Charles C. Jones, Jr. at Camp Claghorn. The two visited back and forth. Hanleiter kept a diary of his wartime experiences that survived the war and is now housed in the archives of the Atlanta Historical Society.[42]

Hanleiter had four children by his first wife; she died in 1848, and the children had grown up by the time the Civil War ended. By his second wife, Anna Shaw, he had eight children, at least one of whom accompanied her parents to Bethesda to work as a teacher. The Hanleiters had the nearly impossible task of reconstructing Bethesda, paralleling the reconstruction of Savannah in particular and Georgia in general. Unfortunately for the Hanleiters, but agreeably to his stockholders, President William Wadley concerned himself more with the reconstruction of his railroad, the Central of Georgia. In fact, Wadley's instructions to Hanleiter helped create an impossible situation. Wadley told the new superintendent that he need not undertake a farming operation; a vegetable garden would suffice. Hanleiter inquired about fencing in the fields against encroaching cattle and other animals. Wadley promised to have a plank fence constructed.[43]

---

[42] Cornelius Redding Hanleiter, "War Diary," manuscript at Atlanta Historical Society, 19, 51.

[43] Elma S. Kurtz, "War Diary of Cornelius R. Hanleiter," *Atlanta Historical Bulletin*, no. 14 (September 1969) 12; *Dictionary of Georgia*, 2:1025.

Hanleiter went to work with all the enthusiasm of a new director and motivated the twenty-two boys who returned from Bethany to Bethesda to share the responsibility of restoring the home to its pre-war condition. President Wadley and the Board of Managers wished Hanleiter well, suggested that he call if he needed help, and went about their business. On the first of every month, the zealous superintendent reported his progress and repeatedly invited the board to send inspectors out to monitor his administration. The president and his board seemed satisfied that Hanleiter had things under control. The president paid an occasional Sunday visit, usually a social call for an hour or so.[44]

Hanleiter had no trouble managing the boys, and his daughter proved to be an excellent teacher. Though the boys fared well, the crops did not. Wadley's promised fencing never materialized and cattle trampled down the corn, peas, and other crops. Heavy late summer rains ruined the vegetable garden and Hanleiter had to ask for funds to purchase provisions. The number of boys dwindled from twenty-two to nineteen, not unusual or alarming in itself; however, Hanleiter took strong objection to the president's arbitrary removal of a boy from Bethesda and later abandonment of him in Savannah.

Pent-up feelings caused an explosion when Wadley and the officers visited Bethesda on November 24, 1867. Instead of congratulations, Hanleiter heard criticism. Where were the products of the farm, Wadley demanded. Where were the stacks of hay; why had no fencing been done? Wadley accused Hanleiter of failing as a farmer. The superintendent could not contain his anger at what he considered to be unfair charges. He accused Wadley of not carrying out his promise to build proper fences and of shirking responsibility for the administration of the House. William Wadley has been characterized by a

[44] C. R. Hanleiter to William Wadley, February 1, 1868, Bethesda Archives.

biographer as a "gruff, demanding Yankee and a tight-fisted financial manager."[45] He did not take kindly to insubordination. Hanleiter's days at Bethesda were numbered after the confrontation on November 24.

On January 15, 1868, President Wadley received an application from an acceptable candidate, a mild-mannered clergyman with the necessary requisites of a wife who could qualify as matron and a daughter who could teach. Three days later, President Wadley notified the unlucky Hanleiter that the board of managers had accepted his resignation. The Reverend E. P. Brown would take charge on February 1, 1868.[46]

Hanleiter's reply was eloquent in its outrage. He began by noting for the record that he should have had the courtesy of an interview with the board to give his side of the story, especially because he was a member of the society. As it was, he and his family had to vacate the premises on a cruelly short notice. "You should remember that your comfortable salary of $10,000 a year (and how much more in perquisites I do not know) is not a whit more necessary for the support of your family, than was the modest sum of $1,000 for the support of mine," Hanleiter wrote. He ended on a note of majestic scorn:

> Permit me, sir, to say that however profound your judgment and great your ability as a Railroad Manager, you lack one very important and essential attribute to fit you for the responsible position of President of our Union Society—a position rendered honorable if not illustrious by being

---

[45] Ibid. Also, *Dictionary of Georgia,* 1025.

[46] E. P.Brown to William Wadley, January 15, 1868, Bethesda Archives. There is a biographical sketch of Hanleiter in the *Dictionary of Georgia Biography* asserting that Hanleiter helped raise money to benefit Bethesda. If so, it is hard to account for Wadley's harsh attitude.

> associated in times past with the names of such philanthropists as Habersham, Stephens, Jones, Sheftall, Bulloch, Arnold, Cohen, and Fay. I mean that of Charity without which all other virtues are as nothing.[47]

On that note, sad for Hanleiter and sad for the society, one superintendent left and another came. Hanleiter went back to the newspaper business in Atlanta. In 1872 Georgia Governor James Smith named him to a commission investigating advertising done by the Republican administration under Governor Rufus Bullock. When Grover Cleveland became president, Hanleiter was rewarded for his loyalty to the Democratic Party by a position in the Government Printing Office.[48]

The Reverend Mr. Brown began his tenure on February 1, 1868. Scarcely a month passed before Union Society inspectors visited Bethesda. Mr. Brown assembled the boys for the visitors, and daughter Ellen asked the students about geography, mathematics, and English grammar. The boys exhibited their spelling ability and skill in writing. President Wadley might not have liked Miss Brown's modest explanation that the boys owed their progress to the instruction of their previous teacher, Miss Hanleiter. The inspectors commented on the boys' health and their "witty manner." They concluded that their association with the "refined and well bred" Brown family had a wholesome influence. The Hanleiters probably had more to do with their good behavior.[49]

During the tenure of the Browns, the society began an ambitious building program. Two thousand people came out for the 120th anniversary on April 27, 1868, to witness the laying of the cornerstone

---

[47] Hanleiter to Wadley, February 1, 1868, Bethesda Archives.

[48] Kurtz, "War Diary," 11.

[49] S. Boyers and S. F. Lancester to Board of Managers, March 14, Bethesda Archives.

of a new building. Plans called for an imposing central structure first and wings to be added later. The society minutes state that the new structure would be located "as near the site of the original House of Mercy as could be determined." Apparently, the fathers of the society had forgotten, or did not know, that the first buildings faced away from the marsh. The new structure stood at a right angle to the marsh. Considering that in 1870 Union troops still occupied Georgia and that Georgians had not recovered economically from the devastation of war, the aggressive new building campaign indicated bold leadership. Perhaps it also meant that the Union Society held stock in William Wadley's Central of Georgia Railroad, one of the few securities to gain in value after the war. During the next three years, expenditures at Bethesda cost the society $33,000, an astronomical sum for that time.[50]

For reasons not chronicled, the Browns did not stay long at Bethesda. Augustus S. Quarterman began a new ledger on June 30, 1870, and we may suppose he had assumed the post of superintendent by that date. President Wadley had Quarterman's application for the position dated January 2, 1868, and Quarterman had the endorsement of influential members of the Union Society, including Colonel Charles C. Jones, Jr. Quarterman, age thirty-seven, was a native of Liberty County, Georgia, and a neighbor of the Charles C. Jones family. He married Anna Matilda Moultrie of Macon in 1852. He and his wife taught at Glynn Academy in Brunswick before the war. He served as a private in the Liberty Independent Troop during the war and resumed teaching afterward.[51]

Thanks to Quarterman's entries in his ledger, we know more about the daily routine at Bethesda than at any earlier period of its history.

---

[50] WPA, Bethesda Collection, item 1894, 17.

[51] A. R. Lawton to William Wadley, January 20, 1868; Joseph J. West to A. Sims, January 1868, Bethesda Archives; Myers, *Children of Pride*, 1651.

Whatever Quarterman's literary qualities might have been, prolixity was not one of them. Most of his comments concerned farm work done by Lewis the handyman. Lewis and the boys spent an inordinate amount of time at "Binah's Field," fencing, mowing, raking, to what purpose is not clear. If Quarterman had differences with the gruff President Wadley, they are muted in the journal. There is a hint of criticism on January 11, 1874, when Wadley ordered the front lawn plowed up and sown with oats.

The boys, who appear collectively as little angels in earlier reports, suddenly seem all too human. The pages of the journal tell of repeated runaways. A champion of sorts in the game of runaway was a boy named Morris Pittman, admitted at the age of seven on January 18, 1870, with his brother John, two years older. On January 7, 1874, Morris ran away. Two days later Quarterman sent out for and caught young Morris. However, on January 27 Morris and four others, including his brother John, ran away. On February 1 Morris and John returned, apparently of their own volition. Two days later, Morris was off again; this time Quarterman went after the escapee himself and caught him. After six attempted escapes, Quarterman appealed to the board of managers and received permission on February 4, 1874, to dismiss the eleven-year-old Pittman.[52]

Another recalcitrant who achieved the dubious fame of frequent mention in Quarterman's ledger was one Musgrove Morrison, admitted on June 11, 1872, at the age of eleven. Morrison ran away on March 6, April 6, May 25, and June 12, 1874. On March 23, the boy not only "resisted" the teacher, Miss Ward, but "fought" with her. Two of the bigger boys defended her. She sent for Superintendent Quarterman. In the presence of the other students, Quarterman made

[52] The ledger in Bethesda Archives is titled "Quarterman's Journal," although two of his successors also wrote in it. The first entry was December 18, 1873; the last August 25, 1876.

the boy take off his shirt and Miss Ward whipped him over the shoulders with a stick. The lesson had an unintended effect. When Henry Bunch disobeyed Miss Ward later in the year, she reminded him of Morrison's punishment. Bunch swore an oath that no man would strip him; he would kill anyone who tried. Nevertheless, Bunch received a flogging with a "chinquapin switch." Henry Bunch had entered Bethesda on July 28, 1869, at the age of eight. On September 22, 1874, he was sent home to his father at Waynesboro "as unworthy of charity."[53]

After seven boys ran away on April 6, 1874, Vice President Cunningham came out from Savannah and demanded to know why so many tried to get away. He blamed the bad examples among the boys, not the administration. However, there must have been a private agreement between Cunningham and the Quartermans, because Mr. and Mrs. Quarterman resigned later the same month, after the celebration of the 124th anniversary of the Union Society. The Quartermans stayed on until a replacement could take over the institution. Augustus Quarterman's last entry is fraught with thoughts not expressed: "This closes my connection with the Union Society," he wrote on June 30, 1874. He and his wife returned to Walthourville in Liberty County and taught school there. Mary Ann Quarterman died in 1896, and in 1901 Augustus reported that he was "still teaching: it has been the business of my life." He died in 1908 at the age of seventy-seven and was buried next to his wife in the Walthourville Cemetery.[54] It is curious that he did not comment in his Bethesda ledger about his teaching, the business of his life, but concentrated on farming. The fact may have something to do with President Wadley's priorities.

---

[53] Quarterman's Journal, 53. Another treasure in the Bethesda Archives is a "Register of Boys" with dates of admission, ages upon admission, and the places and dates of placement. The ledger was begun on January 1, 1870.

[54] Quarterman's Journal, 43; Myers, *Children of Pride*, 1651.

"The Boys Are Somewhat Mutinous"

J. E. Davies began his tenure on July 1, 1874. The most charitable description of his administration is that it was a disaster. One is reminded of William Golding's novel *The Lord of the Flies,* in which a group of boys turn savage. Because it is instructive of what can go wrong in an institution like Bethesda and in the belief that knowing what has happened makes it possible to avoid repetition, Mr. Davies's career will be followed in some detail. In the first place, he had trouble with "the help." Only five days after he arrived, he accused Phoebe, the cook, of pretending to be sick. He discharged the hired man Lewis, who served Quarterman well, "for having created a disturbance on the place."[55] Later in the same month, he dismissed Phoebe. He had difficulty finding suitable replacements.

Running away became a favorite pastime with many of the boys. On July 10, the teacher reported four boys for disobedience. It was on this occasion that Henry Bunch, the ringleader swore that he would kill anyone who tried to flog him. Davies applied the "chinquapin switch" anyhow. This prompted the other three disobedient boys to run away, accompanied by three others. The next day one of the boys returned with two boys "notoriously bad as to character"; all three had supper and afterward all three left the premises before Davies said anything to them.[56]

On Sunday, July 12, Mr. Wadley himself came out to talk to the boys, accompanied by Colonel J. F. Waring. The president insisted that discipline would be strictly enforced. Davies recorded Wadley's message in his journal and commented that it placed him in a bad position. He accused Quarterman of having been "rather lax" and

---

[55] Quarterman's Journal, 58.

[56] Quarterman's Journal, 53.

that was why the boys had become "somewhat mutinous." He tried to gain their goodwill, but "I find it difficult to gratify them and at the same time meet the views of the President and Managers."[57]

Wadley's admonition had little effect. Davies noted the next day that "the spirit of insubordination seems still rife among them, so that their conduct today has been outrageous in the extreme." On July 19 six boys ran away, and the next day twelve more left the premises. One-third of the total population of fifty boys were missing. Most of them straggled back or were sent back by parents or guardians after a few days. Davies blamed the discontent on Miss Ward, the teacher, for prolonging classes.[58]

The boys began to vandalize the property. On Sunday, July 19, the same day six boys left without permission, "quite a number" of the boys went into the melon patch and began to break open the melons. Davies remonstrated with them, but as he noted, "they became very mutinous and defiant." They started breaking windows in the wash room and doing other destruction. On September 5, 1874, total chaos threatened. Davies explained the situation without seeming to realize that he bore responsibility for letting things get out of control. "Several of the boys on the place had guns in their possession and finding that they were making too promiscuous a use of the same, shooting them off on the premises at all hours of the day to the detriment of others, and fearing such conduct on their part might bring censure upon me, I required them to leave their guns with me." Davies thus described an incredible situation, boys having been allowed for an unstated time to bring guns with them, to keep guns in their possession, and to fire guns anywhere and at any time. At some point it occurred to Davies that with guns going off randomly,

[57] Quarterman's Journal, 54.
[58] Quarterman's Journal, 57.

someone would likely be shot. However, equally important to him, he might then be accused of failing in proper supervision.

The critical moment occurred when Davies lay down a new rule, that boys could not recover their weapons any time they felt like it. At that point, he noted that "they became outrageously defiant, making all manner of insolent remarks in my presence and threatening mob force."[59] The moment deserves to be remembered as the most bizarre in Bethesda's long history.

Davies might have responded to the threat of mob violence in any of several ways. He decided to go to Savannah and complain to the redoubtable President Wadley. Understandably, Wadley expressed indignation at the state of affairs at Bethesda and promised to come out the next day. In fact, the president did not go to Bethesda. Vice President Cunningham, General Alexander Lawton, and Colonel Joseph Estill formed the delegation. They called the boys together, questioned them, and then hurried off to catch the train back to Savannah. Mr. Davies was flabbergasted: "They hurriedly left (to be in time for the cars) without giving me the benefit of their views and decision in this case. Bidding the insurgents a kindly good-bye, telling them to be good boys!!!"[60]

A week later Davies received a note inviting him to attend a special meeting of the board of managers. He went with a certain trepidation, not knowing what the agenda might be. He recorded in his journal that President Wadley blamed the boys, not himself. The board of managers agreed with the president and authorized the dismissal of nine boys by name. However, there must have been an understanding unrecorded in Davies's ledger that he would be replaced as soon as another candidate could be recruited. Davies's entries thereafter became non-committal.

---

[59] Quarterman's Journal, 61.

[60] Quarterman's Journal, 62.

There were no further descriptions of misbehavior on the part of the boys. By January, Davies began carting wagonloads of his possessions to his property on the Isle of Hope. Clearly, President Wadley had decided that Davies must go the way of Quarterman and Hanleiter. Davies's last entry on February 28 was anti-climactic: "Sabbath school exercises as usual conducted by Rev. A. J. Hughes Supt-elect at Bethesda."[61]

On March 1, 1875, the Reverend Andrew J. Hughes assumed the troubled post of superintendent of Bethesda. On the second day, he revealed his method of gaining control of the students: "I commenced today to drill the boys in the school of the soldier." The conversion of Bethesda into a semi-military school was a bold innovation and it must have had President Wadley's prior approval. The drilling continued for two weeks and the boys responded well. After that, the superintendent drilled them less often, but assigned meaningful tasks to the boys to occupy their spare time. He worked with the boys, white washing, planting vegetables, and cleaning up the premises. Hughes won the cooperation and respect of the boys and the workmen. Running away became a rare occurrence.

At the end of his first month, Hughes noted with satisfaction, "The boys have conducted themselves very well, this is the last day of the month and I am happy to say that I have not found it necessary to punish a boy since I have been here, one month." He spoke too soon. On April 2, he had to whip three boys, the first spankings he ever administered. That afternoon he drilled the boys again.[62]

On April 17, a delegation from the Union Society came out to examine the students and pronounced themselves satisfied. Miss Ward must have been grateful for the restoration of discipline in the house. In October she brought her furniture from her Savannah apartment

---

[61] Quarterman's Journal, 65, 73.

[62] Quarterman's Journal, 73.

to Bethesda. She intended to stay. The society's anniversary was observed on April 28, pleasantly but without much ceremony. The boys behaved well. Most of the superintendent's entries concerned routine agricultural work done by the two hired men, Smith and Jones. President Wadley had expressed keen interest in Bethesda's ability to sustain itself, and that may explain the emphasis in the Hughes journal on agriculture and the minimal attention to schooling.

In August Hughes and the boys spent a great amount of time and effort building a bridge, presumably to Skidaway Island. Fencing in the field also occupied their attention. On occasion Hughes gave the boys a holiday for their good work. On November 26, 1875, the superintendent went to Savannah to recover the body of Oliver Suttles, who died in a Savannah hospital of lockjaw. Little Ollie had come to Bethesda two years earlier at the age of six. Hughes provided a military funeral for the boy and buried him in the old graveyard to the south of the main building. Hughes indicated that several other boys had been buried there in the past. Charles Schultz, three years a Bethesda boy, died at the age of nine in 1876 and was interred near Suttles. Hughes fenced in the little cemetery for better protection.[63]

The first flare-up of unusual behavior occurred on January 2, 1876, when three outsiders caused the trouble by showing up at Bethesda armed and intoxicated. The leader, a boy named Levese, announced his presence by firing off his pistol outside the main building. Superintendent Hughes confronted the boy and told him to stop. Instead of leaving, Levese lingered and tried to incite the boys to disobey the superintendent. The situation could have become ugly if the boys had followed his example. They did not. Apparently, the

[63] Quarterman's Journal, 107. (The specific location of the cemetery is not known at the time of this writing.)

troublemakers left without doing further mischief because nothing more is said about them.[64]

On the rare occasion when a boy ran away, as two did on March 5, 1876, Hughes trusted the older boys to go fetch them back. He varied the boys' routine by celebrating special days, Lee's Birthday on January 19, and the founding of Georgia on February 22. On July 4 he loaded the boys into wagons and took them to the Isle of Hope to see a regatta and enjoy a cookout. The last entry in Andrew Hughes ledger reads, "Men cut wood again today. Boys policed premises and raked straw." The date is August 26, 1876. The ledger begun by Quarterman and ended by Hughes is a precious relic of an era of Bethesda's history about which little else is known. Even the names Hanleiter, Quarterman, Davies, and Hughes have been forgotten. If Hughes's successor, Albert Vernon Chaplain, kept such a detailed record, its location is not known. Probably the President of the Union Society decided that he had read enough about plowing, planting, raking, and fencing. Truth to tell, though the ledger contains some interesting glimpses into life at Bethesda, in general the notations are dull to the extreme. The point was made by some smart-aleck boy who managed to get access to the journal. After reading details he considered insignificant, he scrawled "Boy had a boil on his rump and wouldn't work." A few pages later, he added a disparaging comment: "You had better saved the money you paid for this Book than use it for such foolishness."[65]

A separate ledger of enormous value in Bethesda's archives is titled "Register of Boys Union Society." Augustus Quarterman began the record on January 1, 1870. He listed the boys by their names, their dates of admission, their ages upon admission, and the final disposition of each boy. The first name in the registry was that of

[64] Quarterman's Journal, 111.

[65] Quarterman's Journal, 118, 124.

Frank Bolan, admitted on October 2, 1868, at the age of eight. By consent of President Wadley, the boy was placed at D. G. Patton's on May 1, 1875. Andrew Hughes added that comment.[66]

By noting the date of admission and that of placement or dismissal, trends can be determined. In 1868 ten boys were admitted, nine were successfully placed, only one sent away. The average stay for this group was over five years, longer than usual. Five entered in 1869, three were placed, and two dismissed. Eight came to Bethesda in 1870 and only three were placed in employment. Five had to be sent away. The average stay was under four years. Of the eleven members of the class of 1871, four were placed, six given up to mothers, and one ran away to New Orleans. The longest stay was an unusual ten years, the shortest one week, the average four years. Some of those "given up" to mothers actually ran away to mothers. The average residency of the class of 1872 was three years; of thirteen admitted, five found jobs, four were expelled, three "given up," and one ran away. The largest entry group during 1870–1877 was twenty-two in the year 1875; the smallest was one boy admitted in 1877—and he ran away! The overall picture one gets is an average stay of less than four years for each boy with the considerable commotion of boys coming and going at unpredictable times.

A. V. Chaplin and Calm

With the advent of Albert Vernon Chaplin, calm settled over Bethesda. In several places in the records, Chaplin is listed as beginning his tenure in June 1876. However Andrew J. Hughes's last notation in the

[66] The Register of Boys begins with Quarterman's entry on January 1, 1870, and concludes with the release of a student on March 5, 1962. It contains the names of all boys admitted from October 2, 1868, to August 18, 1946.

Register of Boys is December 30, 1876, so Chaplin must have taken up his duties with the New Year. Chaplin liked Bethesda and Bethesda liked him, and he stayed on as superintendent until October 6, 1914, from age thirty-two to sixty-nine. A. V. Chaplin's annual reports resembled the entries in the ledger his predecessors kept: they told of planting, fencing, harvesting, and other agricultural topics. The president's annual reports conveyed news of the important and unusual. Beginning in 1879, the dynamic Colonel Joseph Estill, publisher of the *Savannah Morning News*, served as president. He reported, for example, that the west wing was added in 1883, costing $4,055 in mostly donated monies. In 1895 the east wing and new stables were constructed for a cost of $15,000. This completed the master plan drawn up in 1870 when the society began work on the central building. Bethesda could house 125 boys in the finished structure. By 1900 successive purchases of adjoining property raised the land holding to 513 acres, about the size of the trustees' grant to James Habersham and George Whitefield.[67]

In 1893 only one wing had been built adjoining the central hall. (Courtesy Bethesda Museum.)

[67] WPA, Bethesda Collection, item 1894, 16–17.

One of President Estill's more imaginative innovations involved the construction of a technological school with funds donated by a wealthy New Yorker named Edwin Parsons. Completed in 1890, the facility contained a manual training school equipped for carpentry, smithery, ironmongering, printing, and other skills. Although a bold experiment, Parsons Technological School failed for two reasons. First, competent instructors could not be found, or retained when hired. The second reason might have been foreseen. Most of Bethesda's boys were too young to learn certain skills, and most left before they reached the age to undertake the jobs they trained for. President Estill announced the closing of the school three years after it started. In 1899 the building burned down.[68]

Estill acted as Bethesda's best public relations spokesman, using his newspaper to build community interest and involvement in the home. The annual anniversary days took on the aspect of festivals. In 1880 fifteen hundred persons ventured out on the Skidaway line, or arrived in buggies and carriages, for the April 23 celebration. Governor Alfred Colquitt gave the principal talk. Major James C. C. Black, president of the Augusta Orphan Asylum and future congressman, paid his compliments. The Savannah Guards Band serenaded the gathering and everyone enjoyed the day. Estill's overt purpose in dressing up the anniversary celebrations was to enlarge the contributing membership of the Union Society.[69]

He also began the public promotion of former Bethesda boys. At the 1882 anniversary he presented the alumni as living examples of the Bethesda training. "A kind, paternal superintendence, seasoned with the discipline of the school room is our method of managing boys," he said, "and that it is the best evinced by the number of prosperous

[68] WPA, Bethesda Collection, item 1894, 16–17.

[69] *Proceedings of the 130th Anniversary of the Union Society at Bethesda, April 23, 1880* (Savannah: Morning News Steam Printing House, 1880) 5.

young men to be found in every walk in life, who are proud to say that they were 'Bethesda Boys.'" Twenty-three alumni attended the 1885 anniversary. They formed the "Bethesda Union."[70] Thereafter the superintendents made a conscious effort to maintain contact with former boys. The Bethesda Union took charge of organizing the dancing for the anniversary celebrations.

President Estill added another social element to the anniversary days. Girls from the Savannah Female Orphan Asylum came out as guests of the Union Society. The appearance and the demeanor of the boys improved remarkably as a result. Estill attempted in 1879 to attach Bethesda to Chatham County's public school system without success. However, after some discreet lobbying by his friends, he announced in 1885 that the Board of Education would incorporate the school and pay the salary of the teachers.[71]

Tranquil Bethesda as viewed from the Back River at the end of the nineteenth century. (Courtesy Bethesda Museum.)

[70] *Proceedings* for the years 1882, 1885, 1886. The 1885 Anniversary Day marked the first formation of an alumni association, the "Bethesda Union."

[71] Thomas Gamble Jr., *Bethesda: An Historical Sketch of Whitefield's House of Mercy in Georgia and of the Union Society* (Savannah: Morning News Printers, 1902) 144–45.

The annual proceedings reveal the historic highlights, but do not allow the reader a glimpse into life at Bethesda. They are minutes of meetings, not histories of people. Friends of Bethesda are fortunate that an interesting manuscript exists in the archives of the Home and in the collections of the Georgia Historical Society. The story nearly became a motion picture; it should some day be published as a book. Lillian Chaplin Bragg, the author, was born at Bethesda in 1885, the daughter of Superintendent Chaplin and Helen Flora Wallis Chaplin. She grew up at Bethesda and had happy memories of a childhood as a girl among dozens of boys. She recalled riding next to her father in a buggy going to visit Wormsloe, about four miles away on the Isle of Hope. Mr. Wymberly Jones DeRenne, who lived there, served on the Union Society Board and visited Bethesda on occasion. She remembered the tall, dignified black man, Frank Jenkins, who wore the livery of Wormsloe. He tended the horses when DeRenne and Chaplin went indoors to talk. "It was then that I, along with a half dozen little orphan boys, swarmed about Frank, chatting uninhibitedly."[72]

Lillian Bragg's manuscript is a chronicle of her mother's recollections of her first days at Bethesda. The stories provide random glimpses of how life was and, in some ways, how life still is carried out at Bethesda. Her style is reminiscent of Booth Tarkington's "Penrod and Sam" or Mark Twain's "Tom Sawyer." The account begins when Helen, or Nellie, as everyone called her, put an ad in Col. Estill's *Savannah Morning News* seeking a position as governess. On September 22, 1887, she received a letter from A. V. Chaplin: "I am in need of a seamstress for boys' clothing. Salary $8.00 a month and room and board." Her family strongly objected to her going to a place

---

[72] Lillian Bragg to Mrs. Craig Barrow, September 1, 1965, Elfrida DeRenne Barrow Collection, Wormsloe. I am indebted to William Harris Bragg, the historian of Wormsloe, for a copy of the letter.

they had never heard of called Bethesda. "If there was such a person as A. V. Chaplin, he in all probability was a seducer of innocent girls," they said. Despite the tears and protests of her mother, Nellie caught the train from Grahamville, South Carolina, to Savannah, then changed to the Skidaway train.[73]

The train came to a halt in the middle of a forest and the conductor told her this was Bethesda, her destination. A cheerful boy driving a horse and buggy greeted her as she stepped from the car. They rode companionably through what seemed to her a dense forest for a mile and a half. Suddenly, they came in sight of a noble building crowned by a cupola and a swarm of boys wearing uniforms of blue denim shirts, brown pants, and navy blue caps. They ran alongside the buggy shouting, "She's come!"

When Mr. Chaplin greeted her, she thought him handsome and a bit reserved. She met the teacher Mr. Lee and the matron Mrs. Sams and then went right to work sewing. The previous seamstress had left three weeks before so there was accumulated work to be done. She had no chance to be lonesome; besides, the boys kept popping in to say hello.

She learned the daily eating routine on her first day. At 1:00 P.M. a bell rang, a signal for the dining room crew to set tables in the dining room on the second floor of the west wing. At 1:15 P.M. the bell was tapped, not rung, to tell the boys to wash hands. Mr. Chaplin had introduced three hand pumps: one in the kitchen, one in the washroom, and one outside in "the burn." There was not enough soap to go around, so the boys used black dirt as an abrasive. The roller towels got dirty fast. At 1:30 P.M. the dinner bell sounded. At the entrance to the dining room a line formed where faces and hands were inspected. The older boys did the inspection; grimy hands or necks got

---

[73] The typewritten manuscript titled "Memories of Nellie Wallis Chaplin" is in the Lillian Chaplin Bragg Papers at the Georgia Historical Society.

Albert Vernon Chaplin, the "grand old man" of Bethesda before his retirement as superintendent in 1915. (Courtesy Bethesda Museum.)

sent back for a second washing. Then the boys marched into the dining hall, followed by the superintendent and staff.

After the blessing, the boys dug in to the dinner: sweet potatoes with syrup, rice, backbone stew, turnip greens, and cornbread. Nellie noted the low hum of conversation and learned to judge the appeal of the menu by the tone of conversation. She admired the way Mr. Chaplin had rigged up overhead frames of green cloth that, when pulled by a rope, fanned away the flies. The breeze mussed her hair, something the close-cropped boys did not have to worry about. Mr. Chaplin tapped a bell to allow those who had finished to leave. They dropped their plates and utensils into a pan at the door.

She learned that the boys really liked the handsome superintendent, just as he genuinely liked them. He acted as advisor, father, doctor, and farmer. He lanced boils, extracted splinters, bandaged cuts, and even spanked them if they deserved it. He would not punish immediately and usually did not have to at all. A wide strap hung menacingly near his door next to a "cooling off" bench for those called on the carpet or "burn." The boys showed her around the campus. The shallow creek was called the "little fellas'" and the deep creek the "big fellas'" to designate who could swim where.[74] They showed her how to cook stew by an open fire, calling it "cush." Ingredients might be oysters, crab, potatoes, and eels. They tried to frighten her with stories of escaped lions in the woods, and once as a kind of indoctrination took her "snipe hunting" and left her alone in the woods holding a bag for the non-existent snipe. She soon liked the boys as much as did the superintendent.

The supper routine went much like dinner's: "Medicine Chest Bells" rang after meals for all kind of ailments, bandages on cuts, or medication for minor pains. The bedtime bell sounded at 9:00 PM.

---

[74] The places were pointed out to this writer by old Bethesda boys on Anniversary Day 1999.

The older boys made sure their charges were tucked in, then each called, "All right, Mr. Chaplin." Saturday was a day off from school. The boys liked to go crabbing, even though they sank to their knees in the mush of the marsh. Crabs made good "cush." The boys discovered that heart of marsh grass tasted delicious. During the summer, swarms of sand flies pestered humans in the outdoors. The boys tied cloths to wires and set them on fire, so the smoke helped a bit to drive off the flies. Saturday night was bath night. Water was heated in large black cauldrons and poured into long troughs in the wash room. Every boy washed in the trough, trousers rolled up and one foot in, then the other, with some boys down the line splashing water over their faces, arms, and chests, trying to disregard what might float by. Older boys checked younger ones assigned to them. Nellie marveled at the way the older boys acted as substitute parents for the little ones, carrying them on their backs through the omnipresent cock-spur patches, generally acting like big brothers and learning valuable lessons in responsibility every day. In return, the young ones served as "lackeys" for their older "buddies." The buddy system made sense; in addition to teaching bigger boys responsibility, it also taught the little boys discipline. As a practice, it lasted at Bethesda until the 1950s.

After supper on Saturdays, halls in the main building were scrubbed in preparation for Sunday visitors. Following breakfast on Sundays, the superintendent held a general inspection. Older boys checked the younger ones while Mr. Chaplin supervised. Nellie helped adjust ties. Visitors arrived on the eleven o'clock train. Most boys had at least one parent who visited occasionally, or if the parent could not come, another relative—perhaps an aunt or an uncle—would substitute. The visitors stayed for dinner, attended Sunday services at 4:00 PM, and caught the 5:30 PM train back to town. The boys who did not have visitors played baseball in the summer. There were the usual children's games in their season: cops and robbers, prisoner's base, or shinny. Shinny resembled field hockey; the boys knocked a ball about using bent saplings. Other activities included kites in March, marbles in spring, jacks in summer.

Nellie looked forward to the festival days, especially when winter set in. The big buildings looked handsome but were drafty and cold, and the boys came down with colds and "the grippe." Most went home for Christmas. Nellie felt sorry for the boys who could not go home. She thought she would give them a nice surprise for Christmas, so she dressed up in an outfit resembling that of Mother Goose. Actually, she looked more like a witch and the smaller boys ran out of the room, terrified. On future Christmases, the superintendent dressed like Santa and things went better.

For Valentine's Day, the boys made their own valentines for Mr. Chaplin. He would leave his door open a crack and they would sneak down the hall and slip the cards through the opening. Some of the drawings had little to do with love. Nellie mentioned one showing Mr. Chaplin shooting a Yankee. If not the usual valentine message, there was genuine sentiment in the gesture.

The most important event of the year was (and still is) Anniversary Day on April 23. Visitors arrived with picnic baskets. A band composed of Savannah firemen greeted the 11:00 A.M. train. Former boys returned and the girls from the Savannah Female Orphan Home came out as guests of the Union Society. The Board of Managers held their annual meetings, then came the outdoor speeches—not the favorite moment for the boys, but the occasion for the state of the home speech by the president. During most of the long Chaplin tenure, Colonel Joseph Estill served as president. In recent years, the pageantry has dwindled from the annual meetings, but alumni still gather, the Union Board still meets, and the important reports are read.

Nellie witnessed one of Colonel Estill's most important and daring decisions. He had a continual struggle raising money for Bethesda, a chronic problem for all presidents from Whitefield to the present. He and Chaplin discussed the unpromising future. Then he had an idea.

The number of boys at the home hovered around fifty. "We won't starve them, no," said Estill, "but we'll make them look pitiful. We'll make the public weep when they hear the name Bethesda. We'll wring their hearts, that's what we'll do. Every issue of the *News* will carry a line about the terrible conditions at the Home." He and Chaplin decided to admit every boy on the waiting list. So much the better if they had to sleep on the floor. "I'd like to see a picture, Bethesda horribly overcrowded," said the Colonel. The plan seemed reckless, even institutionally suicidal. But strangely enough, it worked. The number of boys quickly rose from fifty to a hundred fifty. Chaplin coped as best he could. The *Morning News* carried horror stories about intolerable conditions and overcrowded orphans. Savannahians responded generously with contributions; several persons even donated downtown property to Bethesda. In fact, the campaign attracted the attention of a New York newspaper which sent a reporter to cover the story. Estill's gamble made Bethesda solvent until the Great Depression.[75]

Nellie's story sounded so much like a Hollywood movie that Lillian actually decided to send it to Hollywood. Lillian was one of two children born to the Chaplins at Bethesda; her brother, Wallace, grew up to be a successful medical doctor. Lillian married Kendrick Bragg, also a doctor; they had two sons, Kendrick and Vernon. The Bragg family achieved local fame during the second World War when Kendrick Jr. entered the Air Force, Vernon acted as a civilian flight instructor for the Army Air Force, while Lillian joined the Women's Auxiliary Air Corps. Their dog Duke was enrolled in the "Dogs for Defense" program and did sentry duty at an air base. Captain Kendrick Bragg achieved more than local notice as the pilot of a famed "flying fortress" bomber. On a flight from England to North Africa, his place absorbed countless rounds of ammunition from German planes; then

[75] The above material is gleaned from Lillian Bragg's manuscript.

a suicidal pilot crashed into Bragg's bomber, but—incredibly—it kept flying. Bragg landed safely in North Africa. The classic war song "Coming in on a Wing and a Prayer" was written about this very episode. For his efforts, Bragg received a Flying Cross with four clusters.[76]

Lillian remained attached at Bethesda all her life. She wrote stories about the history of the home for the *Savannah Morning News* while preparing her mother's reminiscences. In 1948 she finished the story to her satisfaction. She asked Charles Coburn—a distinguished character actor, a native of Savannah, and a member of the Union Society—if he would read the manuscript. He replied from Hollywood on June 22, 1948, that he would be glad to do so. She promptly mailed the hefty package to the actor. Lillian fidgeted as he took his time. On September 1 he gave her the good news that he liked it. Now, a scriptwriter had to go to work on the story; did Lillian want Coburn's agent to handle it? Coburn advised Lillian to get Bethesda's permission to do the filming there.

Excited now, Lillian agreed to Coburn's suggestion and immediately wrote to Tom Johnson, then Union Society president, asking permission to use the premises for the movie, reminding him of what Spencer Tracy and Mickey Rooney had done for Boys Town. Mr. Johnson replied cautiously, reserved the right to go over the final script, and asked for a financial benefit.

Coburn's agent Irving Salkow kept the excitement going. He, too, liked the story. He would represent Lillian for 10% of the profits. He recommended scriptwriter Bradbury Foote. Lillian promptly agreed. All this happened fast, Coburn wrote his reply on September 1, and Lillian's last letter was dated September 24, 1948. Events slowed and Lillian chafed. On November 3, 1948, Salkow sent the contracts. Under the terms of the contract, Foote would have the rights to profits

---

[76] *Savannah Morning News*, October 28, 1943.

from the printed story as well as from the film. Lillian expressed dismay: "Have you thought about my side of it? Now that you're my agent I expect you to sort of look out for my interests a bit."[77]

Salkow could play rough. He replied rudely that Lillian could take it or leave it. He took the job as a favor to Coburn anyhow. Lillian immediately signed the contracts, saying she did not want to deprive Bethesda of any benefits it might receive. "It is a noble institution and needs all the help it can get." Salkow then referred Lillian to Foote, the writer. That gentleman informed Lillian that "our" story would make a "sweet, humble and very human motion picture." But he would like a little conflict, a touch of the dramatic. Lillian disliked combining fiction with her history, but she tried to be accommodating. The matron could be a rival with Nellie for Mr. Chaplin's affections, she suggested. Nellie might tease Chaplin by flirting with George, a neighbor on the Isle of Hope. Nellie and George would go out for a boat ride, wreck, and be rescued by Chaplin!

Three months elapsed while Lillian waited for the scriptwriter's reaction. She could not contain her impatience. On April 13, 1949, she called his failure to respond "a slap in the face." Foote deigned to reply two weeks later. He would not apologize because he had nothing for which to apologize, he said. Perhaps the delay would be an advantage. After all, it had not been rejected yet. Lillian submitted quietly until October 29, 1949. "Have you felt inclined to start on the Bethesda story?" she asked politely. No response. She wrote again, three months later, sarcastically asking Foote to drop her a line. Finally, she gave up. On April 18, 1850, she informed Coburn that nothing had been done; she wanted to void the contracts altogether. Lillian managed a

---

[77] The correspondence is in the Lillian Chaplin Bragg Papers, Georgia Historical Society.

courteous note to the recalcitrant Foote on May 3, 1950, saying she regretted that their efforts came to naught.[78]

In retrospect, Lillian should not have gone the Hollywood route. She should have tried to publish her manuscript first, then approached her friend Coburn. As it is, the story remains unread in the archives of the Georgia Historical Society with Lillian's other papers. Her narrative captures the lasting appeal of Bethesda: the magical world of little boys in a place of natural beauty in contact with good compassionate adults who act as surrogate parents.

Most Bethesda boys retained fond memories of their stay at the home. Ninety-year-old Robert Snead wrote Lillian that he had lived at Bethesda from 1880–1888, adding, "I want to tell you again how much I loved your Mother and Father; they were two of the best people I have met in all my life." John Albert Martin entered Bethesda in 1907. He remembered Lillian as a "tomboy"; meanwhile, he remembered her parents affectionately: "They cared for us boys, the same as their own, from the time we wore dresses, until we were grown." Among his memories were the boyhood activities, swimming in the creek, bogging for crabs, stealing pears from a neighbor, hunting squirrels. "If I had my wish," he wrote, "it would be for some good old rabbit cush." He remembered Barney Diamond in a dress.[79] Barney Diamond entered Bethesda under the Chaplins in 1909, and he became the most celebrated of the Bethesda alumni. His story belongs in another chapter.

The Chaplin years (1877–1914) were good ones, though there were runaways. The reports in the annual proceedings began referring to them as boys "absent without permission" instead of "runaways." In

---

[78] The correspondence is in the Lillian Chaplin Bragg Papers, Georgia Historical Society.

[79] Robert Snead to Lillian Bragg, September 17, 1961, Lillian Chaplin Bragg Papers, Georgia Historical Society; Reminiscences by John Albert Martin, *Bethesda News* (July 1942) 4.

1896 thirty-two boys were admitted, and of those, eight left without permission. Because some of them left after a brief stay, the average residency at Bethesda was four and one-third years, but many boys remained longer.

The society's proceedings for the 1910 anniversary provide a final portrait of the Chaplin era. Several hundred friends of Bethesda attended the Anniversary Day activities on April 28. A string orchestra furnished music for dancing on a spacious pavilion set up for the day. The officers retired to the library where Mrs. Chaplin served a well-prepared meal. President D. R. Thomas presided over the business meeting, ending his thirty-one years of membership in the society. He reported 101 boys enrolled at Bethesda, forty in the first and second grades, thirty in the third and fourth, and thirty-one in grades five through eight. A committee of ladies prepared supper. According to the enthusiastic secretary recording the proceedings, "[t]he tables groaned beneath a superfluity of viands sufficient to delight the hearts and appetites of a jaded Epicurean as well as a hearty and growing lad."[80]

[80] Minutes of the Union Society, April 28, 1910, in *Bethesda News* (October 1954) 2.

CHAPTER SEVEN

THE BURROUGHS YEARS

A hiatus in administration occurred between A. V. Chaplin's retirement at the age of seventy on October 6, 1914, and May 2, 1915, when forty-two-year-old Ole Wycliff Burroughs assumed office. The boys took unusual liberties during Professor W. J. Hoxie's interim administration and tested the discipline of the new man when he came. Ole Burroughs proved more than equal to the task. A native of Pittsburgh with degrees from two colleges and a successful career as principal of Pittsburgh's Boys Industrial School, Burroughs came to Bethesda well qualified for the task before him. With him were his wife, Henrietta, and their children: John, age five; and Mary, age twelve. Mary remembered that they arrived in a record-breaking heat wave and, though the place looked dilapidated, she liked the idea of living on a farm.[1]

Henrietta Burroughs experienced a culture shock in coming to the South. She confided to her diary that the boys showed a lack of discipline, laxness in work, and a general shiftlessness, all of which she imputed to their southern heritage. Nor did she care for the superintendent Hoxie who blamed the poor condition of the premises on the Chaplins. Hoxie removed his belongings on June 28 and Henrietta noted, "We wish him good riddance." When the Burroughs visited the Chaplins on the Isle of Hope, she formed a better opinion of them: "We have heard so much good and so much bad about them, but I feel that the bad was painted blacker that it should have been." The

[1] Interview with Mary Burroughs Scandrett, no date given, clipping in Bethesda Archives.

Chaplins told them that Hoxie had begun to talk badly about the Burroughs.[2]

Whereas Henrietta saw a grimy place full of mean-spirited boys, Ole Burroughs saw potential. The men of the Union Society promised their support; the people Burroughs met in Savannah were friendly, and he genuinely liked the boys. He thus began a tenure that lasted until 1945, and even after that he continued to be affiliated with the home until his death in 1958. The Chaplin and Burroughs years covered almost a century, and the home enjoyed stability under the two gentlemen whose talents differed, but who both were so well suited to the work of raising boys into young manhood. Chaplin had a quiet inner dignity that commanded respect, while Burroughs had a creative imagination, a flair for writing, and a lively sense of humor. In other words, although Chaplin enjoyed a good joke, Burroughs would have been more likely to tell one.

Before the boys accepted Ole Burroughs, they tested him. The new superintendent had bought a supply of new brooms intended for the boys' use. On August 4, 1915, twelve of the brooms were missing. Burroughs realized that his authority was in question. He announced that there would be no supper until the brooms were returned. After the brooms reappeared, Ole rang the bell for supper, but about twenty rebellious boys remained outside the hall, yelling and beating on tin pans. Burroughs went out and told them to apologize or leave. Seven apologized that night, but the others remained defiant. At breakfast Burroughs stated that he would give the offenders until supper to make amends. Several did, but seven refused to apologize and even resorted to using insulting language. Henrietta Burroughs noted, "It made me feel sort of sick. Ole and I had never anticipated such impudence." Burroughs dismissed the boys. That night Ole and Henrietta met with

---

[2] Diary of Henrietta Burroughs, April 4, 1915–December 31, 1915, Burroughs Collection, Georgia Historical Society.

the teachers and all agreed to leave Bethesda if the Board of Managers of the Union Society refused to back them up. They need not have worried, though, for they were *fully* supported.[3]

Although Burroughs on other occasions demonstrated he could use the wide strap that A. V. Chaplin left hanging on the wall, he preferred persuasion and inspiration. He established a system of awards for effort and accomplishment and gave the boys a voice in selecting those who deserved the awards. He loved dramatic presentations, and in one of his most successful and significant innovations, he appealed to the ladies to act as auxiliaries to the teachers. A. V. Chaplin had always relied on volunteers among the wives of Union Society members, but Burroughs cultivated their cooperation in new ways. During the hiatus between administrations, Union Society President Henry Cunningham recommended the formation of the Women's Advisory Board. As first chairlady, Mrs. George Baldwin worked closely with Superintendent Burroughs. The committee structure indicated the kind of help Bethesda needed: house and furnishings, water supply, cattle and fowl, school, social life, table and food, and alumni. The appearance of the home received immediate attention. The house and furnishing committee turned its attention to the library, play room, study, and teachers' rooms. By 1917 Mrs. Alexander R. Lawton, the new chairperson, could say that the first floor of the main building was no longer an embarrassment.[4]

Ole Burroughs arranged a football game in the fall of his first year with Savannah's YMCA. Bethesda won 24–8. Fifteen-year-old Barney Diamond starred. Diamond also performed in black face in Burroughs's first minstrel show on May 19, 1916, along with Clifford Richardson and John Laroche. When the United States went to war

[3] Diary of Henrietta Burroughs, April 4, 1915–December 31, 1915, Burroughs Collection, Georgia Historical Society.

[4] Catherine Charlton, History of the Women's Advisory Board, Union Society Minutes, April 23, 1945.

with Germany, Burroughs arranged for a local army veteran to drill the boys.[5]

Bethesda alumni had formed a habit of returning for anniversary day, and in 1885 during the Chaplin administration had attempted a permanent organization, the Bethesda Union. Burroughs later claimed to have sponsored the first organization of former boys on November 16, 1917. Sixteen alumni attended the first meeting. In a few years that organization lapsed, and the alumni wouldn't be re-formed again until 1935.

Ole Burroughs began the practice of marching in the Boar's Head for the Christmas meal. The boys were properly solemn for this 1930 Christmas procession. (Courtesy Georgia Historical Society.)

[5] "Bethesda Diary," *Bethesda News* (June 1947) 3.

In 1920 the Women's Board introduced the tradition of celebrating an old English Christmas. Mrs. Hortense Orcutt suggested that the Women's Board buy two presents for each boy, one for him to keep, one to give another boy. Both gifts would be wrapped and given out by Santa. The Burroughs started the custom of bringing in the boar's head, the riding in on the yule log by the smallest boys, serving from the wassail bowl, then to the gym for Santa's distribution of gifts. Burroughs asked for the help of the Women's Board in recreation and social life. They responded by organizing programs in folk dancing, ballroom dancing, and handicrafts, all taught by volunteers. The Women's Board helped organize a drum and bugle corps, a Boy Scout troop, and parties every month with girls in attendance. Burroughs loved music and singing, and the women volunteers began tutoring individuals. Lee Jones, a Bethesda boy, discovered a talent for music and went on to the Yale School of Music and a successful career with the National Broadcasting Company.[6]

In 1922 the Cooper Harris legacy made improvements on the main building possible. The dining room was moved from the second floor to the first floor and the second floor made into a gymnasium. The ladies donated new chinaware and utensils for the refectory. Cooperation accomplishes wonderful results, and it produced a jewel in the construction of the Whitefield Chapel, begun in 1916 and dedicated in 1925. Burroughs's good angel in this case was Mrs. W. L. Wilson of the Women's Board, who also happened to be the President of the National Society of Colonial Dames. Through her mediation, the Colonial Dames presented the chapel to Bethesda as their gift. The simple, dignified, meeting-house style designed by Albert Simons of Charleston would have pleased George Whitefield in whose memory it was dedicated on Anniversary Day 1925. The architect used All Hallows Church at Snow Hill, Maryland, built in 1748 as his model. The

[6] "Women's Advisory Board of Bethesda," *Bethesda News* (January 1942).

beautiful stained glass window, fabricated by the Willet Studio of Philadelphia, was contributed by Mrs. Clarence Anderson and Mrs. J. A. P. Crisfield of Philadelphia, descendants of James Habersham in honor of their ancestor, Bethesda's co-founder. The window is a replica of one in the Carthusian Church near Florence. Flourishing unconsumed, the burning bush symbolizes Bethesda, once even described by Whitefield in that way. The Willet Company did the windows in the Military Chapel at West Point, the Princeton Theological Seminary, and other nationally significant places. Mrs. Craig Barrow contributed the pulpit in memory of Noble Jones, her forebear. Mrs. Bullard donated the altar to honor John Wesley, while the Georgia Society of Colonial Wars gave the pews. The entire project was a triumph of cooperation and a credit to Burroughs's skills in management and diplomacy.[7]

Ole Burroughs loved pageants and plays, and the Women's Board had the talent to produce unusually ambitious performances. The standards were set by an historical pageant on Anniversary Day 1919. The program featured the "Spirit of the Savannah River" attended by nymphs and dryads, Lady Huntingdon, George Whitefield, John Wesley, James Edward Oglethorpe, Tomochichi, six Indians, and eight ladies and gentlemen of the court of George II. In short, everyone who was anyone was represented.[8] In other years, the boys appeared in a surprising variety of plays: "Little Black Sambo and the Kings in Nomania" in 1926, "Gammar Gurton's Needle" in 1927, "Damon and Pythius" in 1931, "Ali Baba and the Forty Thieves" in 1932, Moliere's "A Doctor in Spite of Himself" in 1933. When girls' roles were called for, the boys played the part in a reversal of the custom

---

[7] *Savannah Press*, December 29, 1924, clipping in Scrapbook 1919–1951, Bethesda Archives.

[8] *Savannah Press*, December 29, 1924, clipping in Scrapbook 1919–1951, Bethesda Archives.

from Shakespeare's day. Misses Sarah Cunningham and Lillie West acted as directors with Ole Burroughs as impressario.[9]

Posing for their picture in 1925 on the occasion of the dedication of the Whitefield Chapel are (left to right) Clifford Jebey, a staff member, Ole and Henrietta Burroughs, George Elton, Savannah Mayor Robert M. Hull, and Union Society President George A. Mercer. (Courtesy Georgia Historical Society.)

Then again, the pageant put on for the 200th anniversary in 1940 dwarfed all earlier celebrations. Martha G. Waring wrote the script; Sarah Cunningham, Mrs. George Butler, and Henrietta Burroughs directed. The performance was staged in the open-air theater, a contribution of the Trustees' Garden Club designed by Hugh Tallant in 1934. The amphitheater was packed for the April 23 pageant. Miss

[9] *Savannah Press*, December 29, 1924, clipping in Scrapbook 1919–1951, Bethesda Archives.

Margaret Gilchrist, dressed as "the Spirit of Bethesda" and hooded in gray robes, narrated the story of the home. In the first scene, boys romped about to represent the Indians, the first residents. Other scenes showed George Whitefield talking to the first orphans, Whitefield explaining Bethesda to Lady Huntingdon, the founders organizing the Union Society, the removal of the boys during the Civil War, the "Spirit of Womanhood" featuring the work of the women's auxiliaries, the "Spirit of Youth" a parade of boys carrying tools they used in their chores around the home. Never had there been such an extravaganza staged by Ole Burroughs and his friends.[10] Some plays were put on after 1940, but the glory days of pageantry ended with the outbreak of World War II. The fanfare accompanying the 200th belied the fact that Bethesda had fallen upon hard times financially.

The man who worked most closely with Ole Burroughs during the 1920s was George Anderson Mercer, president of the Union Society from 1921–1933. Mercer, a nineteen-year member of the Union Society who never missed attending Anniversary Day during those years, was a neighbor of Bethesda and a close friend of the Burroughs family. Mercer's realty company bought the island of Vernon View; he built and his family lived in the first house on the island. George Mercer's youngest of four sons, Johnny, was about the same age as John Burroughs, and they spent some happy growing-up times together. Mary, a few years older, remembered the picnics on Skidaway Island when there was nothing there but a caretaker's house, birthday parties at the old Bannon's lodge in Thunderbolt, and the rides to Savannah on the streetcar. Johnny Mercer loved music and formed a friendship with Bethesda's gifted Lee Jones, but Johnny never learned to read music. Nevertheless, he grew up to be one of the most prolific and successful songwriters in America. He wrote 1,500 songs,

---

[10] *Savannah Morning News*, April 24, 1940; *Savannah Evening Press*, April 24, 1940.

seventy-five which were hits and four that won Oscars. In 1962 Chatham County honored Johnny Mercer by renaming Back River, which flowed near his home and behind Bethesda, Moon River in honor of one of Mercer's best known songs.[11]

While the children played, George Mercer and Ole Burroughs worried about financing. The home barely met expenses in 1923. The income derived from the society's real estate rental ($19,881), the Bethesda farm ($3,395), donations ($6,364), interest and dividends ($7,827), and Union Society membership dues ($4,946) totaled $42, 415. With income and expenditure so closely balanced, Bethesda could not afford repairs, a badly needed heating plant, a new barn, or anything at all of significance. Burroughs and Mercer decided to do what Bethesda had always done since Whitefield's détente with Savannah: they would appeal to the generosity of their fellow citizens. Advertising came of age during the '20s, and Bethesda embraced this new trend in order to raise $50,000 between December 3–12, 1923. Ole Burroughs wrote the script for the newspaper campaign and sentiment has seldom served so well. "Beloved Bethesda" became his theme: "The heart of every true Savannahian swells with pride because of the honor Bethesda, which has been Home for several thousand orphan boys (1500 of them in the last fifty-five years) has brought to us throughout the length and breadth of the land."[12]

Burroughs certainly played the economic card. "Bethesda is a producer of producers." He appealed to pity, telling how a widowed mother sickened and died, leaving her sons orphans. "The same thing

---

[11] Johnny Mercer's award-winning numbers were "On the Atchinson, Topeka, and Santa Fe," "In the Cool, Cool, Cool of the Evening," "Moon River," and "Days of Wine and Roses." There is a sketch of Mercer in *DGB*, 2:708–709.

[12] "Citizens Campaign Committee Bethesda Home for Boys Improvement and Expansion Fund $50,000 or More by December 12," A. R. Lawton Chairman, 1923, letterhead in Scrapbook 1919–1951.

could happen to you." He used his best magic, a photograph of twelve very small—some snaggle-toothed—all smiling boys, with the caption, "Bethesda is not an institution; it's a home of happiness." The campaign raised $56,000, more than the anticipated $50,000. Coincidentally, after the success of the drive was assured, Albert V. Chaplin died. The *Morning News* of December 9, 1923, paid him an appropriate compliment, calling him "one of the most zealous, patient, and affectionate workers that Bethesda has ever known."[13]

Having scored with the first advertising effort, the team of Mercer and Burroughs kept it going. Burroughs wrote a series of "Heart to Heart Talks," again heavy with sentiment and calculated to wring the heartstrings of Savannahians. One story told of a Bethesda alumnus, Cyrus Taylor, who died in France during the Great War. He had written to his mother, "If I do not come back, give one-half of what I have to Bethesda." Another challenged Savannahians to go out to the home and mingle with the boys, for "you will find your heartbeats begin to quicken and your tenderness stowing for the mastery, and your whole spiritual nature will be uplifted."[14]

Each story carried the notice that George Mercer stood ready to draw the will of anyone free of charge who would include a bequest to Bethesda. The offer resulted in a number of properties falling to Bethesda during the next twenty years. However, except for a generous legacy of $63,000 bequeathed by Percival R. Cohen in May 1927, few of them brought immediate returns. Unfortunately, the real estate market turned sour after the collapse of the Florida boom in 1926, and George Mercer's real estate investment company had to be liquidated in 1927. Twenty-eight years later, Johnny Mercer paid off all of the investors in his father's company in the amount of $300,000. The Union Society displayed its admiration for George Mercer by re-

[13] *Savannah Morning News*, December 9, 1923.

[14] *Savannah Morning News*, March 21, 1926.

electing him president, in spite of his earlier resignation. George Mercer died in 1940 at the age of seventy-two. In 1954 Bethesda erected a flagpole in his honor.[15]

Advertising could neither prevent the Great Depression nor sustain Bethesda. During the 1930s, the Union Society was rich in property but strapped for cash. The real estate brought in enough rent to allow

The imposing entrance to Bethesda, constructed in 1940 for the 200th anniversary of the home. The boys carted the bricks from the old swimming pool to the site. (Courtesy Bethesda Museum.)

[15] Scrapbook, 1923–1927; *Bethesda News* (July 1954) 2.

Bethesda to scrape along—just barely. Mayor Thomas Gamble, who wrote a history of Bethesda, expressed the frustration felt by many friends of the home. He addressed 200 Bethesda alumni at the bicentennial banquet in 1940: "It is a reflection on Savannah that...this magnificent home, whose history should awaken pride in every breast and rally to its aid the support of thousands of Georgians, must struggle so hard with its problems and finds its services to our youth sadly impaired by lack of enthusiastic encouragement and adequate financial aid."[16] The time had come for the Bethesda boys to rescue their home.

The Rise of Barney Diamond

The economic depression brought on a psychological depression, and the last ten years of Ole Burroughs's tenure seem somber in comparison to the first two decades. The Union Society had to foreclose on eleven parcels of realty by 1934. Unpaid city taxes loomed as a problem. Even those who needed special care could not get the help they needed. Ole Burroughs wanted to place a sick boy with his aunt and pay the aunt $5.00 a month. The board declined in favor of placing the boys in an Atlanta charity sanitarium. Society President Alexander R. Lawton canceled publication of the society's proceedings for 1932–1935. He reported in 1936 that the society owed $14,000 in back taxes to the city.[17]

Ole Burroughs worried about increasing vandalism by outsiders and suggested to the Trustees' Garden Club that an entrance gate would afford protection. The club had just contributed an open-air theater and the women accepted the challenge. Mrs. George Garmany

[16] *Savannah Morning News*, April 24, 1940.
[17] Union Society Minutes, August 26, 1935.

raised the money to pay the architect Hugh Tallant to design the gate and contractor George Clarke to do the construction. The boys did their part by carting bricks from the old swimming pool to the site. Since 1936, the handsome entrance has welcomed visitors and proclaimed Bethesda's founding date, all while providing better security. The New Deal WPA provided a marker reciting the history of the home.[18]

By 1937 the society owed the city $25,000 in taxes. President Lawton told the board of managers on December 10, 1937, that Bethesda faced a crisis. It cost the society $2,500 a month to run the home, and that exceeded the society's income. The society managed to struggle along by selling properties to the Federal Housing Commission. Beachfront property bequeathed to the society was sold for $15,000 in 1940.[19] The number of boys at Bethesda dwindled as the waiting list grew longer. This accumulation of problems served as a background for Mayor Thomas Gamble's appeal to 200 Bethesda alumni to rescue the home from its worsening plight. The man chiefly responsible for the large gathering of former boys was Barney Diamond. He modestly credited Tom Moore, Eugene Torrance, Charlie Vaden, and Harry Carter, but they and everyone else knew that Diamond was the main man. He led a whole generation of Bethesda men who followed in assuming responsibility for Bethesda's future. Integral to their renewed association with the home was the affection they felt for Ole and Henrietta Burroughs.

If Lillian Chaplin Bragg had not decided to write a book about her mother, she might have done well with the story of Barney Diamond. He and his brother Raleigh entered Bethesda in 1908, Barney at the age of eight and Raleigh at age ten. A. V. Chaplin held the post of superintendent at the time. Oral tradition has it that young Barney

[18] Union Society Minutes, April 16, 1936.

[19] Union Society Minutes, October 25, 1937, April 8, 1940.

was dismissed as incorrigible. Not so, according to the register of boys in Bethesda's archives. Older brother Raleigh was one of the ringleaders in the "broom" incident in 1915, and for his efforts, was dismissed and sent back to his aunt. We have seen earlier that Ole Burroughs mentioned Barney as one of the home's best football players in 1915 and a performer in a minstrel show in 1916. When Barney left Bethesda in 1917, he had one streetcar token. His first job was driving a wagon for the American Express Company. When the war broke out, he joined the merchant marine and remained a sailor for four years. In 1923 he happened to meet Ole Burroughs in Pittsburgh. Ole had gone there for the funeral of his father M. C. Burroughs. Very likely, Barney had heard of the death of the elder Burroughs and made it a point to attend the funeral. He told Ole that at the time he worked as the foreman of a construction gang in Cincinnati. Barney kept in touch with Burroughs as he improved his situation in life, marrying his wife Helen in 1925, founding his own construction company, securing government contracts during Franklin Roosevelt's New Deal, and moving to Washington, DC. He renewed personal contact with Bethesda and the Burroughs on his way back from Jamaica to Washington in 1940. He learned about Tom Moore's efforts to organize the alumni and, more immediately, that the bicentennial of Bethesda's founding was at hand. The meeting began his intense commitment to Bethesda. He mailed out invitations to the alumni to come to the 1940 Anniversary Day, arranging a reception at the Hotel Savannah and an alumni ball. Two hundred Bethesda men answered the invitation and attended the celebration. In fact, Diamond participated in the elaborate bicentennial pageant as part of the Civil War tableau. It was at a banquet sponsored by Diamond that Mayor Thomas Gamble aimed his challenge. Bethesda was in financial trouble; what would the men of Bethesda do about it?[20]

---

[20] *Bethesda News* (December 1970); *Savannah Morning News*, April 23, 1940.

Tom Moore credited Barney Diamond with raising the number of members in the alumni club from twenty-three to two hundred in 1942. Eighty-six members of the club served their country in World War II. Six gave their lives: Staff Sergeant George Henriot; Lieutenant Tom Jesup; Edwin Tapley of the US Navy; and three men of the merchant marine, John Coccia, Frank Sims, and Arthur Hand. Tom Moore counted 161 alumni in all in the service and he guessed that there were about fifty more.[21] Union President Charles Sanford took the Bethesda boys to the Savannah shipyards to observe the launching of the liberty ship, the *S. S. George Whitefield*. A few months later, the boys watched the launching of the *S. S. James Habersham*.[22]

Ole Burroughs loved to put on pageants. In 1951 Bethesda boys posed as signers of the Declaration of Independence. (Courtesy Bethesda Museum.)

---

[21] *Bethesda News*, January 1944, July 1944.
[22] *Bethesda News*, October 1943, January 1944.

The war years were quiet at Bethesda. Gas rationing limited the number of visitors for Anniversary Days. Ole and Henrietta Burroughs faithfully answered the mail they received from the Bethesda men in the service. Son John served as a lieutenant in the navy, while daughter Mary taught at Bethesda. The number of boys at the home dwindled to forty-eight, but the number in the Alumni Club climbed to nearly three hundred by 1945. Bethesda alumni took ads in Tom Moore's Newsletter: M. O. Seckinger, a plumbing contractor; Eugene Torrance, insurance; Leo Shearouse, Southeastern Radio Parts.[23]

As the war neared its end in April 1945, so did the long administration of Ole Burroughs. In his final report to the Union Society on Anniversary Day, he explained that his increasing deafness at age seventy-two made it more difficult to relate to the boys as he would like. Thirty years had taken a toll on his wife as well: "Neither of us is as patient as we were. It is only fair to the boys to bring in new blood." Mary Burroughs had returned to help her parents after graduation from the University of North Carolina. She said that her father turned down a job offer from a prestigious northern school to realize his ambitions at Bethesda, an active alumni, a cottage system, and a healthy endowment. In 1945, at least he had an active alumni.[24]

Sixty alumni attended the farewell banquet Barney Diamond gave for the Burroughs on August 14, 1945, at the Hotel Savannah. Diamond collected enough money from the alumni to give Bethesda a station wagon. The Burroughs moved only a mile away from the home and continued to help in any way they could. Ole contributed articles to the newsletter about incidents in Bethesda's history. But he had to come out of retirement sooner than he expected because his successor, Max Livingston, lasted only three years as superintendent. Livingston

[23] *Bethesda News*, February 1945, August 1945.
[24] *Bethesda News*, June 1945.

was able and left without hard feelings; everyone understood that he needed a better paying position for his growing family. Ole Burroughs agreed to return until a new person could be employed.[25]

A forceful voice during the three years of the Livingston superintendence belonged to Women's Board chairlady Mrs. Catherine Charlton. She objected strongly to Livingston's spending so much time with the farming operation and too little with the boys. The influx of small boys after the war, increasing the total to seventy-six in 1947, required more supervision and more space. Catherine Charlton reminded the officers of the Society that the Women's Board had set aside a small sum in 1921 for a cottage. She stressed the need for more casework prior to the admission of new boys, boldly insisted that the women be included in the long range planning for Bethesda: "Unless some of the members of the Board of Managers are informed along these lines, you are not in a position to give either intelligent approval, or intelligent disapproval, to the suggestions we have to make." The men paid attention; no other chairlady had accomplished that feat in the history of the Women's Advisory Board. She and Mrs. Thomas Hilton were named to a joint committee with two nominees from the Union Society. Catherine Charlton continued to push for a separation of farm duties from those of the superintendent, for an increase in the number of house mothers to a greater emphasis on counseling by trained social workers.[26]

The fact that Barney Diamond chaired the committee on Building and Grounds helped the Women's Board realize their dream of a new cottage. Diamond Construction Company made the low bid in 1947 for the Cohen Cottage, named for Percival Cohen, who left a legacy for Bethesda in 1927. The long invested funds accrued to $64,000. Tom

---

[25] *Bethesda News*, December 1946; the Livingston family is featured in *Bethesda News*, April 1946.

[26] Catherine Charlton's comments are in Union Society Minutes, April 2 and 23, 1946; April 3, 1947; and October 7, 1948.

Moore, representing the Bethesda alumni, contributed $10,000 in addition and the building was completed in 1948. The society named Claud Corry, manager of the Bethesda farm for eight years, as superintendent; Tom White, an alumnus, class of 1922 and in 1948 a Presbyterian minister at White Bluff Church, joined the faculty. Mrs. Charlton noted that neither had social work experience. The men of the Union Society answered that Bethesda was a home, not an asylum.[27]

The "Big House" as it looked before the central hall was removed in 1953. (Courtesy Bethesda Museum.)

To emphasize the ascendancy of Bethesda alumni, Barney Diamond was elected vice-president of the Union Society in 1949. Other Bethesda alums, Harry M. Carter and George Vaden, were treasurer and assistant treasurer respectively. Within a few years Harry Carter

---

[27] *Union Society Minutes*, October 7, 1948.

went on to the presidency to be followed by a fellow alumnus, Edward Perkins. History sometimes repeats. Bethesda alumni Peter Tondee and Richard Milledge helped start the society. It was particularly fitting that Bethesda boys again assumed responsibility for the home.

The Search for Direction

After World War II everything seemed to be in flux. Bethesda had changed very little in purpose, management, or appearance since the first World War when Ole Burroughs took charge. The city of Savannah remained static during that time, excited by the ballyhoo of the '20s but dispirited by the Great Depression of the '30s. After the wartime gas rationing ended and automobiles multiplied, downtown businesses moved out to the highways, travel increased, the suburbs mushroomed, and everyone rushed about either because they had to or because they could. City planners would have put streets through Savannah's venerable squares except that there were enough sensible people to squelch that bad idea.

The decade of the 1950s was one of almost continual change for Bethesda and the Union Society. Symbolically, the stately central hall of the main building was demolished. High winds had buffeted the building, damaging the cupola and roof so badly that the painful decision was made to take it down. By 1953 the deed was done; ever since then the central building has been conspicuous by its absence. The demolition of the old structure coincided with the end of the equally old tradition of a school at Bethesda. Superintendent Claud Corry hinted at the possibility in his 1950 report. He thought the school had done well over the years, but that the public schools would do better. The outside contact, he believed, would be beneficial for the boys. During the year, with the consent of President Tom Johnson and the Board of Managers, the school was phased out. A victim of sorts was Elizabeth Johnson, beloved Miss Lizzie, who had taught at

Bethesda for thirty years. The Society granted her wish to remain at Bethesda and helped her with a pension.[28]

Though academics were phased out, a manual training class was started in 1951, providing an outlet for the older boys' energies when home from school. The youngest boys in grades one through three attended the Isle of Hope School, beginning in the Fall of 1952. Earlier, in February of that year the fourth through six-graders transferred to Montgomery. A total of forty-three boys attended Montgomery, and twelve at the Isle of Hope. Twenty-two older boys attended three area high schools. Like many other Georgians, the boys of Bethesda spent a great amount of time riding around.[29]

In 1953 Claud Corry began to doubt the wisdom of the move off campus, but did not say so openly. Corry labored under the disadvantage that he had no professional training in social work or counseling. Catherine Charlton, during her fifteen years as chair of the Women's Board had dunned the Board of Managers with the need for professional house parents, counselors and social workers so that, though they were not as convinced as she would have liked, they were willing to experiment. The cottage plan meant small group living arrangements. Cohen Cottage, opened in 1949, was a step in the right direction. Another cottage, donated by alumni and friends, and named Alumni Cottage, and built gratis by Barney Diamond, was ready in 1953 when the central building was removed. In that year the Society named the remaining west wing Burroughs Hall, and the east wing the Ella Beckwith Lawton Building, honoring Mrs. Alexander R. Lawton, longtime chairlady of the Women's Board.[30]

A bequest from Emma Nagle permitted the construction of a new superintendent's house on the campus. The old frame house was

[28] *Bethesda News,* April 23, 1950.
[29] *Bethesda News,* April 23, 1952.
[30] *Bethesda News,* April 23, 1953.

moved to Ferguson Avenue, to be used as a farm house. Marvelous to relate, the farm showed a profit in 1954. However, Corry thought it a risky business, as he well knew from his eight years managing the farm. He remembered the criticism leveled at the Home, especially by the Women's Board that farming operations took too much of the supervisor's attention and too much of the boys' time. He leaned toward closing it.[31]

Another frequent criticism by the Women's Board, the need for caseworkers, led Corry into closer involvement with other Chatham County agencies. The need for counseling was more pressing than ever before because thirty-two of the seventy-three boys at Bethesda in 1954 were wards of Juvenile Court. The other boys had been placed by parents or relatives. Chatham County instituted Children's Services, Inc. in 1947 specifically to provide casework services to agencies like Bethesda. In 1953 twenty-seven of the seventy-three boys received casework services. In 1954 the United Community Services of Chatham County authorized a comprehensive study of twelve institutions housing children, three foster home placement and adoptive agencies.

The study was carried out under the supervision of out-of-state childcare professionals and resulted in a 1955 publication entitled *Children of Change*. An underlying premise of the experts worried some of the institutions, as well as some members of the Union Society; "any plan which involves a child's removal from his own home should be regarded as a drastic step" to be taken only after "a careful diagnostic study," according to the study. Another finding must have been equally troubling to the traditionalists, the study found that 109 children in the four major institutions (Bethesda, Savannah Home for Girls, Gould Cottage and Kings Daughters

[31] *Bethesda News*, October 16, 1953, April 23, 1954.

Nursery Home) were in care for more than one year. That fact the experts called "most startling."[32]

Among the most important conclusions of the study concerning Bethesda was that Bethesda, the Savannah Home for Girls, Gould Cottage, and Children's Services should join under a new umbrella agency providing institutional services for white boys and girls from ages seven to eighteen, foster care for white and black children of all ages, casework service for unmarried mothers and adoption services for white and black children.

The study found fault with Bethesda in its policy of accepting only boys, and urged a return to the pre-1801 co-educational policy. The Board of Managers met on January 18, 1956 to consider the proposal. It proved to be a lively session. The usually non-committal minutes contained unusual language, Dr. Sproull voiced "impassioned" objections, Mr. Artley "vehemently" opposed the notion of putting Bethesda under another agency. Mr. Middleton called the entire report "a disgrace." Former President Alexander Lawton "flatly opposed" any consideration of losing Bethesda's independence.[33]

Only the fact that key Union Society members had participated in the study prevented the outright rejection of the proposed merger. Outgoing President Tom Johnson, incoming President Harry Carter, Secretary Malcolm Bell, and future President Julian Space, had been involved in the study, and they argued for a trial of the new arrangement, and they prevailed. Harry Carter, Barney Diamond and Reuben Clark were named to represent Bethesda on a "Joint Review

[32] *Bethesda News*, December 8, 1955; Savannah Benevolent Association, *Children of Change: An Appraisal of Child Welfare Services in Savannah and Chatham County, Georgia* (Savannah: United Community Services, Inc., 1955).

[33] *Bethesda News*, January 18, 1956.

Council." The Women's Board supported the notion of improved access to caseworkers, but strongly opposed admitting girls.[34]

The Union Society delegation won several concessions from the council. They insisted that, because the Union Society had the largest capital endowment as well as the prestige of a long tradition, the combined agency be under the control of the Union Society, that the new agency be called "Bethesda-Savannah Children's Center," and that Bethesda continue operating as it always had under the Center. The Union Society named fourteen members to the Center's board of directors, compared the two by Gould Cottage, two by the Savannah Home for Girls, four by Children's Services and three by United Community Services. On June 14, 1956 the Board of Managers adopted the report of the Joint Council, despite the misgivings of many. It was understood that after two years, the arrangement could be canceled.

To add to the confusion of change, Claud Corry decided that he needed to go back to school to learn more about social work and counseling. The Board of Managers declined his request for financial assistance. He cannot be faulted for feeling unqualified, with all of the contemporary emphasis on psychological counseling. In his six years, he had been party to more profound changes than Ole Burroughs in his forty years.[35]

The Board of Managers hired an experienced social worker to head the Bethesda-Savannah Children's Center in the person of Anton Vlcek (pronounced "Val-chek"). He had the responsibility of managing Bethesda, Savannah Home for Girls and Gould Cottage. Long-term care was provided by the first two institutions and short-term by Gould Cottage. Despite the cumbersome organization, the system worked better than its critics thought it would, and the two

---

[34] *Bethesda News,* March 23, 1956, June 14, 1956.

[35] *Bethesda News,* June 14, 1956.

years of experimentation turned into thirteen. Much of the credit for maintaining the cooperative effort must go to Vlcek, to Union Society Presidents Julian Space and Edward Perkins, and to Tom Johnson, president of the Board of Bethesda-Savannah.[36]

If there was a flaw in the arrangement, it was that an efficient administrator like Vlcek obviated the need for a strong superintendent at Bethesda. A. H. McMillan, the first to be employed in the new scheme, lasted only ten months. Robert Branning, hired as a caseworker, succeeded McMillan in 1957. He remained for almost six years, giving way in November 1962 to Kenneth Tutweiler. In 1966 Harry Dunagan assumed the job and held it until 1970.[37]

Tom Johnson as president of the Board of Bethesda-Savannah acted as chief cheerleader, insisting in his yearly reports that the new arrangement worked wonderfully.[38] Anton Vlcek resembled a secular version of George Whitefield in that he excelled at exhortation to nobler efforts in a way that made many of the Union Society's Board of Managers uncomfortable.[39]

President Johnson stressed the fact that greater numbers of children were cared for by the combined agencies and more children were being adopted. The new measure of success was in returning children to their families. Although the restoration of boys to parents or relatives had always been a fact of Bethesda's history, far more had been returned to families than placed in jobs, it had never been regarded as a matter for boasting. No previous superintendent had pointed with pride to boys who went home during the year. A new dimension was added in 1961 when the Florence Crittenton Maternity Home for unmarried mothers joined the Bethesda-

---

[36] *Bethesda News*, August 9, 1956.

[37] *Bethesda News*, April 20, 1957, June 4, 1957, February 14, 1963, September 21, 1966.

[38] *Bethesda News*, April 28, 1961.

[39] *Bethesda News*, April 28, 1961.

Savannah Home consortium. Traditionalists in the Union Society began to feel unfocused.[40]

A stronger argument for maintaining the connection with the other agencies, at least to some who disliked other aspects of the arrangement, was the fact that Bethesda-Savannah received $100,000 annually from the United Fund. However, Bethesda needed that kind of assistance less in the 1960s than ever before. The improved financial condition stemmed from a rebounding post-war economy that allowed the Union Society to sell a number of properties bequeathed to the Society during the George Mercer campaign of the 1920s. Real estate broker William Lynes, a member of the Society, handled the sales without commission.

Anton Vlcek had a greater administrative challenge than any previous Bethesda supervisor. In 1962 he had to oversee fifty-five people, including caseworkers, cottage "parents," cooks, laundresses, maintenance and clerical personnel in the various sub-agencies of Bethesda-Savannah. Thoroughly committed to the goal of creating a better society, he stressed the need in his annual reports of doing more to correct existing evils and alleviate the suffering caused by those evils. In 1962 he pointed out the irony that "on the very day our brave astronaut was orbiting the globe in space at a cost of millions and millions of dollars, I saw a colored man eating out of a garbage can in back of one of our business establishments." He lectured his listeners for "a selfish interest in ourselves rather than an interest in others." He chided them for their lack of support for public schools, for their assumed opposition to slum clearance and for their complaints about high taxes. He noted that in 1962 there were only five orphans in all the allied institutions, but all his charges needed counseling. Bethesda, the Savannah Home and Gould Cottage housed 208 children, 106 children were in foster homes, ninety-nine in adoptive homes, and

[40] *Bethesda News*, April 18, 26, 1958.

144 in the Florence Crittenton Home, the numbers added to 560, a staggering total to those who preferred the simple days of the Ole Burroughs administration.[41]

Ole Burroughs himself remained loyal to Bethesda through the changes. He contributed well-written historical sketches to editor Tom Moore's *Bethesda News*. The articles radiated the nostalgia of a genuine fondness for Bethesda. Readers might have contrasted the happy days of plays and pageants with the new age of trauma and anxiety. Ole Burroughs died in 1958 at the age of eighty-five, emphasizing the break with the past. The Board of Managers resolved that "In the termination of his fruitful life the Union Society of Savannah and Bethesda Home for the Boys have lost one the like of whom we may not again see." The Board voted pensions for Henrietta Burroughs and Elizabeth "Miss Lizzie" Johnson.[42]

Anton Vlcek pressed on for further departures from the past. In 1963 he invoked the memory of Catherine Charlton, who fifteen years earlier had recommended affiliation with the Child Welfare League, an accrediting agency. Standards for childcare agencies were monitored by Governor Carl Sanders's new Division of Children and Youth in the Georgia Department of Welfare. Vlcek received the support of Elizabeth Lee, Tom Johnson's successor as president of the Bethesda–Savannah Center. The center applied for membership in the Child Welfare League, underwent inspection of its member institutions, and received accreditation as of January 1, 1965. The principal shortcoming, a chronic one, was the lack of a sufficient number of caseworkers.[43]

An ambitious experiment during the Vlcek regime involved a "Halfway House" at 120 West Harris Street for boys considered too

---

[41] *Bethesda News*, April 28, 1962.

[42] *Bethesda News*, April 18, 26, 1958.

[43] *Bethesda News*, April 20, 1963.

old to reside at Bethesda and too young to be on their own. However, there were too few boys of that age and description to warrant continuing and after a six-year period of trial from 1960 to 1966 the house was sold.[44]

In 1969 the Board of Governors of the Union Society voted to withdraw Bethesda from the coalition of agencies. The only reason mentioned in the society's minutes was that "the time had arrived." The vote was a lopsided 14–2, with Tom Johnson and Roy Gordon on the negative side. No one had fought harder for affiliation with the other childcare agencies than Tom Johnson. Perhaps the fact that two other powerful supporters of the combined agencies, Harry Carter and Julian Space, had died recently had something to do with the decision to withdraw. If so, the society made amends for the slight to their wishes by naming the new recreation building the "Carter-Space" Building.[45]

To dramatize the return of Bethesda to its traditions, the Board of Managers chose a Bethesda boy to supervise the home after Harry Dunagan resigned as of June 1, 1970. The appointment of Bill Ford was historic in that he was the first Bethesda alumnus to become superintendent and a further indication of the important role the alumni played in the operations of the Union Society. The hiring of Bill Ford represented "a return to normalcy," analogous to the United States electorate turning to the comfortable Warren Harding after trying to measure up the idealism of Woodrow Wilson. Bill Ford was born in a blighted section of Savannah on February 24, 1934, and placed in the Kings Daughters Nursery Home when six months old. He entered Bethesda at age six and remained almost twelve years. In 1974 he reminisced on his first days at the home. He felt alone and sorry for himself in this strange place with its huge oaks and pines. All the other

[44] *Bethesda News*, April 24, 1965, September 21, 1966.
[45] *Bethesda News*, March 3, 1969.

boys seemed bigger and stronger, and all busied themselves with work. Gradually, though, he became aware of a sense of community, even of a family. He particularly remembered an elderly neighbor who would take him to church on Sundays and treat him as a son. Bill starred in athletics and did well in his studies. Aided by a $65.00 per month stipend from the Union Society, he attended Toccoa College and graduated from Asbury College, then went on to Emory for a Master's Degree in Divinity. After serving for twelve years in the South Georgia Methodist Conference, Bill was asked by a fellow alumnus, Ed Perkins, President of the Union Society, to return to Bethesda. He readily accepted.[46] The year 1969 marked not only the end of the long experiment with the allied agencies, but also the day when Bethesda lost its principal benefactor, Barney Diamond.

[46] *Bethesda News*, April 25, 1970; Bill Ford reminisced about his first days in a radio interview on April 23, 1974, transcript in Bethesda Archives.

CHAPTER EIGHT

REACHING FOR THE MILLENNIUM

No one knew exactly how much Barney Diamond was worth when he died on October 13, 1969, but Savannahians whispered to one another that his legacy amounted to millions. Those who knew Barney well and were aware of his devotion to Bethesda were not surprised to hear that he had left the bulk of his estate to the home. For the Bethesda family, it seemed too good to be true. For years the annual reports of the Union Society faithfully chronicled Diamond's benefactions. In 1947 he supervised construction of a new dairy barn, and in 1950 he gave $20,000 to an alumni endowment. Later his company constructed the Alumni Cottage in 1952 and erected the flagpole honoring George Mercer in 1953. In 1956 he donated property worth $51,000 in St. Mary's, Georgia, to the Union Society.[1]

The *Bethesda News*, edited by Tom Moore (whose salary was paid by Barney Diamond), recorded the Diamond Company's achievements. In 1951 Diamond won contracts for building US Navy docks at Norfolk; the substructure of a Jacksonville, Florida, bridge; a bridge over the Patuxent River in Maryland; and a pier for port terminals at Wilmington, North Carolina. In 1953 Diamond constructed a sewer system for Miami, Florida; and in 1955 a wharf at King's Bay near St. Mary's, Georgia. In 1956 Diamond's company began building port facilities in Grand Bahama Island, a $33 million project.[2]

In 1952 Barney, Frank Jackson, Charles Sanford, and Julian F. Corish formed the Bernard F. Diamond Foundation for the specific

---

[1] *Bethesda News*, December 7, 1947; Union Society Minutes, April 23, 1950; April 23, 1953; August 9, 1956.

[2] *Bethesda News*, December 11, 1951; December 13, 1953; July 15, 1955; November 16, 1956.

support of the Union Society and other charitable organizations. To be precise, Diamond left most of his wealth in the form of his company's stock to the Diamond Foundation. The newspaper estimates put the estate worth at $35 million. Diamond's first wife, Helen, died in 1964. Two years later he married Dolores Austin, twenty-four years his junior. According to Diamond's will, Dolores Diamond received the income from a $150,000 trust fund, a house at 309 Paradise Drive, and a car. Son Jack Diamond was awarded the two-story stucco residence overlooking the Vernon River and its marshes.[3]

Portrait of Barney Diamond, Bethesda alumnus and Bethesda's most generous benefactor. (Courtesy Jack Diamond, son of Barney Diamond.)

[3] *Savannah Morning News,* October 11, 1969; *Bethesda News,* January 1976.

Enter Melvin Belli

Jack Diamond admits today that he should have agreed to adjust the monthly stipend upward instead of insisting that it stand as written. "I wanted Bethesda to have the money," he said.[4] Dolores astonished Jack Diamond and everyone else in Savannah by hiring one of the most famous attorneys in America, Melvin Belli. Belli had won several well publicized "palimony suits" involving Hollywood movie people. Belli fired the opening salvo in a legal battle by challenging Diamond's will, arguing that Diamond was mentally unfit when he signed the will and that he was under the "overreaching" influence of his attorney and employees, all four of them trustees of the Bernard Diamond Foundation. Dolores Diamond added that Barney was "mentally unfit" because of his drinking.[5]

The response of the executors printed in the October 13, 1969, newspapers indicated that they intended to stand firm. Belli, they said, made "an irresponsible and reprehensible attack on the character, integrity, and intelligence of Mr. Diamond." They protested Dolores Diamond's depiction of Barney as an alcoholic as equally reprehensible. The debate delighted the news media and titillated the public. Dolores struck back at the trustees of the Bernard Diamond Foundation: Tom Adams, Frank Jackson, Dale Hendrix, and Ken Stewart. She said they milked the Foundation by charging living expenses and bar bills to the trust, "as they have done for years." She dearly loved her husband, she said, even if he did drink too much.[6]

The headlines of the *Savannah Morning News* on October 22, 1969, read "Belli Storms into Town $30–$60 Million at Stake." Belli looked more like a circus impresario than a lawyer. He cultivated a long,

---

[4] Interview with Jack Diamond, February 1, 1999.

[5] *Savannah Morning News*, October 14, 1969.

[6] *Savannah Morning News*, October 14, 1969.

white hairstyle and issued pontifications rather than statements. He told the awed reporters that the $150,000 trust Barney left would not be enough to take care of Dolores and her dogs—"and he liked the dogs," he added. He inferred that Barney treated Dolores worse than his dogs.

Belli's first move bordered on the bizarre. He obtained a court order for the exhumation of Diamond's body and brought down a medical crony from New York to look for signs of brain damage, even hiring a photographer to take pictures of the brain at the doctor's direction. The photographer took 150 shots and later sued Dolores Diamond for $2,500 in payment. Unfortunately for Belli's case, the examination failed to show damage to the brain. The real damage in this case was done to the memory of a dignified, reserved, and generous man who all his life had tried to avoid publicity.[7]

Judge Shelby Myrick, Jr. set January 19 as the date for probate hearing to test the will. However, Belli managed to get a delay of a few days, so the hearing actually began on January 23, 1970. Belli complained that the "conspirators" objected to his requests for further delay because they knew he would "expose their nefarious schemes." He intended to prove that Diamond's brain was "incapable of prolonged rational thought" and the will was drawn up by "the conspirators."[8]

The defense put forth three witnesses who testified that Diamond was mentally alert till the end and that no one made him sign a will. Nevertheless, the judge permitted Belli a two-month delay so he could gather his evidence. When the hearing began on March 23, 1970, Belli did not attend, sending his assistant Bill Choulos as a substitute. Most of the questioning was conducted by Belli's co-counsel on this case, Donald Austin, who happened to be the brother of Dolores Austin

---

[7] *Savannah Morning News*, October 22, 1969.
[8] *Savannah Morning News*, January 24, 1970.

Diamond. He cross-examined Ned Adams, the lead attorney for the Diamond Foundation, for fourteen hours over the course of two days. At one point Donald Austin argued that even if his sister was "a red-neck cracker," Barney should have done better by her. Nothing was said about brain damage; Belli's expensive medical expert did not appear in court. Belli's extravagant claims about mental incompetency proved groundless.[9]

Judge Myrick ruled on March 28 that Diamond's will was valid. He noted that Diamond had taken out an insurance policy shortly before he died and that he would have been certified to be of sound mind to satisfy the insurance company. The judge praised Ned Adams for his "knowledge, composure, and frankness" under the grueling cross-examination. The friends of Bethesda rejoiced when they learned of the judge's decision. That should have been the end of it. However, Belli had not lost interest in the case that had such rich potential in fees. He flew into town to appeal the decision, demanding a jury trial. He impressed reporters by telling them that he was in New York Tuesday, San Francisco Wednesday, and Savannah Thursday, and that he would be in Atlanta on Friday and Miami on Monday.[10]

One judge disqualified himself because of his connection with Diamond's attorneys and Judge Dunbar Harrison heard Belli's appeal. Belli estimated that the trial might take up to six months. He would prove that there was an oral contract—hitherto not mentioned by anyone—that took precedence over the written will. To the amazement of the friends of Bethesda, Judge Harrison agreed to try the validity of the alleged oral contract before taking up the appeal on the validity of the written will.[11]

---

[9] *Savannah Morning News*, February 12 and March 25–27, 1970.

[10] *Savannah Morning News*, March 28 and July 24, 1970.

[11] *Savannah Morning News*, January 11, 1971.

An entire year elapsed between the initial hearing and the beginning of the trial on March 23, 1971. Huge expenses were billed by the lawyers. Bethesda's adherents worried that Belli, rather than Bethesda, would profit most from Barney Diamond's legacy. A circus atmosphere prevailed as the trial began with Belli as the ringmaster. He put William Edward Sharp on the stand. Sharp testified that Dolores and Barney were happy in their marriage before Barney began to drink heavily. Barney would use abusive language to his wife in the hearing of Sharp and his wife. "Was it embarrassing?" asked Belli. "Yes, it would embarrass her and embarrass us, too," answered the witness. Sharp continued his story, reaching the climax as the jury and spectators hung on every word. Late in 1967 Dolores left their Vernonburg house in tears and came to stay with the Sharps. Barney, she said, had been mean to her. Next morning Barney himself came to their house, "Sweetie," he said, "you know I'm always mean to you when I'm drinking." There and then he promised to leave her one-third of his estate if she would come home with him. Dolores called upon Sharp and his wife to witness what Barney said. Mrs. Sharp later confirmed Willard Sharp's testimony. The astonishing aspect about the court's permitting this testimony and the serious attention the jury gave it was the fact that Joyce Sharp was Dolores Diamond's sister and Willard Sharp, the main witness, was Dolores's brother-in-law, who certainly had a vested interest in Dolores's inheritance. The testimony of these in-laws proved to be the substance of Belli's case, though he prolonged the trial as long as he could.[12]

Belli put Barney's son Jack on the stand. Jack testified that he never heard his father talk about dividing his estate into thirds. He believed that Dolores had married Barney for his money. "There was always something she wanted," he said. Belli seized upon Jack Diamond's statement that his father told him four days before he died, "We've got

---

[12] *Savannah Morning News*, March 23, 1971.

to provide for Dolores." In a complete reversal of his contention a year before, Belli contended that Barney was lucid when he made that statement and that he meant that Dolores should get one-third of his estate.[13]

To the jury it did not matter what Diamond's lawyers said. They were hometown folks familiar to the jurors. Marvin Belli dazzled the jurors with his histrionics. It did not matter that Diamond's attorneys put up a witness who testified that Dolores had said she didn't expect anything from Barney because he wanted to leave everything to Bethesda, not to mention others who said Dolores cursed at her husband and used vulgar language generally. The trial dragged on for two months. On May 24, 1971, the jury delivered its verdict in favor of Dolores Diamond. They upheld the oral contract; Dolores would receive one-third of the Diamond estate.[14]

Diamond's lawyers contended that Judge Harrison failed to see the obvious fraud in the last-minute improvised testimony of the sister and brother-in-law of the plaintiff. The lawyers appealed to the Georgia Supreme Court. Dolores filed to block the appeal, but she need not have bothered. The Georgia Supreme Court upheld the verdict of the jury in her favor. The trustees of what remained of the Diamond legacy merged their foundation with the Union Society to form a new legal entity, the Bethesda Union Society. Dolores, disappointed at her share of the diminished legacy, sued the trustees for $9 million in damages, claiming she had been defrauded. However, she lost this one. In truth, Barney Diamond's once wealthy estate, composed mostly of stock in his companies, had been drained by the long trial while the publicity adversely affected the value of the stock. Dolores received over a million dollars and Bethesda slightly over three million—a handsome sum and much appreciated by officers of the Union Society.

---

[13] *Savannah Morning News*, March 24, 1971.

[14] *Savannah Morning News*, March 26 and May 25, 1971.

But the friends of Bethesda could not help thinking of "what might have been."[15]

The entire episode is so bizarre that it would have been great for John Berendt's gothic novel about Savannah, *Midnight in the Garden of Good and Evil.* The central character of Berendt's book was Jim Williams, a wealthy dealer in antiques, who shot and killed his youthful lover, Danny Hansford, in 1981. Hansford, a child of a severely dysfunctional family, was for a time one of Bill Ford's charges at Bethesda. He and his brothers, Johnny and Billy, entered Bethesda in 1971. Bill McIlrath remembers the three Hansford boys; they were there when Bill Ford invited him to join the faculty at Bethesda. Bill Ford and Bill McIlrath had attended Asbury College and Ford married McIlrath's sister. As superintendent, Bill Ford handled external affairs such as fund raising, public relations and dealings with the Union Society; "Mr. Mac" acted as father figure to the staff as well as to the boys. The Hansford boys had been at Bethesda one year before he joined the staff. He recalls all three as having a chip on their shoulder. Johnny liked to saunter around wearing an army jacket with a swastika emblazoned on the back. Of the three, Danny had the most violent temper and would fly into tantrums, but behaved himself most of the time. The brothers left Bethesda in 1974 and returned to live with their mother. In his teens, Danny turned to drugs and sex. His tumultuous relation with Jim Williams and his violent death form the crux of John Berendt's perennial best selling novel.[16]

Danny Hansford and his brother represented a nagging problem for Bill Ford and his staff. Some boys referred to the home by the juvenile court had problems too deep even for the magic of Bethesda. Bill Ford expressed the thought in one of his annual reports, "More chilling is

---

[15] *Savannah Morning News,* November 13, 1971; October 12, 1974.

[16] *Bethesda News,* April 27 1972; interview with Bill McIlrath, February 1, 1999.

the evidence that many of our children are unable to respond to love." According to Glaen Richards, President of the Bethesda Alumni in 1999, the alumni persuaded the juvenile court not to send its worst cases to Bethesda. The home was not intended to be a place of punishment.[17]

The refrain appeared as a troubling undercurrent in the superintendent's annual reports, in spite of the addition of two new cottages and the smaller number of boys housed in each cottage. The Perkins Cottage opened in 1977 and the Robinson in 1979. In the 1977 report, Ford pointed to problems associated with the boys attending outside schools, in which drugs and racial unrest caused turmoil, and the busing that consumed so much time. He suggested returning the school to the campus; he wanted to create "an atmosphere of love."[18]

Hurricane David caused $100,000 worth of damage in September 1979. The Home had no electricity for a week; the National Guard supplied a generator. Ford spoke of "tremendous pressure and hard work" during the year. Evidently, he had begun to hear criticism of his management of the institution. He defended his administration in his annual report to the Union Society. He stressed the difficulty of rearing children in the troubled times, adding, "the battle cannot be won from the critical armchair of those not actually involved with the work on campus at Bethesda." The same parents who could not control their children expected Bethesda to solve their problem. In an unusual plea for support from the Board of Managers in 1980, he said, "We have been second-guessed many times, and I would be remiss if I did not say that we have been depressed and hurt from time to time because of it, even to the verge of resignation."[19]

---

[17] Union Society Minutes, April 23, 1983.
[18] Union Society Minutes, April 23, 1977.
[19] Union Society Minutes, April 26, 1980.

President Ed Perkins supported Ford, a fellow Bethesda alumnus. The Society established a "policy committee" to work with the administration on problems. However in the same year, 1980, a complaint about corporal punishment to the Georgia Department of Human Resources brought on further doubts about the administration. In 1983, Ford lost his most stout defender with the retirement of Ed Perkins. In his report on Anniversary Day of that year, Ford repeated an earlier frustration, some boys expressed appreciation, while others blamed Bethesda for trying to help them. Numbers dwindled as referral agencies sent children to other homes that accommodated boys and girls. Staff turnover at Bethesda fostered a climate of uncertainty, even confusion. The use of corporal punishment brought on a fine of $500 by the Georgia Department of Human Resources in 1988. The Department removed a boy from Bethesda because of "improper" treatment by a house parent.[20]

Wiley Ellis, the new Union Society president, proposed that an outside agency, the Lutheran Family Services, investigate conditions at Bethesda. The Board of Managers agreed on June 8, 1988. The proposed study lasted twenty-three months and cost $36,925. The expense indicated the seriousness of concern of the Board of Managers. Meanwhile, Wiley Ellis informed Bill Ford that there would be no more corporal punishment for the present.[21]

Finding a Direction

The report by the Lutheran Family Services exploded upon Bethesda, causing a major shake-up in the organization. President Wiley Ellis called a special meeting on January 5, 1989, to discuss the findings. He

[20] Union Society Minutes, April 23, 1983; January 27, 1988.

[21] Union Society Minutes, October 18, 1988.

told the Union Society Board of Directors that the reason for the meeting was of the utmost importance; the Society must determine "how to go forward and what to do about the current superintendent, William Ford." The report faulted the superintendent for a lack of leadership, for a poor selection of house parents, and for the low morale of the staff. The report recommended hiring a professional in child care as superintendent, greater staff training, more recreational activities, a different work program, less emphasis on religion and corporal punishment, and a restructuring of the Union Society's oversight committees. Those at the meeting spoke frankly. Wiley Ellis said that when he took over the presidency from Ed Perkins he recognized that the Board of Managers had lost touch with operations at Bethesda.

Something drastic must be done to reassert control of the home; nothing less severe than a change of administrations. Bill Ford was a fine man, an excellent spokesman, a father figure for the boys, but there were too many problems with his administration. Jenny Lynn Bradley, representing the Women's Board, said that she knew that there were issues involving house parents, but did not know the severity of the problems until she read the report. The directors agreed that Bill Ford must go and allowed him to resign. Wiley Ellis had already contacted a replacement in the person of Robert Noble who had agreed to take over as interim director on May 1, 1989.[22]

At a second meeting of the board of directors on March 11, 1989, Ellis introduced Bob Noble. The occasion proved historic because of two resolutions proposed by Ellis and adopted by the directors. The first opened membership on the Board of Directors to women. The board promptly elected Jenny Lynn Bradley and Rhea Sparkman. Ellis's second proposal caused more soul-searching. He asked the board to open Bethesda to boys of any race, color or national origin. In view

[22] Union Society Minutes, January 5 and March 11, 1989.

of the Civil Rights Acts of the mid-sixties, the resolution was overdue. Nevertheless, even a delayed change causes trauma. Would Bethesda lose something of its precious uniqueness? What new and unknown problems might be encountered at a time when Bethesda had so many other problems to address? Ed Perkins, as a Bethesda alumnus, knew how other Bethesda men felt about tampering with traditions; he asked for a year's delay in the adoption of the resolution. After a spirited debate, the board voted nine to five against delay, with one abstention. Then Ellis's motion carried by a vote of eleven to two, with two abstentions.[23]

Wiley Ellis told Bill McIlrath he would have to leave with Ford. McIlrath had been at Bethesda seventeen years. His wife Sally served as a nurse at the Home. They had raised their three boys at Bethesda and loved the place. However, McIlrath accepted the dismissal with good grace. A plainspoken man, he told his colleagues he had been fired. To his surprise, they all signed a petition, threatening to quit if McIlrath left. They sent the petition to every member of the Board of Directors. Wiley Ellis and Bob Noble met with them as they aired their opinions. They sang McIlrath's praises; they disliked the consultant's de-emphasis on religious practices; they insisted on retaining some form of corporal punishment. Wiley Ellis let Noble make the decision. McIlrath would stay. Bethesda would continue non-denominational religious services. Corporal punishment would be administered as a last resort, and in Noble's presence. With the consent of the Board, Wiley Ellis offered Bill Ford the post of chaplain for $500 a month and $10,000 severance pay.[24]

Bill Ford's Anniversary Day report represented his farewell address. Most of the visitors did not know the circumstances of his leaving, and his report was a veiled but poignant response to his critics. He stressed

---

[23] Union Society Minutes, March 11, 1989.

[24] Union Society Minutes, April 21, 1989.

the breakdown of family values in modern society. Now, more than ever, children needed the anchor and stability of religion. "Many who offer themselves as child care specialists boldly state that you cannot reconcile religious values with methods of modern child care, George Whitefield did and so has Bethesda for 250 years." He accused those who objected to corporal punishment of over-reacting. "Shall we all stop eating because there are some among the human race who practice abusive eating habits?" The number of childcare centers who upheld traditional practices diminished every year. He hoped Bethesda would not join the trend. Ford achieved passages of eloquence in his address: "I can also report that this great children's home has become a focus on negatives; what is wrong, not what is right; what is missing, not what is present; what is ugly, not what is beautiful; what is destructive, not what is constructive; what hurts, not what helps; what we lack, not what we have."

In a voice heavy with emotion he argued for fairness, "Deception and untruth have magnified problems and no one seems to care. Misguided over-reaction and thoughtless action by those who lead...could become a most destructive force for Bethesda in days to come." He called upon the alumni to take a more active interest and participation in the Union Society. He knew that some alumni opposed the new initiatives, the admission of women to the Board of the Society, the proposed admission of black youth to Bethesda, but he made it clear that he did not mean to encourage divisiveness: "Not one here can justify bigotry in race or religion. God is not the author of confusion."

He discounted the importance of his departure. He knew that Whitefield's work would endure: "Battered by war, stormy winds of hurricane, fires and financial difficulties, this mighty work has withstood every obstacle." He would take his leave after spending twelve years at Bethesda as a child and nineteen as superintendent. He thanked Bill McIlrath, the staff, the Women's Board, and the officers of the Union Society on behalf of himself; his wife, Bonnie; and their children, Dawn, Charles, Rollin, and Bill, Jr., "for whom my beloved Bethesda has also become home." He closed by saying that Bethesda's finest hour was yet to come. Bill Ford's talk on that Anniversary Day moved his listeners to tears. It was his finest hour. He had given Bethesda two decades of his life and the boys his unstinting devotion. He had helped provide stability. However, what some saw as stability, others viewed as stagnation. His critics decided that Ford's love of Bethesda could not compensate for perceived shortcomings in administration. For those shortcomings, he paid the price of having to leave the place he loved.[25]

Bethesda welcomed Bob Noble, a friendly, cheerful man with the experience needed to reform the home. Noble later said that he found a staff "worn out, discouraged, confused, and just barely hanging on." They were not sure of which way to turn or which way to head. "There was a sense of desperation," he said. His first priority was to improve morale by talking and listening to each staff member. He made an immediate request to the Union Board for a badly needed increase in salaries for all employees. He, with the help of consultants from the Lutheran Family Services, wrote handbooks for the management of the cottage units. He restored family style meals, and emphasized cleanliness and good manners. He secured a van for each cottage, easing transportation problems. By July, Wiley Ellis announced to his board that "things were back under control." Bob Noble hired twelve part-time personnel, mostly college students, to work with house-parents. He held weekly staff meetings and encouraged the staff to attend workshops. Counselors evaluated the boys, and several whose emotional problems were too severe were placed elsewhere.[26]

[25] Superintendent's Report, April 21, 1989.
[26] Union Society Minutes, July 21, 1989.

Meanwhile, the Union Society struggled with the problem of finding its direction. In spite of all the positive changes during the year, the number of boys dwindled to thirty-five. None had been referred by Juvenile Court; all attended Bethesda by parental choice. History does not repeat itself exactly, but it does hold lessons for those who study it. George Whitefield first faced the dilemma of formulating a mission for Bethesda when he realized that there were too few orphans to sustain the operation. Even though the small number of orphaned and neglected children could not justify the expense of maintaining the great house he had built for them, he remained committed to the necessity of providing for them. His solution to the problem was to start a school for "young gentlemen." His needy children and the young gentlemen would benefit together from a good education. Whitefield's plans soared to the heights of his imagination, and he nearly turned his school into one of America's earliest colonial colleges.

Perhaps the members of the planning committee of the Union Society thought of Whitefield's example when they made their report on December 15, 1989. Bethesda's mission statement had said that the Home supported and educated orphans and indigent boys and fitted them to maintain themselves honorably in society. The newly proposed statement read that the "object shall be to provide residential, educational and social services of the highest quality to youth and families." The Board of Directors met on December 16 to discuss the committee report. They saw their alternatives, an emphasis on reforming problem children or a stress on education. The Board opted for education. Their decision influenced the search for a permanent director, a search to be conducted on a national scale for a professional with experience in education and in residential childcare.[27]

[27] Union Society Minutes, December 16, 1989.

During the year 1990 while the search went on, Frank Kuhn of the Family Services Institute (formerly Lutheran Family Services) acted as a consultant in revamping the organization. The Union Society's committees were charged with setting annual goals, meeting regularly, keeping minutes. Community relations needed to be improved; an "isolationist" attitude had to be replaced by an "involved and cooperative" approach. The board's signing of the Civil Rights Compliance Act implied accepting referrals from the Department of Family and Children's Services.

If the transition from Anton Vlcek to Bill Ford could be compared of the nation's choice of Warren Harding to succeed Woodrow Wilson, a return to comfortable isolation after troublesome involvement, the decision to hire David Tribble echoed the country's turning to Franklin Roosevelt and a policy of bold experimentation and involvement. President Samuel Zemurray introduced Tribble on Anniversary Day, 1991. Zemurray thanked Bob Noble for his interim leadership, "When he arrived on the scene we were shipwrecked, and now we are sailing smoothly with the wind at our stern." The Union Society officers felt much better, largely because they delivered the larger question of finding a direction for Bethesda to David Tribble. By August of his first year Tribble narrowed his objectives to five, the developing of an independent living program, a volunteer organization, an educational program, an individualized residential program and a community outreach. He needed a clearer focus, a better mission statement. In his words, they needed "a niche that is true to Bethesda's historic mission." Nothing could be more appropriate than an adoption of George Whitefield's idea of converting Bethesda into a school of excellence.[28]

President Sam Zemurray echoed this sentiment in a called meeting on January 9, 1992. "Are we satisfied with mediocrity or do we expect

---

[28] Union Society Minutes, April 9, 20, 21, 1900.

excellence?" he asked, adding, "Bethesda should be preparing our boys for college, for a vocation, or for the military." He asked each Board member for an opinion on whether to start a school at Bethesda. Several invoked the memory of George Whitefield in answering in the affirmative. A crucial question was whether a school could be supported? The endowment amounted to $16,123,615 as of January 2, 1992. That should spin off enough revenue to support a school. Some saw the school as an opportunity to attract outside students. The fourteen board members voted unanimously to start the school and charged David Tribble with the task.[29]

The Union Society chose David Tribble to lead Bethesda into the new millennium.

[29] Union Society Minutes, January 9, 1992.

With the essential point settled, that Bethesda would become a residential school, Tribble proposed a new mission statement, "Bethesda is an alternative school for boys, within a structured residential environment. Our aim is to bolster academic performance while grooming a boy's overall readiness for continuing education. Bethesda will admit students of any race, color, and national or ethnic origin." He believed that a loving, structured environment would turn problem children around. Boys need and want discipline. He would insist on proper dress and grooming, courtesy and respect in conduct. George Whitefield would have said amen to that.[30]

Fifty-two teachers applied for positions of lead teacher on the faculty. Tribble hired Tom Wuest as lead teacher, Nancy Davidson and Debbie Moore as instructors. They arrived at Bethesda July 1, 1992 to prepare for opening in September. They would offer classes in grades four to eight, beginning at 8:00 A.M. and ending at 3:30 P.M. The school year stretched from September 9–August 13. School opened on time, despite the resignation of three houseparents in August. In David Tribble's words the boys "were not too thrilled with school." Two years later Tom Wuest confessed that his first reaction was complete discouragement. The boys could not play together without fighting. Now that the boys lived and studied on campus twenty-four hours a day, the staff felt over-burdened and drained of energy. To the credit of the teachers and houseparents, the boys began to settle into the new routine. Union Society President Tom Potterfield could report on Anniversary Day 1993 that after a slow start, the school was a success. The Women's Board improved the library and the Alumni supported an active sports program.[31]

Some psychic hurts were healed when Bill Ford returned as President of the Bethesda alumni in 1993. He promised on behalf of

---

[30] Executive Director's Report, February 6, 1992.

[31] Executive Director's Report, October 1, 1992; April 23, 1994.

the alumni to work with the Home and with the Union Society. On Anniversary Day 1994, Bill Ford put into words a sentiment that many had felt, "There seems to be a spirit about this historic place that keeps Whitefield's vision alive in spite of human frailties and weakness."[32]

Nearing the Millennium

The attempt to start a school of excellence for about fifty boys was risky business. Whitefield himself had not succeeded at it, nor had the noble Lady Huntingdon, or the distinguished gentlemen who formed the post-Revolutionary War Trustees. President Joseph Fay and Superintendent S. Z. Murphy had better results, in spite of the inconveniences of the Civil War, and the school once begun had been carried along by the always powerful force of tradition through the Chaplin and Burroughs years for very nearly a century until 1952 when the boys were sent out to public schools. The times were so different, the challenges different, even if the boys were much the same. A. V. Chaplin and Nellie were father, mother, counselor, disciplinarian, doctor, nurse, psychologist, and general factotum for the boys. So were Ole and Henrietta Burroughs, aided by the forty years "Miss Lizzie" Johnson taught school. Now half as many boys needed ten times the staff of teachers, social workers, counselors, houseparents, with various county, state and federal oversight agencies hovering about. The process of growing up had become a community business.

David Tribble credited Debbie Moore, first an instructor then principal of the school, for the progress toward accreditation by the prestigious Southern Association of Colleges and Schools. The

---

[32] Alumni President's Report, April 23, 1994.

evaluation process began in 1996 and culminated in certification in December 1998. Beginning with the 4th through 8th grades in 1992, the school subsequently added grades one through three, conducted a self-study, underwent close scrutiny by a visiting team of educators, and received an unusually high number of commendations. Among the strong points cited were the ten to one ratio of students to teachers, a faculty of dedicated educators, strong parental involvement and the financial commitment of the Union Society. "Most of our students are behind and we can't afford to back up and remediate," said Principal Moore, "So we must accelerate their curriculum so they will be able to go to high school and do well." The fact that boys who were failing elsewhere managed to succeed at Bethesda represented the realization of the fondest hopes of those who dared to revive Whitefield's dream.[33]

Some friends of Bethesda feared that the admission of young black students might generate new problems. In 1999, David Tribble could recall only one fight that had racial overtones. If anything, black youth appreciated Bethesda more than white; they responded more positively to personal attention. Tribble said that he had found that boys generally were more accepting of others than adults were. Black students won as many academic awards as did the white students at Anniversary Day 1999. A black student, Jonathan Taylor from Atlanta, was valedictorian of the eighth-grade graduating class.

Bethesda has had a farm for more years than it had a school. George Whitefield realized he could not maintain the home on donations alone, and he excelled all those who came later in fund-raising. He acquired land for farms, or plantations, as gentlemen once called their farms. Whitefield felt he needed farm revenue so much that he argued with the Georgia Trustees to admit Negro slavery. William Piercy

---

[33] *Savannah Morning News*, August 31, 1998; Union Society Minutes, April 2 and June 4, 1992.

kept the proceeds of the plantations for himself. After the Revolution the Bethesda Trustees struggled to make the farm a paying proposition before moving the children out to Bethesda. The wind and fire of 1805 dashed their hopes. For want of farm revenue, the Union Society kept its charges in Savannah until 1854 when school and farm began operations at the old site.

After the Civil War, President William Wadley fired Cornelius Hanleiter for neglecting the farm, even though the boys were being taught well by Miss Hanleiter. The Quartermans, who prided themselves on their teaching, could not produce farm revenue. One of the reasons for A. V. Chaplin's long tenure was that he made the farm profitable. The Women's Board began to object, during the Burroughs years, to the superintendent's having to spend so much time on farm matters. However, the farm helped Bethesda survive the Depression. During the '50s, the farm generated $6,000 annually, but by then the Union Society began to build up an endowment from the sale of donated property. Claud Corry, a farm manager for eight years, advised shutting down the farm operation but operations continued under farm manager Drew Chapman until his death in 1982. Under Bill McIlrath, and with the restoration of the school, the farm acquired new clout as a learning laboratory in "agribusiness."

In 1992 Bethesda had about 100 head of cattle and only a few boys interested in farming. In 1997 McIlrath attended a trade show and got the idea of breeding registered cattle. The bloodline of registered cattle can be traced, making them more valuable. President Sam Zemurray liked the idea and donated seven registered cattle. The word spread and during 1998 forty other valuable animals were donated by breeders in Georgia, Tennessee, Alabama, and Florida. Donors hoped that some of Bethesda's students might become cattlemen. The boys became intrigued with the idea of adopting their own animal, learning how to take care of it, and entering it in competitive cattle fairs. In the November Coastal Empire Fair, Bethesda entries won two firsts, two seconds, and its bull rated grand champion.[34]

David Tribble inherited a controversial issue, the restoration of the historic John Russell painting of the Countess of Huntingdon. The painter John Russell (1745–1806), admired Selina's spirituality and very nearly abandoned his career as an artist at her suggestion. Though the Countess urged him to join her co-religionists at Treveca, he was reluctant to abandon the Church of England. He continued to admire the Countess and painted two portraits of her. She sat for the first on October 20, 1772. The portrait showed her standing, a crown of thorns in her hand and her foot crushing her coronet. Russell refused payment for the portrait, "I intend making the orphan home in Georgia a present of it," he wrote.[35] According to Russell's biography at the Royal Academy Library, the painting was sent to Georgia and lost in a shipwreck. This writer was happy to inform the curators at the Royal Academy that the painting had survived the crossing, wars, fires, hurricanes, faulty restorations and the Lady still stands triumphantly at Bethesda where John Russell intended it to be. Lady Huntingdon sat for another portrait, this one half-length, her cheek resting on her right arm, her head in a bonnet with an expression much like the Bethesda painting. This second portrait belongs to the Cheshunt collection. John Russell did a portrait of George Whitefield showing the Itinerant standing with his arms raised in the attitude of preaching. An engraving enjoyed wide circulation, but the original has been lost. Curiously, Russell's original portrait of John Wesley is also lost. In 1785 Russell was named "Crayon painter" to the Prince of Wales and in 1788 was elected to the Royal Academy.

---

[34] *Savannah Morning News*, August 20, 1998; interview with Bill McIlrath, April 24, 1999.

[35] George Williamson, *John Russell* (London: George Bell and Sons, 1893) 45, 139; Mark Pomeroy of the Royal Academy Library, Burlington House, London, was helpful in the research on John Russell.

The Countess gave the portrait to Bethesda during the early Piercy administration when her great expectations of Bethesda as a seminary for the conversion of America were at their highest. The painting survived the ravages of the Hessians and then the French who passed through Bethesda, taking what they wanted. More surprising, it survived the fires of 1773 and 1805. The Union Society housed the portrait at Chatham Academy until 1852 when the officers decided that the Georgia Historical Society could take better care of it and conveyed it to the Society on indefinite loan.

The historic John Russell portrait of the Countess of Huntingdon as it hangs in the Bethesda Museum. (Courtesy Bethesda Museum.)

When the Women's Board took over the management of the Bethesda museum, Anne White Leitch, chairlady of the museum committee, took a special interest in Lady Huntingdon. Through the services of a professional genealogist, she established contact with the current Lord and Lady Huntingdon. They not only contributed valuable artifacts, including Lady Huntingdon's prayer-book and family photographs, but Margaret Hastings, Countess of Huntingdon, actually visited Bethesda on October 10, 1978. The Women's Board defrayed her expenses from Boston where she had gone on a business trip. Anne Leitch tells the story about how the modern Lady Huntingdon expressed unkindly feelings toward her ancestor for selling off the family jewels to finance her charitable works. Anne Leitch could show her Bethesda and say, "Well here are your jewels." Lady Huntingdon felt overwhelmed by the beauty of Bethesda and its children, and assured her hostess that she no longer felt sorry for the sale of the jewelry. Her delightfully witty and informative talk to the Women's Board members assembled in the Whitefield Chapel is a valuable addition to the museum holdings.[36]

In 1991 President Samuel Zemurray arranged to have the historic painting of Lady Huntingdon returned to Bethesda. The years had taken their toll of the portrait, the Countess faded into the gloom of a darkened canvas. The Board of Directors authorized Zemurray to have the work restored. Zemurray obtained bids and settled on John Swope of Florida. Swope studied the painting and found serious problems. The canvas was pitted with holes, and had a large slash forty-seven inches long and seven and a half inches wide that marred the center of the dress and left sleeve. Worse, the face suffered holes in the left corner of the lips, the right cheek and the right eye. The original had been painted over and the overpaint was flaking and

---

[36] I am indebted to Nita Williams of Savannah, a member of the Women's Board, for a copy of the countess's remarks.

would have to be removed. In Swope's opinion the garments had been done by one of Russell's assistants. He initially estimated that his time and labor would cost the Society $15,000, but the final bill exceeded $20,000. Some members questioned the cost. The most outspoken was a Bethesda alumnus, J. Everett Flowers, who said that Swope should have kept a photographic progress report. He found fault with the retouching of the jaw line and said that Swope had used too little color in the face, so "as to render her as the living dead." The restoration of the canvas he approved, but he thought that the repaint showed little artistic ability and should be rejected. Despite his objections, the Board voted to pay the restorer the full amount. More recently, Nita Williams, a member of the Woman's Board, has arranged to have some color restored to the cheeks of the Lady. Regardless of its imperfections, the painting is a treasure, one of the few artifacts traceable to Bethesda's colonial origins. Although Selina cannot be called lovely, there is a majesty in her demeanor. The artist succeeded in capturing on canvas her dominating personality.[37]

Remarkably, the trust established by Lady Huntingdon for the maintenance of her twenty-nine chapels has lasted through the years. For a time after her death the "Huntingdon Connexion" flourished. In 1828 some 35,000 persons attended the Connexion's 200 chapels which were cared for by seventy-two ministers. Her followers, like Whitefield's, gradually merged with the Congregational Church. The "arminian" Methodists who followed Wesley in rejecting predestination dominated the Methodist Church. Today the "Lady Huntingdon Connexion" exists as a self-perpetuating trust with limited funds. In 1990 there were only 1,000 members of the Connexion. However, the Countess is well remembered in England. Her dresses in their muted tones are at the Costume Museum in Bath, and her chapel in the heart of the same city is now the "Building of

[37] *Bethesda News* (Fall 1991); Union Society Minutes, June 6, 1991.

Bath Museum." The Lady herself rests peacefully at the Hastings Chapel near her ancestral home in Ashby de la Zouch in Leicestershire. In 1991 two members of Lady Huntingdon's Connexion visited Bethesda in the persons of Mr. and Mrs. Staplehurst of England. Their visit, together with the restoration of the painting, linked modern Bethesda to its past.[38]

The most contentious incident during David Tribble's tenure concerned the proposed leasing of Bethesda property for use as a supermarket. On April 23, 1994, the Society's board of directors approved the concept of leasing of thirty-seven acres on the northwest corner of Ferguson and the Diamond Causeway for commercial purposes. The plan called for a supermarket, drugstore and fifteen other retail stories including a restaurant and a bank. Further negotiations with developers narrowed the proposal to a lease of 11.83 acres on the same site to Kroger Food Stores. President Tom Potterfield, who initiated the proposal, left it to his successor, Jenny Lynn Bradley, to carry out. Mrs. Bradley, the first woman to be elected President of the Union Society, had to face a storm of criticism when the news of the lease became public. The protestors argued that they liked to see the green trees along the road. Glaen Richards, who headed the Bethesda Alumni, replied that the property was already zoned for agriculture and that Bethesda just might start a hog farm on it.[39]

Robert Savadge of Orlando, Florida, who represented Kroger, and who was an expert in community planning, expressed astonishment at the "Babel of voices and conflicting statements." Savadge ungenerously blamed much of the adverse reaction on Bethesda. He said that the Home needed to clearly express its mission and to focus both its

---

[38] Edwin Welch, "Two Calvinist Methodist Chapels, 1743–1811," *London Record Society*, 1975; *Bethesda News* (Fall 1991).

[39] Union Society Minutes, April 23 and September 8, 1994; May 5, 1995; Interview with Glaen Richards, April 24, 1999.

self-image and its public image. David Tribble might have replied that they had just gone through all that.

The Chatham County Zoning Commission, responding to the objections of property owners in the neighborhood, turned down the proposal. The Union Society appealed to the County Commission. The emotion in the commission room was intense, as usually happens when property values are in question. Bethesda had always been the darling of Savannah and Chatham County, but many of their friends deserted the Society on this issue. The County turned down the proposal on September 25, 1995.

Now the majority members of the Society Board had their dander up. They considered expelling Society members who had opposed the lease, but saner heads prevailed. Former President Tom Potterfield moved a resolution to appeal to the Superior Court. In a fighting mood, the Board agreed to appeal. On April 20, 1996, the Court decided against the Society. Jenny Lynn Bradley expressed a "post mortem" opinion: "While we were in the limelight a little more than we would have wished, we felt the rezoning petition, though denied, brought Bethesda's story and efforts to expand its program to the attention of many."[40]

The controversy produced two results, both in response to the consultant's challenge to present a clearer image to the public. On February 1, 1996, Tom Potterfield proposed to the Board of Governors that Bethesda hire a development director, one who would get out the Bethesda message and help build the endowment. The Board agreed and in 1998 David Tribble hired John Gerhm, former development director at Armstrong Atlantic State University. The second outcome involved the dissemination of David Tribble's explanation of Bethesda's purpose and plans under the title "Bethesda Model: A

[40] Union Society Minutes, August 17 and 21; September 7, 1995; April 20, 1996.

Hybrid of Educational and Residential Programs with a Holistic Focus."

On Anniversary Day 1999, President Lane Morrison reported that the endowment had soared from $16 million in 1991 to $28 million in 1999, thanks to the rising stock market. Alumni President Glaen Richards commented on the "Boys Town" methods of positive reinforcement practiced by David Tribble and his staff. He said he saw "lots of hugging going on." Thinking back to his stay at Bethesda, he would have liked some hugs. The Alumni continued to contribute the Thanksgiving dinner to the boys, and to sponsor the athletic program. On behalf of the Alumni, Richards began a "Bible program," giving each boy a personal Bible to keep when he left.

The Women's Board continued to hover like protective angels over the boys. Some members of the Board have felt that their Board showed as great and continuing commitment to the supervision of the boys as even some of the superintendents. Mrs. Sallylu Sipple gave the 85th annual report of the Board on April 24, 1999. She told how board members took boys on field trips, provided Christmas presents, paid expenses of five boys who went to Washington, DC, and continued long running projects, the refurbishing of the cottages, landscape beautification, the upgrading of the museum and the maintenance of the chapel. Since 1914 the Women's Board has acted as a guardian angel for the boys of Bethesda.[41]

David Tribble gave his annual report on the occasion of the 1999 Anniversary Day against the background of intense media attention to the Littleton, Colorado high school massacre and to the issue of teen violence. He did not refer to that tragedy, nor did he have to say that Bethesda deliberately took in boys who had the potential to do violent

---

[41] Union Society Minutes, February 1, 1996; Women's Board Report, April 24, 1999; I am indebted to Mrs. Sallylu Sipple, Women's Board president, for sending me her report.

acts. He said that boys "lacked skills in expressing concerns" and the staff worked with the boys on that fundamental problem, encouraging and supporting. Many boys came to Bethesda having been rejected or having felt rejection. They had to learn how to bond with themselves first, then with their Bethesda family, then with God.[42]

The Flavor of Bethesda

George Whitefield called it the most delightful place on earth. The physical setting itself is an important aspect of the mystique of Bethesda. The huge oak trees with their great branches draped in Spanish moss convey a feeling of timelessness. The green-brown marsh grass stretches away from the sandbank to the meandering waterway now called Moon River, and in the distance the woods of the Isle of Hope define the horizon. The sea breeze carries the singular slightly pungent smell of the marshes. The two stately wings, over a century old, lend dignity to the campus. The conspicuous gap where the central hall once loomed recalls an even more imposing past and silently appeals to the friends of Bethesda for a restoration. The modest brick cottages nestle here and there amid the trees, all with names honoring benefactors. Most of the boys who come to Bethesda have never seen such a natural setting, with a forest on one side and tidal wetlands on the other, and in both woodlands and marsh mysterious living creatures waiting to be discovered. The pervading quiet of the place is gentle, calming.

Newcomers and even strangers soon learn that unseen aspects are ingredients in the flavor of Bethesda. George Whitefield still hovers over his home; his will still drives Bethesda toward excellence. At least it motivates those who strive so earnestly to perpetuate the work he

---

[42] Executive Director's Report, April 24, 1999.

started. James Habersham is present in memory, less intimidating than the Great Itinerant. The countess, Lady Huntingdon guaranteed her continued presence in the Home by sending over her life-size portrait, out of which she glares at small boys the way she once did at the noble Count Henri d'Estaing.

The faces of Bethesda. Jimmy Bragg, Paul Leddy, Lee Freeland, David Leddy and Donald Freeland pose for their picture in September 1970. (Courtesy Bethesda Museum.)

Boys add the essential element in the Bethesda mix. Bethesda is and always has been a community of children and, most of the time, a home for boys. It shares many characteristics of traditional boys' boarding schools. New boys must adjust to the expectations of the authority figures and must find acceptance among their peers. For most of its history, the big brother system acted as part of the process of indoctrination. The big brother explained the rules to the new boy, and at times enforced them by a spanking. Big brothers watched out for their charges in swimming, checked their appearance at meal times, carried them on their back over cock-spur fields, and generally looked after them. In return, the little brothers ran errands and did chores for the older boys.

Boys can be cruel to one another, especially in the early testing process. Bill Ford remembers his first experience. Still new, lonesome, and friendless, he walked about the grounds and stopped under a tree to watch two boys trying to catch a squirrel. Henrietta Burroughs came by. "You are the new boy?" "Yes'm." "Are those boys chasing squirrels?" "Yes'm," he said again. She ordered them to stop that foolishness and come down, then walked off. They climbed down from the tree and the bigger boy promptly knocked Bill Ford flat with a punch in the nose. The lesson was that one should not tattle and also that a small boy had to expect an occasional unfair hard knock in life.[43]

The assigning of nicknames was part of the process of acquiring a Bethesda identity. Joe Moseley entered the Home on July 20, 1941 and remained until January 1, 1946. On his first day a bigger boy called him "Mooseface." Joe asked why. "Because you are so damned ugly," was the less than satisfactory answer. Nevertheless, the name stuck, as did so many others. Albert Hucks was "Potgut," then simply "Guts." Years later many wore their names like badges of honor: Jughead, Milkbottle, Jug-O-Rum, Old Gator, Bones, PeeWee King. John Henry Dean, at Bethesda from 1936 until 1944, said that the older boys taught him to be a man. The result was a bonding among them that lasted all his adult life. Albert Hucks said simply, "I learned to get along." He meant that he learned how to socialize, not only at the home, but in his later life.

Some boys were identified by their laundry numbers. Each boy had a bin with a number on it; he wrote the number on his washable

---

[43] Interview with Bill Ford, April 24, 1999.

clothing. Luke Sims, at the home from 1933–1942, could remember who had what number over a half-century later. Glaen Richards, '39 to '44, recalls his attempt to steal a watermelon. When surprised by a farmer, he ran away leaving the melon wrapped in his shirt. Of course, the laundry mark gave him away.[44]

As at all boys' schools, Bethesda boys constantly test the limits of acceptable behavior. John Albert Martin wrote his reminiscences in a 1942 issue of the *Bethesda News*. He recalled bogging for crabs, stealing pears from a nearby farmyard, and making "cush" or stew with rabbits or squirrels as ingredients. Sidney Williams remembered breaking into the pantry and stealing vegetables from the farm. Roy Moulton, a Bethesda boy in the 1890s, wrote in his memoirs about a nearby convict camp. The convicts wore chains that were fastened to a post in their tents at night. "There was nothing the convicts liked to do as much as sing, and we liked to stand around and hear them." Doubtless, A. V. Chaplin and Miss Nellie would have disapproved of the boys' visiting convict camps at night if they had known about it. The chain gangs were still around in the 1940s. Albert Hucks and others would bring spoons to certain prisoners and next day retrieve rings made from the spoons. Ole Burroughs must have wondered about the spoon shortage and ring glut.[45]

The ultimate in limit-testing was and still is running away. There seems to be little or no stigma attached to running away. In fact, boys brag about it. In most instances, the boys voluntarily come back after a few hours or a day or two. Sometimes the parents or guardians return them. It is rare for a boy with no home to run away. One such was John Woodell, who wrote Lillian Bragg about his experience. He arrived at Bethesda on March 20, 1900, at age twelve and left Bethesda

---

[44] Interviews with various alumni, April 24, 1999.

[45] *Bethesda News* (July 1942) (January 1975); interview with Albert Hucks, April 24, 1999.

with Harry Clements, age sixteen; and Hardy Clements, age thirteen; while others were at Sunday supper on June 9, 1901, with the notion of going to the Clements' relatives near Hardeeville, South Carolina. The boys walked the entire way, following the railroad tracks, avoiding neighborhoods where blacks congregated, but getting food from black families on isolated farms. They walked across the Savannah River trestle and up the highway to Hardeeville and the Clements' home. Harry and Hardy could stay, but there was no room for young Woodell. He drifted from hobo villages to railroad work gangs, barefoot, starving, and so dirty he was mistaken for a black child. Running away is not a good idea if there is no place to go. Woodell was lucky; he found a family that took him in and saved his life. He wrote Lillian Bragg in 1963 that he still retained an affection for Bethesda and hoped to return for a visit some day.[46] Bill McIlrath says that instances of running away occur periodically. Someone will try it and for a brief time others will be tempted to follow suit. Then there will be long intervals with no such unauthorized leave-taking.

A key component of the Bethesda mix is the tradition of manual work. From Whitefield's time to David Tribble's, boys have had to work. Work is educative, therapeutic, healthy, and therefore good for the boys, but beyond that fact, their work has always been necessary for the survival of Bethesda. Glaen Richards was accustomed to hard work when he entered the navy from Bethesda in 1944. He remembers rising at 3:30 AM to milk the cows. John Albert Martin put it into rhyme: "I remember each one of us had a detail such as raking, sweeping, and filling the milk pail."[47] Boys learned skills and gained confidence in themselves. Bill Garrison said, " There is something about the whole Bethesda set-up that makes a boy feel he is not having

[46] Woodell's letter is among Lillian Bragg's Papers at the Georgia Historical Society.

[47] Interview with Glaen Richards, April 24, 1999; *Bethesda News* (July 1942).

everything dished out to him by charity." John Winchester expressed a similar thought: "I can say that Bethesda fitted me with a training that is a little better than the average boy gets at home." They felt that they contributed to the support of the home, indeed that they had a *responsibility* to support the home.[48]

Discipline plays a major role in the Bethesda scheme. Glaen Richards said that fear and common sense motivated him. To stay in line, he needed little more than a sight of the wide strap with wicked-looking strips cut in the lower end, a legacy from Chaplin to Burroughs, conspicuously in plain sight outside the superintendent's room. Under Tribble discipline is administered through incentives and positive reinforcement. Many, perhaps most of the boys come from an undisciplined background. They need an orderly environment where there are clear guidelines. Joe Saxon, who entered Bethesda in 1968 and left in 1981, addressed the boys on Anniversary Day, 1999. He told them that he came from a home that had no structure, "the biggest thing we got was discipline." He learned the hard way, by mouthing off to houseparents and suffering the consequences, in his case the patrolling of the horsepasture. He had no father that he knew, but at Bethesda he learned how to be a father to his own children.[49]

There are as many stories as there have been boys at Bethesda, though few are as dramatic as Barney Diamond's. Sidney Williams is another who did well in the world of business. He entered Bethesda December 31, 1917, at the age of eight and remained until September 15, 1928, when he entered Georgia Tech. After graduation he got a job at Coca-Cola and rose to the rank of a major executive. In 1939 he went to Copenhagen, Denmark, to open a new bottling plant and,

---

[48] Garrison to Ole Burroughs, December 23, 1938; Winchester to Burroughs, April 9, 1935, Bethesda Archives.

[49] Saxon's remarks to the Bethesda students, April 24, 1999.

while there, witnessed the Nazi takeover of Denmark. Lee Jones, talented musician and friend of Johnny Mercer, gained prominence in radio broadcasting. He is credited with the introduction of the quiz show. On New York's station WQXR, he arranged for four panelists to answer questions about music and music history. Jones's idea led to Clifton Fadiman's "Information Please," and Jones incorporated his format into bandleader Kay Kyser's "College of Musical Knowledge." Jones became personally acquainted with the "greats" of NBC radio: Jack Benny and his crew, Fred Allen, George Burns, and Gracie Allen. He even recalls encouraging a young and nervous Bob Hope, commenting on Hope's "ad-lib" cards. In his retirement, Jones returned to Savannah and volunteered his services to Bethesda as publicity agent.

If someone tried to imagine a prototypical Bethesda boy, they could do no better than to learn the real story of Tom White. Tom was born in Savannah on April 7, 1916, as Herman Campbell. He never discovered who his real parents were. On November 22, 1916, the six-month-old baby was adopted by Mr. and Mrs. Thomas Joseph White of Savannah, who changed his name to Thomas Joseph White, Jr. Within a year, Mr. White was murdered and a distraught Mrs.White left the infant with a neighbor and never returned to claim him. The neighbor placed Tom in the nursery run by the king's daughters. At the age of six, Tom entered Bethesda and remained there from 1922–1936 when he entered Abraham Baldwin Agricultural College. He said of himself that he was never homesick because he knew no other home than Bethesda. He acquired a strong work ethic, imbued deep moral values, and excelled in his studies and sports alike. Ole Burroughs remembered Tom as a serious lad who walked swiftly, as though he had important work to do. When other boys went home, Tom stayed at Bethesda. On special holidays he was invited to dinner at the residence of Vance Wilson, a neighbor. Soon he became good friends with Mr. Wilson's daughter, Louise.

The Women's Club provides Christmas presents for the boys. Alex Miller (left) and Scott Price open theirs on Christmas Day 1987. (Courtesy Bethesda Museum.)

The boys singing carols on Christmas 1989. The girls belong to Bethesda house parents. (Courtesy Bethesda Museum.)

After finishing studies at Abraham Baldwin, Tom returned to make some money working at the dairy at Bethesda. Two years later Tom entered graduate school at the University of Georgia. Then, feeling a call to the ministry, he entered Columbia Theological Seminary and became a Presbyterian minister. George Whitefield would have been pleased, and Ole Burroughs certainly was. His first assignment was at White Bluff Presbyterian Church, and while there he taught for a time at Bethesda under Claud Corry. He married Louise, who patiently waited for him to finish his studies, and she became a valuable helpmate in his ministry. Tom and Louise served five years at White Bluff; five at Cuthbert, Georgia; five at Quitman, Georgia; and finally settled down at the First Presbyterian Church in Covington, Georgia. His parishioners loved them both and gave them a testimonial in 1975, celebrating the fifteenth anniversary at Covington. The author of Tom White's biographical sketch remarked, "Words can never explain Tom White's devotion to the Bethesda Orphanage; yet, I think one word can explain this devotion; it is 'Home' for a little boy who was left there."[50]

David Tribble understands the impact Bethesda has on young persons. "We forget how powerful a place like this is," he says. "At the home, the boys learn to be part of a community, they practice responsibility, but most importantly, they get close, caring attention. "Everyone needs to have someone who loves him without stint."[51] Ole Burroughs felt the same way. In one of his advertisements for George Mercer's fund-raising campaign, Burroughs wrote, "Go out to Bethesda and mingle with the boys. You will find your heartbeats begin to awaken and your tenderness striving for the mastery, and your whole spiritual nature will be uplifted."

---

[50] The above accounts of Bethesda alumni are taken from folders in the Bethesda Archives.

[51] Interview with David Tribble, February 1, 1999.

At the traditional Anniversary Day alumni banquet, the emotion is palpable as old boys tell what Bethesda has meant to them. Over the years, some have tried to describe their feelings. In 1946, R. N. Stoner submitted a poem to the *Bethesda News*:

A poet I would like to be
For here we have it all.
The trees all draped with Spanish moss
And leaves just tinged with Fall.
The water and the marsh are here
A poet's dream at hand.
The moonlight on the marsh at night
Surpasses that on land.[52]

Joe Moseley attended the home from 1941–1946. He wrote music to accompany his lyrics and gave the song to Bethesda in 1992. In part it reads:

You touched my life.
You marked my way.
You gave me reason
In my life to dream.
You taught me how
To meet the world.
You made my life a
Challenge to fulfill.
You touched my life.
You taught me truth;
How truth would always
Help me find my way.

---

[52] *Bethesda News* (December 1946).

And you taught me to be
All the things I could be.
You touched my life.
You touched my life.[53]

Each anniversary alumni members struggle to express their feelings, and upon occasion distinguished speakers have lavished lengthy encomiums upon the home. Perhaps George Whitefield best captured the feeling many have striven for in his happy expression "Beloved Bethesda."

---

[53] I am indebted to Joe Moseley for sending me a tape recording and a copy of the lyrics to his touching tribute to Bethesda.

INDEX